Strange Deaths

STRANGE DEATHS

John Dunning

MULBERRY EDITIONS

First published in 1981

Copyright © 1981 John Dunning

All rights reserved

This edition published in 1992 for
Mulberry Editions by Cresset Press,
an imprint of Random House UK Limited,
20 Vauxhall Bridge Road, London SW1V 2SA

ISBN 1–873123–13–2

Printed and bound in Great Britain

CONTENTS

INTRODUCTION

Now that I have written considerably more than a thousand accounts of true crimes, it would be nice if I were able to begin this introduction with the statement that many persons have questioned me concerning my theories of crime in general.

Alas! I cannot. In so far as memory serves, no one has ever asked me such a question with the exception of one person who, as it happened, knew far more about the matter than I did.

Perhaps this is just as well for, were I to be questioned on my theories concerning crime, I could not give a clear answer.

To begin with, I find it difficult to define exactly what crime is.

The simplest definition is that crime occurs when there is a violation of the law, a generalization which can comfortably encompass double parking and the dismemberment of one's chosen victim.

There are, however, a number of incompatibilities inherent in such a definition as law is, to some extent, dependent upon time, place and circumstances.

In a house located on a state line in a federal republic such as the United States, an act committed in the living room may be a crime and the same act committed in the kitchen may not.

This may not extend to murder, but even in that case, the location of the scene of the crime may have a profound effect on the severity of the punishment.

So too with the era in which the crime takes place. Until fairly recently murders were all lumped more or less

7

together. There were few degrees. Either the murder was deliberate and premeditated, unintentional or justified – as in the case of the defence of one's self or family – or it was unproved, in which case the accused went free.

Today, courts routinely hand down reduced sentences and even acquittals on the basis of psychological opinion that the accused, although guilty, was not mentally responsible for the act. There have been cases in Europe where the accused was ruled incompetent to stand trial because his crime was so horrible that no sane person could have committed it.

And, finally, there are circumstances which, in today's society, may become very complex indeed, as in the case of the husband who, having fallen asleep in front of the television, awakes to find his wife being raped on the sofa by a burglar.

Indignant and irritated, he seizes the television set and smashes it over the burglar's head, causing the usual contusions, abrasions, shock and, perhaps, trauma. (Even for a burglar, this is not the ideal time to have a television set smashed over the head.)

Now the question is, is the husband guilty of assault?

Many would reply no, that he was acting in defence of his family.

But what if, unbeknown to the husband, his wife was a consenting party to the act? There are, presumably, as many sexually desirable men engaged in the burglar's trade as in any other, and the very fact that the husband had fallen asleep in front of the television could serve as an indication of the boredom of the wife who may suffer from insomnia.

In any case, the husband has now committed a violent act on the person of his wife's lover and not her rapist. Is it assault?

Possibly. It cannot be said that the burglar was engaged in an act detrimental to the husband's property. A liberally constituted society does not regard the wife as the property of her husband. In theory, she is entitled to engage in sex with the casual passing burglar if she so chooses. The most that the husband could ask would be partial payment of the rent by the burglar on the grounds that he was making unauthorized use of the premises.

8

But let us take this a step further. Supposing that the burglar is really the original husband of the wife who has divorced him to marry the husband who is now asleep in front of the television and, realizing her error, now falls with rapture into his arms; and supposing still further (I am not a believer of moderation) that, through a technical error in court procedure, the woman's divorce from her first husband is not valid and she is still legally married to him and not to the television sleeper?

What then? Is the man who believes himself to be the lady's husband guilty of assault?

It would seem that he is. He has smashed a television set over the head of a man engaged in lawful intercourse with his own wife. Whether any of the parties concerned were aware of this state of affairs might or might not affect their actions, but would it affect the pertinent law?

Similar and worse cases have actually taken place. They are not common, but they are not that far-fetched either.

Equally confusing is the application of the concept of law to non-human entities such as corporations.

A corporation is recognized under the law as having an existence and a legal status. It can sue individuals or other corporations, its rights can be violated and, in the United States at least, it has been granted the right to take an active part in political affairs.

Nonetheless, even in those countries with capital punishment, no corporation has ever been executed or even sent to jail, although corporations have, on occasion, been responsible for massacres which compare with those of Attila the Hun.

In some cases, these massacres were carried out with the knowledge of the persons administering the corporation and the corporation was sometimes fined for them. It was, however, usually possible for the corporation to deduct the amount of the fine from taxes as a justifiable business expense, thus transferring the punishment to the other tax-payers.

It would seem that the law is not identical for persons and corporate bodies and, perhaps, this is only reasonable, for corporate murders, even if performed "wilfully, feloniously and with malice aforethought", are not the result of vile passion, but the honest desire to make a profit for the stockholders.

In any case, such impersonal murders are not very interesting. The corporation does not come sneaking about with an axe or, laying its sinewy hands on the victim's throat, strangle his or her eyes out of his or her head. It may poison the food, the water or the air, give people radiation sickness, cancer or blow them up, but there is little drama or conflict in this.

Most of the crimes which I have dealt with contain strong elements of drama and conflict because I have to sell stories about them, and most of them have, therefore, been murder.

Although, as the reader will by now no doubt be aware, I am somewhat confused over the concept of crime in the abstract, I have, over the years, reached certain conclusions concerning homicide.

To begin with, most murders are unintentional. Humans are an unstable lot. When they are placed under sufficient stress, they tend to react violently. Frequently they are astounded and dismayed to discover that they have killed someone and they usually regret it, not simply through fear of punishment, which in our progressive society is seldom very onerous in any case, but because they were attached to the victim or feel sorry for him or her.

Few murders are carefully planned, and fewer still are for money. People who desire money usually try to avoid killing the person from whom they hope to obtain it on the reasonable grounds that, if they are in jail for murder, they will not be able to enjoy it.

Still more rare is the murder for motives of hate or revenge. Modern humans are a rather wishy-washy lot and do not sustain such strong feelings long enough to go around murdering people for some real or fancied wrong.

As a primary motive in most cases, this leaves sex, or rather the differences in the sexes. It is probable that, were there only one sex to the human race, there might be far fewer murders, although it could be that an equal or greater number of people would then die of boredom.

10

There are several categories of sex murders. The most common victim is a married (legally or otherwise) person who is murdered by the spouse or the spouse's lover. There are sometimes sub-motives in such cases – money, fear of exposure, fear of the spouse or simple embarrassment – but the basic force is sexual jealousy.

People who kill their spouses are seldom punished very severely today, no doubt according to the reasoning that, as they only murder spouses, they are no danger to the general public.

Unfortunately, if family-type homicides are not very harshly punished, neither are those of another large and more dangerous class.

This steadily growing group consists of sexually deranged people who prey on women and children, particularly in the larger communities, and provides high proportions of the most appalling crimes against the most pitiful type of victim.

There are few such murders of women and children by sex deviates which could not have been avoided, for the murderers nearly always have long records of previous sexual offences such as led to the murder.

They have been repeatedly convicted, repeatedly declared not responsible for their actions, repeatedly sent for psychiatric treatment, repeatedly pronounced cured and repeatedly released. This process is often continued even after a murder has taken place.

Doubtless, there are sex deviates who do respond to psychiatric treatment, lose their unhealthy obsessions with women or children and become useful members of society, but both courts and psychologists appear to be totally incapable of judging which ones.

However, none of these well-intentioned officials is ever held responsible for the death or suffering resulting from their decisions, based, all too frequently, not upon reality but upon a dogmatic political or social philosophy.

Is the judge or the psychologist, responsible for the release of a dangerously disturbed person who then promptly kills, any less guilty of the murder than the madman who was the immediate instrument?

Ah! But there we are back to the definition of what

constitutes a crime, and that was where we started.

Finally, a few comments concerning the cases treated in this book.

I have, to the best of my ability, tried to retrace actual events as accurately as possible. However, the facts in such cases are often obscure and, not infrequently, known to no living person. If there are errors, I apologize for them.

The names of those people who were not directly involved in the events have been changed, as have those of most of the police officers. Some police departments do not like to make public the names of their criminal investigations officers.

As for the crimes themselves, I personally found them unusual. I can only hope that the reader will agree.

ONE

A VARIATION ON THE SECOND TIME AROUND

Freda Wilson took a long time to die. She was a strong woman, only fifty-three years old, and even the spasms of pain which caused her to moan, tear the bed sheets and writhe like a speared eel brought no relief in unconsciousness.

Nor did the pain-killers which Dr Herbert Roventry prescribed in ever increasing strength and quantity, frustrated by the fact that he had utterly failed to diagnose his patient's illness. The X-rays had shown no sign of an ulcer; there were no indications of gallstones and yet she had these terrible pains in the abdomen and throughout the torso.

They had begun in January 1979 and, Dr Roventry being Freda Wilson's family doctor, she had come to his office in Auckland for help. The Wilsons did not live in the city, but on their prosperous sheep farm some thirty-five miles distant.

James Wilson, Freda's fifty-four-year-old husband, had driven her in. He was a handsome man who had come out to New Zealand from England in 1947 and had made his fortune there.

Without very much effort really. He had been in the country less than a year when he married Norah Harwood, a pleasant woman who was older than him and the only child of one of the biggest landowners in the area. The result had been the sheep farm and an end to Wilson's financial problems.

But, perhaps, the beginning of others, the doctor reflected.

He had been the first Mrs Wilson's doctor too, and he was aware that she had not been capable of bearing children. He was also aware that the Wilsons had not got on well.

Taking that into consideration, it had been James Wilson's second great stroke of luck when Norah died in January 1964, leaving him with the farm.

Six months after Norah had been buried, Wilson married Freda Smart, an employee of a large agricultural-machinery firm where he had bought his farm machines.

There had, of course, been an investigation by the police because Norah had had nothing wrong with her that Dr Roventry knew of and he had not been prepared to issue a death certificate.

He had been quite right, too. The post-mortem had shown that Norah died of strychnine poisoning.

The police had questioned James Wilson and he had readily admitted that he kept strychnine around the place for poisoning pests. He had, he said ruefully, apparently been too careless with it. He had kept it in an old lemonade bottle in the kitchen, and somehow Norah had got it mixed up with the lemonade she drank every afternoon while watching her favourite television programme. He himself had been in the town of Wellington on business at the time.

The facts, as ascertained by the police, corresponded exactly to this statement. Norah had been found dead in front of the television set by a neighbour, and the half-empty bottle of lemonade beside her contained traces of strychnine. Wilson's whereabouts at the time of his wife's death were checked. He had been in Wellington.

Even so, the police had not been convinced that Norah's death was the accident which it appeared to be, and the main reason for this was that their investigations had quickly shown that the affair between James Wilson and Freda Smart had begun long before Norah's death – in April 1962, to be precise. There had been a certain amount of talk and Wilson had been seen visiting Freda's flat.

There had not been very much that the police could do, however. Privately, the inspector in charge of the investigation was one of the opinion that Wilson had deliberately murdered his wife in order to marry his mistress. The less

14

drastic solution of divorcing her was not feasible as the farm was still in her name and he would have lost everything.

By the time that the investigation was concluded, he was also of the opinion that Wilson was going to get away with it. There was simply no evidence to support a murder charge. It was a perfect crime.

It was not only the inspector who was of this opinion. So too were the neighbours in the area where Wilson had his farm, and the second Mrs Wilson found herself practically ostracized. The only person in the district who would have anything to do with her was Jessica Lacey, the owner of a small grocery store and roadhouse near the Wilson farm, and the women soon became good friends.

It was Jessica who was with Freda when she died. James, who had spent a great deal of time at her bedside and seemed sincerely puzzled and concerned by his wife's illness, was in Wellington on business.

Jessica had telephoned Dr Roventry, imploring him to drop everything and come at once.

"She's having a terrible seizure," she wept into the telephone. "The pain is tearing her apart. I think she's dying."

It was an accurate estimate. By the time that Dr Roventry reached the Wilson farm, Freda was dead. She had died in the most hideous agony, but her features, contorted with pain in life, were strangely calm and composed in death. It could have been said that she looked satisfied.

Dr Roventry was not. He still had no idea of what had caused his patient's death, and he not only refused to issue the death certificate, but demanded that a post-mortem be performed immediately.

The police did not oppose this request. Far from it. No one had forgotten about the first Mrs Wilson's mysterious death, and there was a certain amount of exultation inside the Department of Criminal Investigations.

Wilson had pushed his luck too far this time, it was felt, and now he was going to have to pay for one murder, if not both.

While the post-mortem was being performed, investigations began into the identity of James Wilson's current mistress. No one doubted that he had one and, in the police, no one doubted that he had murdered his wife in order to marry her just as he had murdered Norah to marry Freda.

The suspicions were promptly confirmed. Wilson had been having an affair with an extremely beautiful, twenty-six-year-old woman named Ivy Thomas who had taken over a filling station in a nearby village.

The affair had begun in October 1978, and by January 1979 Freda was complaining of stomach pains to Dr Roventry. If it was a coincidence, it was one of the greatest ones that the police had encountered in some time.

But, of course, it had not been a coincidence. The post-mortem showed that Freda Wilson had died of arsenic poisoning. It was in her stomach; it was in her liver; it was in all of her vital organs and, most important, it was in her hair.

It could only have been deposited in her hair if it had been administered over a long period of time, say, from the beginning of 1979 or the end of 1978 up until the time of her death.

This excluded completely any possibility of an accident. Freda Wilson had not merely got hold of a bottle of lemonade containing poison, she had been fed arsenic in small doses over a long period of time, during which it had gradually built up in her body and had killed her.

A rather common way of poisoning a person, but not as undetectable as many murderers have thought.

James Wilson was arrested and formally charged with the murder of his wife Freda.

He denied it.

The police pointed out that he had been having an affair with Ivy Thomas. She was much younger, much prettier than his wife. He had wanted to marry her.

Not at all, said Wilson. He had had no reason to marry her. He was already getting as much sex from her as he could stand, and if he were to marry her, he would have to watch her all the time or end up with a set of horns. Anyway, he added, she was not very well-to-do. He owned a great deal more than she did.

It was, perhaps, indicative of what James Wilson thought about marriage, but unfortunately it was also true. Ivy

Thomas was not as well-off as James Wilson and she confirmed repeatedly in her statement to the police that he had never broached the subject of marriage with her.

In any case, she said, Wilson was old enough to be her father and, while an affair now might be pleasant enough, what would things be like in six years when he was sixty? She was not interested in his sheep farm. A modern, independent sort of girl, she was capable of looking after her own financial needs.

Finally, she raised a point which made the police uncomfortable. Why, she asked, would James Wilson have spent months poisoning his wife when it was a virtual certainty that he would be suspected of it and when all he had to do to get rid of her was to file for divorce?

It was a question that the defence at the trial was going to ask too, and it was a question to which the police had no answer.

In the case of Norah, divorce had been out of the question, for with Norah would have gone the farm and everything else. James Wilson would have been back where he started when he arrived in New Zealand with scarcely more than the clothes he was wearing.

With Freda, however, it was he who owned everything. Granted, Freda might have contested the divorce, might have made trouble over it, but actually there was not much she could have done and there was no question of Wilson losing the property.

The motive seemed to be lacking and, as all efforts by the police to trace where Wilson had bought the arsenic had proved fruitless, a motive was desperately needed.

Wilson himself said that he had bought no arsenic, had had no arsenic anywhere on the farm, and had kept nothing of a poisonous nature in the house since his first wife's tragic death. He had learned his lesson from that.

This was another statement which made the police unhappy. Obviously, the thing for Wilson to have said was that he had had arsenic around the house for use on the farm. Many insect killers contain arsenic and it would have been possible for Freda to have got some of it into her food or drink.

Not, of course, in the quantities and over the period of time which the autopsy had shown that she was ingesting arsenic, but still, this would have been a logical explanation on the part of James Wilson, particularly as he had already used it once in the murder of his first wife.

It was not certain that this was what it had been, for under the unrelenting interrogation, James Wilson finally broke down and confessed to the poisoning of Norah.

"We were unhappy," he said, "and sexually incompatible. The fact that she could not have children destroyed what little feeling there was between us and we had not had sexual relations for some time.

"It was during the annual trade fair in 1962 that I met Freda, when I went to see about buying a new tractor. There was something about her that attracted me tremendously and I asked her to have dinner with me.

"I guess it was what you call love at first sight for both of us. I hadn't really loved Norah and, if it hadn't been for the farm, I wouldn't have married her. I admit that, but I'm not the first man who married for property.

"Anyway, after dinner we went to her flat and we just sort of fell on each other. I had not been having any sex for some time and she told me later that she had only had one or two passing affairs which had not worked out satisfactorily.

"In any case, we were ideally suited, not only as far as sex went, but also in other things. We liked being with each other.

"I used to find every excuse that I could to go into Auckland, and sometimes we were even able to spend a night together, but it was risky because I knew that if Norah found out, she'd divorce me like a shot and I'd be back to working as a farm labourer.

"She didn't have sex with me herself, but she wouldn't have let me get away with having it with anyone else.

"Finally, on this Tuesday afternoon – it was November 12, 1963, I remember it very well – we were lying on the bed in Freda's flat and this thought sort of came to me all by itself.

"It was raining outside, a fine, steady rain, and it was about six-thirty in the evening. I knew I was going to have to get up in a few minutes and go back to the farm and Norah and I didn't want to. All of a sudden, I heard myself saying, 'Norah has to go.'"

Asked what Freda had thought of this idea, Wilson said that she was opposed to it, not, he maintained, because she had any qualms about the murder, but rather because she did not think that he could get away with it.

"You'll be suspected immediately," she had said. "Everybody knows that you and Norah aren't getting on well and everybody believes that you only married her for the farm. The police will investigate and they'll find out about you and me. You'll go to prison for the rest of your life. Can't you just divorce her?"

"I'd be nothing but a farm labourer again," Wilson had replied. "She isn't stupid. I suppose she must have realized that I married her for the farm and she's kept everything in her name. I wouldn't have a penny."

"You could find work of some kind," said Freda. "I've got a job. Money isn't everything."

It had not been everything to Freda and, perhaps, not everything to James Wilson because he was, after all, risking his fine sheep farm by allowing himself to become involved with a mistress, but it was a great deal and he could not bring himself to part with the property.

On the other hand, something had to be done without delay because there was already a certain amount of talk and it was only a matter of time before it got back to Norah's ears. If James Wilson had good and cogent reasons for not wanting to divorce his wife, there was nothing at all to stop her from divorcing him.

Wilson had thought it over for a month and a half and had then come up with what he thought was a foolproof plan.

"Norah has a habit of drinking a bottle of lemonade every afternoon while she's watching television," he told Freda. "If there was a spoonful of strychnine in that bottle, it would kill her like a shot."

Freda had shuddered. She still did not like the idea of murder, but she was hopelessly in love with Wilson and she was prepared to accept almost anything to have him to herself. With her, it was not a matter of money. As she would later tell Jessica Lacey, she would actually have preferred to

19

keep her job in Auckland rather than to live in idleness on the somewhat isolated sheep farm where no one other than Jessica wanted to have anything to do with her.

It was, of course, out of the question. Once she was married to James Wilson, she had to be where she could keep an eye on him as much as possible. Women who marry men who have ridded themselves of a previous wife are seldom so dense that they do not realize that what has happened once could very well happen again.

Nonetheless, she had still tried to dissuade him from his murderous plans, partly because she did not want to be party to the death of another woman, even if it was her rival, and partly because she was certain that he would be caught.

"She probably won't even drink it if the bottle is already open," she had said.

It was something that had not occurred to Wilson and, tragically, it was this somewhat half-hearted attempt to prevent the murder which actually made it successful.

The problem having been brought to his attention, Wilson gave the matter a little more thought and came up with the simple solution of uncapping the bottle, adding the strychnine and putting the cap back on again.

"What's more," he told Freda, "I can arrange it so that I'm not anywhere near the farm when she drinks the stuff. The bottles are standing in a row on the shelf in the pantry and she takes the one on the end. All I have to do is put the doctored one anywhere in the row and I can tell then exactly on what day she'll drink it. On that day, I'll be somewhere else on business."

"You won't get away with it," said Freda. "They'll suspect you immediately."

"They won't be able to prove a thing," said James Wilson.

And, of course, both he and Freda had been right. He had been suspected immediately and the police had been able to prove nothing. They did not believe that the poisoning had been an accident, but they had had no evidence to show that it was not.

As to Freda's other objection that he would not get away with it, she had been only temporarily wrong. He had got

20

away with it for fifteen years, but in the end the truth had come out.

But not all the truth, for James Wilson continued to swear by all that was holy that he had not poisoned his second wife and that he had not even had any inkling that she was poisoned until after the post-mortem report was released.

This was such an illogical attitude that the inspector was tempted to wonder if there might not be some truth in Wilson's statement.

After all, he had confessed to the first murder, and confessing to a second would not worsen his situation much. He was going to get the maximum penalty anyway. Why then continue to suffer the ordeal of continuous interrogation, which the police were forced to maintain because they still did not have all the answers in the case?

If Wilson really had not poisoned his second wife, then there was only one other person who could have done so.

Jessica Lacey.

No one else had been in frequent contact with the dead woman. No one, as a matter of fact, had had any contact with her at all.

Ivy Thomas, who might conceivably have had a motive of sorts for the murder, had, as far as the police could determine, never even met Freda Wilson and she had certainly never been in the Wilson house.

The only person who had been was Jessica Lacey, but once again there was not the slightest trace of a motive.

Unless, of course, Jessica and James. . .?

But Jessica and James had not or, at least, the police could find no trace of evidence that they had had any contacts, other than through Freda, whatsoever.

Nonetheless, a discreet investigation was undertaken. In addition to the other flaws in the case against James Wilson concerning the murder of his second wife, there was the fact that it had never been possible to determine where or when he had bought the arsenic, the analysis of which had indicated that it was a compound which had been intended as an insecticide.

To the inspector's dismay, the investigation promptly produced evidence that Jessica Lacey had bought a package of insect powder containing arsenic, and the quantity was such that it would have been ample for the purpose of poisoning Freda Wilson.

Even more damning was the fact that the insect powder had been bought in the first week of January, less than a month before Freda had come to Dr Roventry complaining of pains in the stomach.

On the other hand, New Zealand is in the southern hemisphere and January is a time when insect powder is required. Hundreds of other people had bought the same insect powder and they could not all be suspected of poisoning Freda Wilson with it.

Granted, Jessica Lacey had often been at the Wilson house and would, perhaps, have had an opportunity to introduce the arsenic into Freda's food or drink, but she was not there every day by any means and seldom at meal times.

Freda had not had the first Mrs Wilson's habit of drinking lemonade while watching television, and it was thought that the arsenic had probably been put into her food.

The inspector was confused. Everything that he had been able to learn concerning Jessica's relationship to Freda indicated that she was not only a good and true friend, but also practically her only friend. She had not had the slightest reason in the world to poison her.

And yet, there was the puzzling fact that Wilson still continued his stubborn denial of all knowledge of the death of his second wife, although he now freely admitted to having murdered the first.

In the end, he was forced to let the matter rest. Wilson would not confess to the murder of his second wife. There was no evidence that anyone else had done it.

James Wilson was brought to trial in spring 1980, not for the murder of Norah, to which he had confessed, but for the murder of Freda, which he denied.

He continued to deny his guilt throughout the trial, but considering that he had admitted to the first murder and that it had been committed with poison, even if not the same poison as that which had killed Freda, the issue was never really in doubt.

In the meantime, the prosecution had developed a theory

to explain the motive for the crime.

Freda Wilson, said the prosecution, had learned of her husband's affair with the lovely and youthful Ivy Thomas. She had probably been particularly alert to such possibilities as it was this same manner in which she had come to be Mrs Wilson in the first place.

She was now in her early fifties and it was conceivable that the romantically-inclined James would tend to stray. Freda Wilson had known or guessed that her husband was involved in an affair with another woman, or he could have told her himself.

Perhaps he had asked for a divorce or threatened to get one against her will, or even if he had not admitted to the affair, Freda might have known of it and suspected that she would eventually be divorced, if not murdered.

After all, she knew very well what James Wilson was capable of.

And that, said the prosecution, was what had been the motive for her murder.

Freda Wilson had not only known of what her husband was capable. She knew what he had actually done, and she had believed that it gave her a hold over him. If she did not have property, she at least had knowledge, and knowledge that could be extremely damaging to James Wilson.

Faced with her replacement in James Wilson's affections and, possibly, house, just as she had once replaced Norah in both, she had seized on a desperate defence – the threat that, if James divorced her or failed to terminate his affair with the other woman, she would expose him to the police as the murderer of his first wife.

James Wilson, said the prosecution, had reacted by murdering her. He had not dared to make further recourse to strychnine, but had chosen arsenic administered over a long period of time in small quantities. Like many laymen, he had undoubtedly not known that arsenic was retained in the body.

Wilson denied these allegations, and the defence pointed out that Freda could not have exposed her husband as a murderer without making herself an accomplice in the crime, but it did no good. Freda or Norah or both, James

Wilson was, by his own admission, a murderer and he was found guilty.

On April 24, 1980, he was sentenced to life imprisonment.

Upon hearing the verdict, he immediately collapsed with a heart attack and was rushed to the hospital. The trial and the long period of interrogation which had preceded it had had a very profound effect on his health in general and, whereas a year earlier he had looked younger than his age, he now looked ten years older, his hair had turned white and he was scarcely able to keep his feet.

After recovering from his heart attack at the hospital, he was transferred to the prison to begin serving his life sentence which, from the appearance of things, would not be very long.

Rather incredibly, he still maintained his innocence of the murder of Freda and seemed very concerned about being convicted of the murder to which he had *not* confessed rather than the one to which he had.

As it turned out, James Wilson's sentence did not last long at all – less than a month after his trial and conviction, he suffered a second heart attack in his prison cell and died on May 20, 1980.

Practically his last words were that he was innocent of the crime for which he had been convicted.

This death-bed statement made the inspector extremely nervous. Wilson had obviously been obsessed with his innocence and it was unlikely that he would have made such a statement if it were untrue when he was undoubtedly aware that he was on the verge of death.

It seemed probable, therefore, that it was true and that James Wilson had murdered only his first wife and not his second. What made the inspector nervous was the question of who had murdered the second woman.

While he was still pondering whether a fresh investigation should be undertaken and, if so, what direction it should take, the report of James Wilson's death appeared in the daily newspapers and, on the following day, the inspector had an unexpected visitor.

It was Jessica Lacey, and she said that she had something important which she wanted to tell him in private.

James Wilson, she said, was innocent of the crime for which he had been convicted.

The inspector had already suspected this, but he was not pleased at the confirmation of his suspicions. He had been hoping that he was wrong. Now, if Miss Lacey had any evidence of Wilson's innocence, Freda Wilson's murder case would have to be reopened.

Unless, of course, Jessica Lacey was about to make a confession.

The inspector waited silently.

"Freda lived in terror of losing her husband," said Jessica Lacey. "She had taken him from his first wife and she feared continually that another woman would take him from her. The older she got, the more fearful she became.

"On Christmas Eve 1978, she had an experience which made a reality of her worst nightmares.

"She was driving home in her own car that afternoon when she saw James' car parked in some bushes beside the road. As she was suspicious of him in any case, she stopped, got out and went to look quietly through the bushes.

"James was on the other side, sitting on the bank of a little stream, and Ivy Thomas was in the water, completely nude. He was begging her to come out and not keep him waiting any longer.

"While Freda watched, she did come out and she did not keep him waiting any longer.

"It was as if she was seeing all of the most terrible fears that she had ever dreamed and, when she came to me, she was white and shaking and she looked twenty years older. I thought she'd had a heart attack.

"Well, it was a sort of heart attack, I guess, and it didn't make her feel better after she'd told me all about it. She kept saying over and over, 'She's beautiful! A girl! A young girl! What am I to do?'"

"I told her there were only two things she could do: forget what she had seen and keep her mouth shut, or file for divorce. She could probably get a good settlement or, if she wanted to continue with the marriage, she could refuse a divorce if James asked for one, and there'd be no way he

25

could free himself to marry the girl, even if she'd have had him.

"She wouldn't hear of it. She didn't want a settlement. She wanted her husband and she didn't want to share him. Besides, she said she was afraid of what might happen if he wanted his freedom and she wouldn't give it to him.

"I asked what she meant and she broke down and told me that James had murdered his first wife to marry her. I said, 'So what's new?' Everybody already believed that he'd murdered her and got away with it. I said that she didn't have anything to worry about on that score. Even James wouldn't have the nerve to keep on murdering wife after wife. Another case like the first one and they'd have his skin.

"I guess that was the wrong thing to say because she looked at me without saying anything for quite a while and then she said, 'If that's what it takes.'

"I asked her what she meant and she said she happened to know that arsenic remained in the body and that it would show up at a post-mortem."

"But surely . . .?" stammered the inspector. "It was terribly painful . . . it went on for months . . . she couldn't have . . .?"

"She made me swear that I wouldn't tell," said Jessica Lacey, "but it doesn't matter now that he's dead. Yes, it's true. Freda poisoned herself with arsenic in order to have her husband convicted of her murder."

TWO

A LITTLE MORE JAM, DEAR?

"I am afraid that I have some very bad news to tell you, Siegfried," said the doctor. He leaned forward over the desk, his eyes fixed on the gold-rimmed glasses which he was holding in both hands. "The tests are positive. Ingeborg has cancer of the liver."

The distinguished-looking man with the silver-grey beard and moustache seated in the chair in front of the doctor's desk cowered back as if he had received a physical blow.

"Oh my God!" he whispered. "Are you certain . . .? Is there nothing . . .?"

"Nothing," said the doctor in a low, firm voice. "There is no hope. Do you want her to know?"

Forty-seven-year-old Siegfried Ruopp hesitated, his head bent forwards and his shoulders bowed with the weight of his grief.

"No," he said finally. "Let her have what happiness is left to her."

He got heavily to his feet, walked to the door and paused, his hand resting on the door handle.

"How long?" he said, not turning to look at the doctor. "What can I tell the children?"

"A year," said the doctor. "A year and a half at the most. She'll have to be hospitalized long before then, of course."

"Of course," repeated Professor Ruopp dully and left the office, the door closing softly behind him.

On the way back to the neat, beautifully maintained but slightly unimaginative house in the Ulm suburb of Wiblingen, however, he apparently decided to say nothing to the children about their mother's incurable illness – not, at least, as yet.

Bernd was twenty and in the final year of his secondary-school education, and Virena was fourteen and in the very middle of hers. Both would, of course, be going on to university. The Ruopps were an academic family, and Siegfried Ruopp held two academic titles – a doctorate in chemistry and the official title of professor at the Schubart secondary school in Ulm, a city of slightly over one hundred thousand people in the south of Germany. As is the German custom, he was invariably addressed by his full title, Professor Doctor Ruopp.

It could be that Professor Doctor Ruopp had come to the conclusion that there was no point in distracting the children from their studies with a tragedy which they and he were powerless to avert.

Nor did he tell Ingeborg, his forty-two-year-old wife. She had, of course, known that he was going to see family doctor, Dr Arnold Weissmann, concerning the results of the laboratory tests which had been run on her that cold and wet autumn of 1976, but, when Siegfried reported that they had been negative, that there was no sign of a malignant growth and that there was nothing to worry about, she accepted the news with relief.

Her mind shied like a terrified horse at the very thought of cancer and she was only too happy to accept the reassurance that it had not, after all, come to her.

On the other hand, she did not feel any better physically either. The vague pains in her back and lower chest continued and, she thought, actually became worse. There was something wrong inside there and, if it was not cancer, what was it?

Dr Weissmann was not very precise. He spoke of obstructions in the intestines, a possible ulcer, inflammation of the stomach lining and he prescribed tranquillizers and pain-killers.

In ever-increasing amounts and strengths. The doctor was trying to ease his patient as gently as possible into the inevitable, ultimate agony which lay before her.

Professor Ruopp did his part. Never had he been so cheerful, so good-humoured. Never had he showered so many attentions on his wife, not even during their courtship a good twenty-five years earlier.

Like some other chemists who find parallels between the two fields of endeavour, the professor was an exceptionally good cook and a veritable master in the preparation of jams, jellies and other sweets and he plied his dying wife with so many good things to eat that she began to put on weight and was scarcely able to get into her clothes.

He was particularly proud of his wild blackberry jam for which he collected the berries during the summer and which was of a richness and sweetness unsurpassed in all of Germany.

Fragrant, delicious, filled with plump, whole fruits, it was of a beautiful, dark-red colour, so dark that it was nearly black.

Rather like the colour of partially dried blood . . . or a rotting liver.

Curiously, the professor himself did not like sweet things and never touched the jams or jellies.

Which did not make them any the less delicious. Ingeborg Ruopp ate heartily and her pains became steadily less endurable.

Eventually she was admitted to the private section of the Ulm University Clinic where, as her case was hopeless, she was given no treatment, but massive amounts of pain-killers.

She was assured by her doctor and her husband that she was there for treatment of an ulcer of the stomach, but, by now, Ingeborg Ruopp knew.

Although she courageously played out her part in the fiction, she knew that she could not have an ulcer. If you are suffering from ulcers, you do not continue to eat quantities of sweet things such as blackberry jam and Siegfried was bringing her a fresh pot almost every day.

Actually, Ingeborg Ruopp was getting a little sick of blackberry jam, but she would never, of course, have mentioned it to her husband. After all, he was so very proud of it and he was trying so hard to do everything that he could for her.

29

It made her feel a trifle guilty. Siegfried had not always had it easy with her and he had had to be very, very patient. She was not at all sure how another husband might have reacted to the madness that had come over her some ten years ago.

Exactly ten years, she thought, lying propped up in the loneliness of the private hospital room and nibbling idly at a spoonful of jam from the pot standing on the little table beside the bed. She was, at the moment, feeling no pain. As a matter of fact, she could feel hardly anything at all and her mind hung suspended in that cosy, slightly woolly cloud which is the result of massive amounts of opiates.

Ten years ago, 1967, and it had truly been madness. He had been married and so had she. They had both had children. There was no question of making a new life together.

And yet, she had loved him so and, as she had never doubted, he had loved her as fervently. Despite everything, they had been happy, even if only for a short time and only when they were actually together.

It had been madness, but a sweet madness and she knew even now, lying there and waiting for death in this cold, white, antiseptic, little room, that, if she had to do it over again, she would do it gladly and pay the price.

The price had, of course, long since been paid. It had been paid when her lover, the handsome distinguished Dr Andreas Boltzer, had lost control of his Porsche sports-car which he loved driving at such high speeds and had spilled his clever, greatly loved brains over the dashboard as the car's nose crumpled like cardboard against the unyielding trunk of the old elm beside the road. He had been thirty-two years old at the time, the same age as herself.

"Dietenheim," she said, speaking the word out loud. It was the name of the village fifteen miles to the south of Ulm where the accident had taken place and where she and Siegfried and Andreas and his family had all lived.

The Ruopps had, however, not been living there when the accident took place for, by that time, Siegfried had learned of the affair between Dr Boltzer and his wife and had sold the house for the first offer he received. They had then moved to Wiblingen on the outskirts of Ulm and would probably have moved further still if Andreas had not been killed. Dr Ruopp had found it extremely humiliating that everyone in Dietenheim knew of his wife's affair with Dr Boltzer.

Yes, reflected Ingeborg, Siegfried had been remarkably patient. They had, of course, spoken of divorce, but, once Andreas was dead, she had had no reason to want a divorce and Siegfried had generously not brought the matter up again.

He had merely punished her by taking a mistress, a very young, very beautiful pupil of his. A professor had to be a great deal less attractive than Siegfried before he encountered any lack of candidates for such liaisons in his classes.

For his sake, she had tried to pretend that she was suffering, but her suffering over the death of Andreas had been so vast, so excruciating that she had had no room for suffering of any other kind and she was afraid that Siegfried had seen through her pretence. In any case, his affair with the nubile chemistry student had not lasted long. The girl had graduated and had gone on to university in another city, though he had probably, she thought, had others since.

However, she did not grudge him his fun. He had been a good husband, a good father and a good provider. If he wanted a bit of extra-marital sex with his students, why not?

All in all, she was satisfied, satisfied with her husband, more than satisfied with her children, satisfied with her life. It was just a pity that it could not last a little longer. Forty-five is a poor time to die. You have barely got used to the idea of being over forty and no longer young and here you are dying already. She did not think for a moment that she had any hope of celebrating her forty-sixth birthday.

Yes, Siegfried had been a dear and would, undoubtedly, make an extremely desirable widower. He was still handsome, well-to-do, distinguished and, heaven knew, an outstanding cook.

Or rather, an outstanding maker of jams and jellies. He was only a competent cook. Being a professor of chemistry, his measurements of the ingredients tended to be a little too exact and cooking, at least great cooking, is more a matter of artistic flair than precise weights and measures.

31

Still, the jam was unquestionably magnificent.

She put another half-spoonful in her mouth, letting it dissolve slowly on her tongue. Perfectly delicious. Siegfried had every right to be proud of it, although he did not eat it himself nor, for that matter, did the children . . . which was probably why he was always urging her to take more . . . funny . . . he never urged her to eat anything else . . . as a matter of fact, he had at times urged her to eat less . . . getting hippy, he had said, she should take off a few pounds . . . strange, he had wanted her to eat less of other things, but not less blackberry jam . . . it seemed to be a sort of obsession with him . . . he had brought her nothing else to eat at the hospital, only jam, the same blackberry jam that he had been pressing on her at home and which he now pressed on her every time he came to visit . . . could it be . . .?

Like a jack-in-the-box, the word poison suddenly popped up into her drugged mind and, in an instinctive gesture of revulsion, she threw the spoon across the room.

Instantly, she was repentant. It was simply too silly. She was compensating, trying to find a scapegoat, someone to blame because she was dying. She was suspecting Siegfried without grounds . . .

And yet, he was a chemist, wasn't he? He did have knowledge of all sorts of poisons and he did have access to them too, didn't he? As the head of his department at the school, he could order any chemical or drug he desired and it would be delivered without question and at school expense.

Curiously enough, hope was beginning to flare in Ingeborg Ruopp's heart. She had assumed that she was dying of cancer, although both her husband and her doctor had denied it, but, perhaps, Dr Weissmann had been telling the truth. It was not cancer, but something wrong with the digestive tract, something which he really did not know how to explain, but which could very easily be explained if Siegfried was feeding her some sort of subtle poison.

How fortunate that she had thought of it before it was too late!

Filled with the exhilaration of a condemned criminal who has just received news of a reprieve, Ingeborg Ruopp reached for the button which would summon a nurse.

32

"I want to speak to my doctor," she said when the nurse appeared. "Immediately. It's very urgent."

Dr Weissman was indulgent.

"Of course, Ingeborg," he said. "I can have the jam analysed. You may be quite right. There may be some substance in it that is causing your digestive troubles."

He was, of course, aware that Ingeborg Ruopp was not suffering from any digestive troubles, but rather from a cancer which had now spread to almost every organ in her body. The important thing was that she kept her spirits up and did not give way to despair and, if it would help her to face her inexorable and now rapidly approaching end, he would cheerfully order everything in the hospital to be analysed.

Ingeborg Ruopp recognized the tone of indulgence.

"I want to see the laboratory report," she said firmly. "On their official stationery and signed by the person in charge. Don't try to treat me like a child, Arnold."

"I won't, Ingeborg, I won't," said the doctor.

Forty-eight hours later, the telephone fell from his hand on to the top of his desk. The chief analyst at the state laboratory had just named such a terrible substance over the telephone that he could hardly believe what he had heard.

"Are you certain?" he had almost shouted into the phone. "Could it have got into the jam accidentally? Oh my God!"

"I would not be making the report if I were not certain," said the analyst coldly. "It is definitely 'X' and the two mice who were given it the day before yesterday are both dead. Perhaps there is some explanation as to how it came to be in the blackberry jam, but, if I were you, I would immediately notify the police. As a matter of fact, we are going to whether you do or not." 'X' was, of course, not the name of the substance which the laboratory had found in Ingeborg Ruopp's jam, but it was the only name that would be given, even to the police.

"It is an extremely potent carcinogen," said Dr Weissmann, making his report behind closed doors in the office of Inspector Gottlob Foerster of the Criminal Investigations Department of the Ulm Police. "Taken internally, it will unfailingly produce cancer of the liver even if the amount is very small. Moreover, it is very rapidly excreted by the body. A post-mortem would probably show no trace of it unless it was performed immediately after death."

The inspector stared silently at him as if he thought that he was insane. He was an elderly man, a year from retirement, with snow-white hair and rather kindly, blue eyes, now wide with shock. The inspector had seen and heard some frightful things during his career as a criminal investigations officer, but nothing to compare to this.

"If I understand you correctly," he said after a long moment's pause, "you are saying that Dr Ruopp has deliberately attempted to murder his wife by infecting her with cancer."

"Not attempted," said the doctor. "If he is responsible for the 'X' in that blackberry jam or if he has knowledge of its presence in the jam, then he has already murdered her as surely as if she were lying in the cemetery at this moment. The cancer has spread throughout her body. Nothing can save her."

"Is this a substance that is commonly present in nature?" said the inspector. "Could it have come into the jam in some innocent manner?"

"In none that I can imagine," said the doctor. "It is not present in nature and, as its effects are well known, it is not available to everyone by any means. No responsible person would even reveal the name to a layman. 'X' is simply too dangerous."

"The perfect murder weapon," said the inspector slowly. "Something which kills by a common disease and leaves no trace in the body. However, I do not think that it is as dangerous as you say."

"Why not?" said the doctor in astonishment.

"There cannot be very many people in this world who are capable of condemning another person to a slow, painful death by cancer," said the inspector. "I have spent my life dealing with criminals. If Professor Ruopp has actually done what you accuse him of, he is the most inhuman monster that I have ever come across."

The doctor attempted to say something, apparently failed

34

to find the words, got abruptly to his feet and left the office. He knew Siegfried Ruopp well.

He also knew what it meant to die of cancer.

So too did the inspector's personnel assistant, Detective-Sergeant Ede Pochert. An earnest, hard-working young man with medium brown hair, brown eyes and an athletic build, he was being groomed to take over the inspector's job when he retired.

"It should be easy enough to trace," he said when the inspector had concluded his account of what he had been told by Dr Weissmann. "A substance as dangerous as that would only be available from a few places and they would surely keep a record of their sales. I expect that I can find out within a few hours whether Professor Ruopp actually bought or had access to any of the stuff, either privately or through the school. The trouble is, how am I going to identify it to the suppliers if I don't know the name?"

"Dr Weissmann said that if you refer to it as Substance 'X', anyone who has a right to know what it is would realize what you were talking about," said the inspector.

"Substance 'X'," repeated the detective-sergeant, making a note. "Anything else?"

"Yes," said the inspector. "So far, you and I are the only ones except Dr Weissmann and the chief of the analysis laboratory who know anything about this. It's to remain that way. Not a word to anyone. Professor Ruopp is a prominent man and a respected academician. At the moment, all the evidence we possess is that the laboratory found this substance, which they say produces cancer, in the jam. There may be a perfectly logical explanation as to how it got there and it may have nothing to do with Professor Ruopp. After all, Mrs Ruopp is in a hospital and it is at least possible that the substance was accidentally introduced into the jam there."

"We would also need a motive," said the sergeant, nodding in understanding.

"You can begin to look for that once you have determined that Professor Ruopp had access to substance 'X'," said the inspector. "If he did not or, if we are unable to prove it, I doubt that we have a case."

The police did, however, have a case.

"The first purchase was in November 1975," the sergeant reported later, reading from his notes. "Thirty grams. There was a second purchase of thirty grams in June 1976 and a final purchase of twenty-five grams in May of this year. Total cost, £34.50. Paid by the school, of course."

"Did the supplier give you any indication of what these quantities mean in lethal terms?" said the inspector.

"He said it was enough to give every man, woman and child in Ulm cancer," said the sergeant. "It makes me feel sick. Doesn't it you?"

"Yes," said the inspector. "It makes you wonder how many other homicidal maniacs with academic titles are running around loose and, perhaps, thinking about dumping something like that in the public water supply. Were you able to establish a motive?"

"Two," said the sergeant. "The first one is named Annegret Beuchert. Twenty-four years old, and very pretty. She's a teacher at the Schubart school, a colleague of Professor Ruopp's. They are also associated more intimately on a non-professional basis."

"Since some time in 1975, I suppose?" said the inspector. "And the others?"

"Since the summer of 1975," said the sergeant, nodding. "The professor has had a number of other close female friends over the years, mostly students from his classes, but he appears to have regarded his affair with Miss Beuchert more seriously."

"I have the impression that you are not much taken with Professor Ruopp," said the inspector. "You mentioned a second motive?"

"I am not," said the sergeant drily. "The second motive was provided by Mrs Ruopp herself. In 1968, she fell madly in love with a Dr Andreas Boltzer who was also married. This was in Dietenheim, down to the south of here and there was a terrible scandal. Both Boltzer and Mrs Ruopp were supposed to be getting divorced from their respective spouses so that they could marry, but then Boltzer was killed in a car accident and that was the end of it."

"Was it really an accident?" said the inspector.

36

"It was really an accident," said the sergeant. "I've seen the traffic police report. He was a notoriously fast driver and he was trying to take a curve at ninety miles an hour which the tests showed cannot be negotiated at any speed over seventy-five. He was alone in the car and there was no mechanical failure."

"Well, it seems to me that we have enough concerning the substance 'X' and the probable motives to proceed to an arrest," said the inspector. "Pick him up. Caution him on his rights. Let him have his lawyer, if he wants, and try to keep this out of the newspapers for the moment. I'll be interested in hearing what he has to say."

"So will I," said the sergeant. "What do we charge him with? Mrs Ruopp is still alive."

"True," said the inspector. "The only charge we can bring now is attempted murder. Once she is dead, of course, we can bring a second charge of murder."

Professor Doktor Ruopp was arrested and brought to police headquarters where he emphatically denied that he had anything whatsoever to do with his wife's cancer.

He also denied knowing that substance 'X' was capable of producing cancer.

He could not deny having had it in his possession as his name was on the order forms to the supplier as well as on the vouchers by means of which he had claimed reimbursement from the school.

"It was merely one of a large number of interesting substances which I purchased routinely for experimentation in my chemistry classes," he said. "I did not know that it was a carcinogen. There may well be many other substances which I have purchased for my classes over the years which are also carcinogens. There are, I am sure, many chemicals that are poisonous in the school laboratory, but that does not mean that I obtained them to poison my wife."

"Nor was your wife poisoned," said the inspector. "She was given a substance which was far worse, for it will inevitably bring about her death by cancer, something more terrible than any poison."

He was attempting to arouse feelings of remorse and guilt in the professor, but he was not having the slightest success.

Dr Ruopp remained calm, unmoved, the detached, objective scientist to the last.

Asked to account for the presence of the cancer-producing agent in the blackberry jam which he had made himself, he said that it must have got into the jam accidentally. He had brought a quantity of the substance home to use in cleaning the algae out of his goldfish pond and some of the household utensils might have become contaminated with it. He had not exercised any special care as he had not known that it was a cancer-producing agent.

The professor was a logical man and he was also able to provide some confirmation of his statements.

He had, indeed, not only applied substance 'X' to the algae in his goldfish pond, but had brought his class home to demonstrate the efficiency of the treatment.

It had been extremely efficient. Within less than three minutes after the addition of a minute quantity of the chemical to the water, every fish in the pond was dead.

The students who had been present at the demonstration reported that the professor had been mildly embarrassed and had muttered something about the amount being too large.

To the horror of everyone concerned with the case, the professor had told his students quite casually the name of the substance and its composition. He had not mentioned that it was particularly dangerous.

The case came to trial in April 1978 with Professor Ruopp still protesting his innocence and his wife in the intensive care unit of the university clinic. He had the best legal counsel that could be obtained in Germany at any price and his defence was simple.

He had not known that substance 'X' was a cancer-producing agent. He had not deliberately introduced it into the jam which he had been feeding his wife, even after her admission to the hospital. He had no idea how it had got there.

The prosecution proceeded to tear this defence to shreds.

Expert witnesses were produced who testified that Dr Ruopp could not possibly have a doctorate in chemistry without knowing what substance 'X' was and what its effects were.

They pointed out that the substance was so lethal that at least one researcher had lost his life when a tiny quantity was spilled without his knowledge on the floor of the laboratory.

They described his use of the substance in the goldfish pond as the height of irresponsibility and pointed out that, had any of the household utensils become contaminated with it, as the professor suggested, the entire Ruopp family would be suffering from terminal cancer by now, which they were not.

Medical testimony was then introduced which showed that Mrs Ruopp's condition and the course of her illness could only be explained if she had been given extremely small doses of the substance over a considerable period of time. A larger dose would have killed her more quickly, but would have left traces of the substance in her body which might have been detected had a post-mortem been ordered immediately following her death.

The reason for this procedure, said the prosecution, was that Professor Ruopp had known that substance 'X' was quickly excreted from the body and, with such small amounts, a post-mortem would have shown nothing.

Although Professor Ruopp never accepted the slightest responsibility for his wife's eventual death and although the charge was only attempted murder, in the minds of the jury the crime was obviously murder and on April 13, 1978, they found him guilty as charged with no extenuating circumstances. He was sentenced to life imprisonment with the stipulation that he never be considered for early release on any grounds.

Three months later, as Professor Doktor Ruopp celebrated his fifty-first birthday in his prison cell, Mrs Ingeborg Ruopp died in great pain.

She was, perhaps, the only woman in criminal history to have been mainly instrumental in the solution of her own murder and to have been a witness to the conviction and imprisonment of her murderer.

THREE

A PERFECT MURDER

It was around September 8, 1975, when forty-four-year-old Frank Bayle left town, and there were few who knew him who had not been expecting it.

Almost everybody in Swansea, the Welsh town located where the Bristol Channel opens out into the grey reaches of the Atlantic, knew that Bayle had been having an outrageously public affair with pretty, twenty-four-year-old Doreen Soupton, his secretary at the import-export office which he was the head of, and when Doreen left it was only logical that Frank would leave too.

It was hard on his forty-three-year-old wife, Blodwen Bayle, of course, but not as hard as the loss of her first husband had been. His name had been John Carsfeld and he had been crushed to death beneath a truckload of stones while at work.

That had been on May 3, 1957, and he had left his wife penniless with three young daughters to support. The oldest, Susan, had been two, Sarah was one, and baby Sheila had been only six months old at the time of their father's death.

Blodwen had done the only thing that she could do. She had moved in with her parents, Paul and Rosaly Morgan, and, in the end, this had proved to be something of a blessing in disguise for a close friend of the Morgan family who came to dinner twice and three times a week was Frank Bayle.

Frank Bayle would have been a great catch for any girl. He was big, charming, handsome, well-built, single and rich. An astute businessman, he was also getting steadily richer.

Blodwen was a beautiful woman of twenty-two, but she

was the mother of three small children and she was, of course, in mourning for her late husband.

Nonetheless, Frank found her so attractive that he left whatever other irons he had in the fire at the time and devoted himself to her courtship.

A little surprisingly perhaps, considering Blodwen's circumstances, this did not turn out to be an easy conquest. The widow remained in mourning for over a year and it was not until January 1959 that she and Frank Bayle finally married.

Despite Frank's good looks, some people thought that she had married him more to provide her children with a father and a source of income than for her own pleasure.

However, the marriage had been a great success by any standards. Frank was fond of the little girls and he was a good and generous father to them. In fact, Susan, Sarah and Sheila, of whom only Susan could remember anything of their real father at all, soon came to regard him as their father in every sense and there was many a happy romp and roughhouse with "Daddy".

The girls were sent to good schools, Blodwen had everything she could ask for in the way of material comfort and Frank was consistently warm, loving and attentive. An ideal marriage.

Except for one thing.

The passage of time.

As Frank and his wife left their twenties, passed through their thirties and began to approach the magic and fatal age of forty, it became apparent that Frank's taste in women had changed but little.

He had liked women in their early twenties when he married Blodwen; he liked women in their early twenties now.

Precisely when he began taking young mistresses is not known nor is the name of the first, but there were certainly several, mostly in succession, but apparently with some overlapping and, curiously, with each succeeding affair becoming a little less discreet.

Eventually, of course, Blodwen had learned of her husband's romantic adventures, but there was not a great deal that she could do about them. The only problem was that she was getting older and there was no way that she could reverse that process. In the meantime Frank remained a good husband, a good provider and an affectionate and generous father. If he found his sexual needs better served by younger women, then perhaps he should be allowed his affairs. Blodwen did not have a jealous nature.

As a matter of fact, she had a remarkably submissive nature and appeared actually to enjoy domination by her male partner, an attitude which would have got her kicked out of the women's liberation movement, had it then existed, and had it ever occurred to her to join it in the first place.

She did not give the impression of being exceptionally passionate or temperamental. Rather, she was a grave, quiet person whose emotions and reactions could best be described as mild. She was a devoted mother.

Her reaction to the desertion of her husband was, therefore, predictable and seemed to bear out the comments made at the time of the marriage – that she had married more to provide her children with a father than herself with a husband.

She found it a puzzling and shameful thing that a man of Frank's age, happily married and the head of a not inconsiderable family, should run off with a woman young enough to be his daughter, and she was much embarrassed by the whole business. She did not, however, appear to be heartbroken and she made no effort to recover her erring spouse.

"As a matter of fact," she told her vicar, Rev. Thomas Richardson, a man as grave and dignified as herself, "I'm not sure that it would be best for the girls if he did come back. It's not really a good example, you know, and then, I suppose he'd only run off again after a time."

The vicar was inclined to agree. Like anyone else with ears in Swansea, he had heard a good deal about Frank Bayle's amorous exploits and the man was hardly a good example for three young girls.

Or anyone else, for that matter. On the other hand, there were the financial considerations . . . The vicar enquired delicately as to what Blodwen's financial situation was

42

and was relieved to learn that her second husband had left her a great deal better off than the first. Nearly everything, it seemed, had been under joint ownership and Frank had left most of it behind. Probably, confident of his business abilities and, perhaps, even a little conscious of his duty towards his family, he had decided to start from scratch with the young Miss Soupton.

Who, the vicar reflected, must still be Miss Soupton as neither Frank nor Blodwen had filed for divorce.

That was, however, a legal consideration, and the vicar's domain lay more in the ethical and moral aspects of the affair as well as in providing comfort to the abandoned wife.

This he did, but apparently with not very much success for Blodwen's visits to the church continued and actually increased in frequency. Although she did not appear to be actually sorrowful, Frank's desertion of his family seemed to prey on her mind so that she could find no peace. By the spring 1978 she was coming to see the vicar almost every day.

On all of these occasions, it was the vicar who did most of the talking. Blodwen had little to say, listening quietly to his words of comfort, thanking him and then going home. She would, he knew by now, be back shortly, but there was nothing that he could say to her that he had not already said many times.

However, April 6, 1978, a Thursday, was different.

Instead of quietly listening to the vicar's reassurances that it was undoubtedly all for the best and, unquestionably if inexplicably, God's will, she sat tensely bolt-upright on her chair, squeezed her hands into delicate fists and blurted out that something was bothering her.

The vicar, who was quite aware of this, but slightly puzzled as to why she saw fit to reiterate it now and with such obvious agitation, suppressed a sigh and ventured that it was hard for a woman still young and left alone in the prime of life . . .

It was possible that he thought Blodwen's distress a result of some new romantic inclination which, as she was still married to Frank and a very moral woman, could result in nothing but frustration for all parties concerned, but she ignored the remark and produced the flat statement that

Frank Bayle was the greatest swine that God had ever created.

The vicar, who was an educated man and knew something about the great swine of history, did not contradict her, but raised his eyebrows in silent, noncommittal inquiry.

Blodwen had, it seemed, reached a sort of psychological breaking point where she was so impelled by the need to pour out all the festering putrescence which had collected in her mind that she would probably have confided in the postman if the vicar had not been available.

Frank, she said, had had nothing on his mind except sex from the moment he saw her at her parent's home. Although her husband had been dead less than three months and she was still in deep mourning, he had immediately begun to court her in a disgustingly passionate manner.

She had not been able to avoid him because he was a family friend of her parents, had eaten there frequently and, following her arrival, had even started spending nights at the house.

Her parents, she added, had known that he was courting her and had approved, regarding him as a highly suitable husband for her.

On January 16, 1958, only a little more than eight months after her husband's death, said Blodwen, who appeared to have a vivid recollection of the exact dates of the events, Frank had come to her room during the night and had subjected her to sexual intercourse.

The startled vicar asked if she meant against her will – had she been literally raped in her own parents home?

Blodwen did not answer directly, leaving the impression that, if she had not exactly approved of the proceedings, she had not resisted very vigorously either.

The correct term was submission. She had submitted and, in so doing, had apparently made a virtual slave of herself to the auburn-haired businessman.

Frank had understood the relationship very well and had presumably delighted in it. He had given her strict orders that from that day on she was never to wear underclothes and he had made frequent tactile and visual checks, sometimes even when she was clearing the dishes off the table in her parents' presence. He had been clever, she said, and they had noticed nothing.

All this time, he had been pressing her to marry him, pointing out that he was wealthy and that he could give her children a good home, but, although they were now engaging in almost daily sexual intercourse, she had refused, considering the time following her husband's death to be too short for a new marriage to be entered into with propriety. It had only been in January 1959, more than a year and a half after becoming a widow, that she had married Frank Bayle.

This was, to say the least, a bewildering account as, far from showing Bayle up as "the greatest swine ever created", it provided a picture of a man who, if sexually obsessed with the young widow and, perhaps, a trifle impetuous, had had nothing but the most honourable intentions. He had asked her to marry him even before the night of January 16, 1958, when he had come to her room for their initial sexual encounter.

The only explanation was that Blodwen had found Frank utterly repulsive, but had married him partially because of her submissive nature and partially to provide a good home and education for her children, but, when the vicar hinted at this, she said that she had loved him after the marriage when she had come to know him better.

The vicar, still striving to comprehend the seeming contradictions in her statements, suggested that Frank's later affairs with young women must have been extremely painful for her, but found himself once again mistaken when Blodwen said that she had not liked it but had found it understandable. She was, she was forced to admit, getting older. Frank liked young women. He had never suggested divorce, not even in the case of Doreen Soupton. The affairs had been distasteful and embarrassing, but they had not really hurt her.

She paused and, after several minutes, said that Frank's relations with her had been embarrassing in any case. He had been in the habit of requiring sex from her at almost any time and in any place which was, she supposed, the reason he had not wanted her to wear underwear.

She fell silent again and seemed to be trying to formulate

45

what she wanted to say next. Whatever it was that was troubling her, she had obviously not yet been able to talk about it.

The vicar said nothing. To begin with, there was nothing that he could think of to say, and secondly, he was not a little bemused at what the citizens of Swansea would have thought had they known that the highly respectable Mrs Blodwen Bayle was running around without a stitch on under her dress and engaging in sex with her husband at odd times and in odd corners.

"Sheila was eighteen in 1975," said Blodwen abruptly and without preamble. "She is my youngest."

The vicar nodded gravely. He knew Sheila and he knew her sisters.

"On June 7, that year," continued Blodwen, apparently now launched on the subject which she had been trying all along to bring to voice, "she came home in the evening and said that she felt ill.

"She went up to her room to go to bed and I followed her. I asked if I should call the doctor."

"She said no, that the doctor could not help and then, after a little time, she said that she believed herself to be pregnant.

"I was shocked. I know that it is common in this day and age for girls to have sex at her age, but it had never occurred to me that my daughters would be so foolish.

"I began to reproach her and she became hysterical and cried out that it was not her fault.

"I thought that she meant she had been raped, which would have been bad enough, but what she then actually told me was so terrible that I could have wished that she had been raped instead.

"She said that one afternoon in March she had been in the upstairs bathroom having a shower. She had thought that she was alone in the house, but while she was still in the shower, Frank came into the bathroom to wash his hands.

"She was not startled because she looked upon him as her father and he had often seen her and her sisters in the nude The bathroom door was never locked and it was quite common for some other member of the family to come in when one or another of us was taking a bath.

46

"Frank had joked with her as he had always done since she was a little girl and had put his hand over the shower head so that it squirted a stream of water into her face.

"Sheila had jumped out of the shower and had stood there naked and laughing without thinking anything about it and, all of a sudden, Frank had grabbed her and had begun to do things to her.

"As I know from personal experience, he understood everything about arousing a woman and he so aroused Sheila that she did not resist when he laid her down on the bathroom floor and subjected her to sexual intercourse for the first time.

"She thought now that she was pregnant as a result of this.

"I was so thunderstruck by this story that I stammered out that it could not be true, that she was saying this only to cover up a liaison with some young man she knew.

"Sheila cried torrents, swore that it was true and then said that her sisters could confirm it.

"I did not see how they possibly could, but I immediately questioned them about it, telling them what Sheila had said and that she thought she was pregnant by Frank.

"When they heard this, they both broke down and said that the same thing had happened to them. Both Susan and Sarah, when they reached the age of eighteen, had been seduced by the monster.

"And not only that. He had continued to have sex with them right up until then, even while he was carrying on affairs with other women.

"And finally, worst of all, he was having sex with them in an abnormal and unnatural manner. He was afraid that they would get pregnant. With Sheila, he had apparently been carried away and had lost control of himself."

The vicar was so shocked and astounded by this recital that he leaped to his feet and began pacing nervously up and down, unable to bring out a word.

"But the police . . .!" he stammered finally. "You should have gone to the police . . .! He couldn't . . . It's illegal . . ."

"Not at all," said Blodwen. "It wasn't incest. He wasn't their father. And he waited until they were eighteen. They weren't even minors. Oh, they could probably have charged him with something, but what would that have done to Susan, Sarah and Sheila? The whole town would have known. Frank was clever. There wasn't anything I could do, not even stop him continuing his dirty games, without harming the girls far more than him."

"But you confronted him?" said the vicar. "You demanded that he cease his relations with your daughters?"

Blodwen did not reply immediately, but sat looking silently down at her hands.

"No," she said finally. "I didn't say a word to him about it. It was too late for anything to be done. Susan, Sarah and Sheila were already irrevocably ruined. I thought it best if Frank did not know that I knew."

"But, my heavens!" he said. "How could you live with such a secret? You must have hated your husband. You must have felt like killing him."

Blodwen raised her head and looked clear-eyed at the vicar.

"I did," she said in a calm, even voice.

"What?" said the vicar. "You . . .?"

"I murdered Frank," said Blodwen. "It's been bothering me ever since."

"But Frank ran away with Miss Soupton," protested the vicar who was beginning to fear that his parishioner was hallucinating.

"No," said Blodwen. "Doreen Soupton simply left town to take another job. I told everyone that Frank had gone with her, but it wasn't true. Frank is lying somewhere at the bottom of the Bristol Channel. Or what is left of him by now. It's been over two and a half years."

The vicar was still not completely convinced that Blodwen was telling the truth. She did not look in the least like a murderess and she was not a large woman. How could she have murdered the big, powerful Frank? And, even if she had, how could she have managed to transport the body to the Bristol Channel and throw it in?

What seemed more probable was that she had, understandably under the circumstances, wanted to murder her husband, had thought a great deal about murdering her

48

husband and had ended by convincing herself that she had murdered her husband, his absence making it possible to sustain the illusion.

As a matter of fact, the whole story could be nothing but a pathological reaction to Frank's desertion of his family. Hurt and unable to accept reality, she had built up a picture of her husband as a totally inhuman monster, guilty of the worst crimes which she could imagine.

It was quite possible that Frank had never laid anything other than a fatherly hand on the girls and that he was now living happily somewhere in England with Doreen Soupton.

The vicar devoutly hoped that this was so, but he had to know the truth and one way to find out was to talk to the girls. If they denied that their stepfather had made any improper advances towards them, then there was probably nothing to the story of the murder either. After all, if nothing had taken place with the daughters, then there would have been no motive for murder.

To the vicar's very great dismay, Susan, Sarah and Sheila confirmed their mother's story about their sexual relations to Frank in every detail.

They did not confirm what she had said about murdering him and all three believed that he had gone off with Doreen Soupton in September 1975, or so it seemed as the vicar did not repeat what Blodwen had told him concerning this and merely asked if they had any idea where Frank was now.

None of them did, other than that it was probably in whatever place Doreen Soupton had gone to, but no one seemed to know where that was.

The vicar had no recourse. He had to know if Frank Bayle was still alive and there was no one in a position to determine this other than the police.

The vicar went to the police, not with Blodwen's story of having murdered Frank, but with a request to help him locate the missing man. There were certain family matters which had to be cleared up, said the vicar.

As might be expected, the police had very little difficulty in locating Doreen Soupton who, as Blodwen had said, had merely left the area to take up a better job and had had no reason to conceal anything about the move.

However, Frank Bayle was not with her and she told a member of the Department of Criminal Investigations that she had not seen him since leaving Swansea on September 9, 1975. She had assumed that he was still there and with his family.

There was no missing person report on Frank Bayle with the police and the information provided by Doreen Soupton was simply passed on to the vicar with no further investigation being undertaken.

However, the vicar was now convinced that Blodwen really had murdered her husband and that the only thing that she could do was to go to the police and confess to it.

He told her this and she immediately agreed. She had wanted to confess to the crime almost from the time it had taken place, she said, but as she assumed that she would receive a long prison sentence for it, she had not wanted to leave her daughters with no parents at all.

In addition, she was afraid that the truth concerning Frank's sexual dealings with them would become known and, she thought, make their lives difficult or impossible.

The vicar replied that the girls were now all in their twenties and that, in any case, no blame could be attributed to them. They had been debauched by their stepfather and were as innocent of any wrongdoing as if they had been raped by a total stranger.

None of them had become pregnant, not even Sheila whose supposed pregnancy had turned out to be a false alarm.

Blodwen then accompanied him to police headquarters where she presented the startled chief of the Swansea murder squad with the solution of a murder before he even knew that there had been one.

In her confession, she said that she had determined to murder her husband immediately that she learned of the corruption of her daughters at his hands, but that she had not been able to find a suitable opportunity.

She did not want to be caught because the subsequent publicity would have destroyed the girls and, in addition, they would have been left completely alone while she went to jail.

50

From June 7 to the first week of September 1975 she had waited patiently and relentlessly for the chance to kill her husband without detection and it had finally come when she learned that Doreen Soupton was to leave town on September 8.

There were many people, she knew, who were aware that Frank was having an extremely passionate affair with his secretary. What more reasonable than that he should go with her when she left? It was the perfect time for him to disappear without arousing anyone's suspicions.

Actually, according to Doreen Soupton's later statement on the matter, Frank Bayle had never for a moment considered leaving town to go with her. He was fond of affairs with young women, but he had had no intention of getting himself involved in a divorce case or leaving his wife or, for reasons now obvious, his stepdaughters.

On Monday, September 8, 1975, Blodwen had bought a bottle of fifty sleeping tablets from her usual chemist and had arranged matters so that there would be no one but she and Frank in the house that evening.

She had then served him his favourite dinner, accompanied by a bottle of excellent wine.

The fifty sleeping tablets had been dissolved in it.

Frank had fallen asleep almost immediately after dinner and, when she was quite certain that nothing would wake him, she had taken a pillow and held it pressed firmly over his face until he died of suffocation.

Being a thorough woman and not wanting to take any chances, she had maintained her pressure on the cushion for nearly an hour.

Certain then that Frank was dead, she had dragged the body, inch by inch, through the house to the garage where she had, with an enormous effort, lifted it into the boot of the car.

It was by now past midnight and she had driven out of Swansea, along the road running parallel to the tops of the cliffs, south of the city.

There she had stopped the car and, with another huge effort, had rolled the body out of the boot and across the strip of grass dividing the road from the edge of the cliff.

51

A hundred feet below, the grey, surging tide, pushed by the waters of the Severn, was boiling out to the Atlantic. She had tipped the corpse over the edge, hearing the splash from below, but unable to see anything in the darkness.

She had then gone home, washed the dishes and replaced the murder weapon, the pillow, on the bed.

There was not the slightest trace of a crime. No one even suspected that Frank Bayle was dead. She had committed a perfect murder.

The confession set in motion an exhaustive check of police records dating back to 1975 in an effort to determine whether any unidentified bodies had been recovered from the Channel or the Severn and, if so, whether any of them might have been that of Frank Bayle.

As it turned out, there had been no identified bodies recovered during that period. Frank's corpse had apparently been carried out into the Atlantic and would never be seen again.

On the basis of her own confession, Blodwen Bayle was formally charged with premeditated murder and held for trial.

Regardless of how compelling her motives might have been, murder was murder and had to be prosecuted under the law.

Brought before the court, Blodwen repeated her confession precisely as she had made it to the vicar and to the police, and said that she was prepared to accept any punishment that the court might deem fit for her act. She did not regret it. Under the same circumstances, she would do the same again.

The defence pleaded extreme extenuating circumstances and reduced responsibility as a result of mental stress brought about by the actions of the victim.

Susan, Sarah and Sheila Carsfeld all testified, confirming in detail what they had told their mother concerning their sexual assaults by their stepfather.

Independent testimony was presented confirming the devotion of Blodwen Bayle to her daughters, and statements concerning Bayle's extramarital affairs were heard.

The picture was completely clear and, in the end, a highly

sympathetic court found Blodwen guilty of premeditated murder with extreme extenuating circumstances and sentenced her to two years' imprisonment. Suspended.

Blodwen Bayle left the court a free woman and to the applause of the spectators.

She had, it turned out, committed a perfect murder after all.

FOUR

TURKISH DELIGHT

It was a little after three-thirty on a Saturday afternoon
when waiter Omar Demir was awakened from his peaceful
after-lunch nap by the sound of a series of explosions.

Startled and confused, he jerked upright on the long
bench running along the wall of the restaurant and stared
about him.

The restaurant was empty, as it should be. The lunch hour
was well past and whatever customers there had been had
gone and were now presumably taking a nap somewhere
themselves.

Had it been a dream then? Had there been no sharp,
cracking sounds except in his mind?

No, it had not been a dream. He could remember very well
what he had been dreaming and it had had no explosions
in it.

Rolling off the bench, he threaded his way through the
tables to the door and peered out into the street. It was June
22, 1974, and there was not a great deal going on outside. In a
medium-sized Turkish town like Adana, the period
immediately following the noon meal is not regarded as
suitable for frenzied activity.

The sounds, it seemed, had not come from outside so they
must have come from within the building itself. Perhaps the
rafters were cracking. In any case, it was not his problem. He
would report it to the owner and let him worry about it.

Walking down the long corridor to the family quarters
where forty-two-year-old Kadir Karayigit would be having
his nap in the little office beside the kitchen, he reflected that

54

the restaurant owner might not appreciate being awakened to be informed that the rafters of his restaurant were cracking, but decided that he did not care. It was not much of a job anyway. No one ever left any tips. If Karayigit did not like it, he could look for another waiter.

Arriving at the door of the office, he saw, however, that Mr Karayigit had other and more serious problems.

Or rather, that he had no problems of any kind any more for, even at first glance, it was obvious that he was dead or, if not, very close to it.

The day was warm and Karayigit was lying on the narrow couch in nothing but his undershorts. They were white and the spreading splotches of red, largely concentrated in the crotch, showed all too plainly where the bullets had entered.

There seemed to have been a great many of them and there was one in his forehead too, just above the left eyebrow. That had, presumably, been the first one for Karayigit did not appear to have moved at all, but lay as peacefully as if he was still sleeping.

For several instants, the thunderstruck Demir stood gaping, his mouth open and his eyes bulging out of his head.

He had grown up in the quarter and he knew all about Kadir Karayigit. He was a poor restaurant owner who, since the death of his wife from tuberculosis six years earlier, did the cooking himself and not particularly well. He was too poor to rob, too poor to have any such bitter enemies that they would murder him. Practically his only claim to fame of any kind was that he was the father of three beautiful daughters.

The three beautiful daughters were, Demir knew, not at home at the moment. Sixteen-year-old Tuerkin and her thirteen-year-old sister, Labdi, had gone for a picnic with an aunt on the shores of Lake Seishun to the north of the city, and eighteen-year-old Guel Sultan no longer lived at home at all, having married her cousin, the twenty-two-year-old Fahri Guenzel, just six days earlier.

This left no one in the big, rambling building other than Omar Demir, the corpse and . . . the murderer!

Demir spun around so fast that he knocked his head against the door jamb and nearly fell over. Recovering, he raced panic-stricken down the corridor, through the restaurant and out into the street.

"Murder!" he shouted. "Help! Murder! Police!"

It had not occurred to him that he himself might be suspected of the crime and he was utterly astounded when the police arrived and took him into custody.

The Turkish police are not noted for their gentle treatment of murder suspects and Omar Demir was in a bad way by the time that Inspector Mustapha Keroglu of the Adana Police Department of Criminal Investigations arrived and suggested that it would be easier to question the suspect if he were still conscious.

He then turned Omar over to his assistant, Detective-Sergeant Ali Oeztuerk, and went back to take a look at the corpse.

He was joined there a few moments later by the Adana coroner, Dr Mahmet Degali, who carried out an examination of the body and reported that Karayigit had received seven bullet wounds in the groin and one through the head.

The head-wound had been instantly fatal and had apparently been received while he was sleeping – there were no indications that he had had any inkling of his approaching death.

The gun from which these bullets had apparently been fired was a black, 7.65 calibre automatic with a clip holding eight rounds, which lay between the dead man's legs. So far, the inspector had left it lying there as he wanted his fingerprint expert to examine it for prints before it was disturbed.

"Well?" he said when the doctor had completed his examination.

"Well, what?" said the doctor. "He was shot, murdered. You can see it yourself. The entire clip fired at close range. There are powder burns on the skin of the forehead. Time was less than an hour ago."

"I meant, well, what is your opinion?" said the inspector mildly. The exception to the rule, he was a gentle, intelligent man whose treatment of suspects would have passed muster with any human rights commission.

"All that I can suggest," said the doctor, who was short, fat and inclined to irascibility, "is that the motive was sexual jealousy. The first shot killed him. There was no need to shoot him seven times in the groin. The murderer was punishing the offending parts."

"Or murderess," said the inspector absently. "Women can fire a pistol quite as well as men and a 7.65 is not a heavy weapon."

The doctor shrugged and said nothing.

"There will have to be a post-mortem, said the inspector. "I will have the body brought to the morgue as soon as the people from the laboratory have finished with their examination of the scene."

The doctor shrugged again and left without making any further comment.

The inspector followed him out into the restaurant where the sergeant was silently smoking a cigarette and eyeing the very nervous Omar Demir.

"What does he say?" said the inspector.

"He says that he knows nothing about it," said the sergeant. "Don't you, you dog?"

"I am a poor man," whined Demir. "Why would I kill my employer? Now I am unemployed."

"To rob him?" said the inspector.

"He had hardly more than I," said Demir. "And I do not know where he kept it."

"Well, we shall see," said the inspector. "Take him to the station, Ali, and do not treat him harshly. The fingerprint expert will soon be here and, if Mr Demir's prints are on the gun, I am sure he will be reasonable and confess."

Omar Demir's fingerprints were not on the gun, however. No one's were. It had been wiped clean of everything before being thrown on to the couch between Karayigit's legs.

"At least it shows that the murderer or murderess knows what fingerprints are, and that it is possible to identify people from them," said the inspector.

"It also shows that it was someone who was familiar with the building," said the sergeant. "Mrs Guenzel says that he kept the gun in the drawer of the night table beside the couch where he was killed. Not everyone would know that it was there."

The murder weapon had been identified by all the Karayigit daughters as the property of Kadir Karayigit himself, and the Ballistics Department had reported that the bullets which had been recovered from the body by Dr Degali had been fired from it.

"I think it must have been a woman," said the inspector. "He had been a widower for six years and he was a healthy man in the prime of life. He undoubtedly took up with some woman and then, for one reason or another, attempted to break off the relationship. The woman was not in agreement and she came around and murdered him."

"You don't think that Demir had anything to do with it?" said the sergeant. "Perhaps, if we were a little more persuasive . . .?" He was substantially less gentle in his attitude towards prisoners than was his chief.

"No," said the inspector. "Demir is not clever enough to commit a murder and then run out into the street yelling, 'Murder! Police!' That would be much too sophisticated an act. You can release him."

"Then we will have no suspect at all," said the sergeant.

"The purpose of the investigation is to determine who murdered Kadir Karayigit," said the inspector. "Not to have suspects in the detention cells whether they are guilty of anything or not."

"Very well," said the sergeant. "I will have him released. What do you want me to do then?"

"Several things," said the inspector. "To begin with, put four or five of our men on to interrogating the people living in the houses near the restaurant. It is quite possible that someone saw the murderess enter or leave the building at the time that Karayigit was murdered. It may be that persons other than Demir heard the sound of the shots."

"If they only heard the shots and did not see the murderess, that would not help us," said the sergeant. "Anything else?"

"Yes," said the inspector. "Talk to the policewomen and the wives of the other members of the department and see if any of them has any connections in that area so that they could go there and listen to the gossip without arousing suspicion. If Karayigit was having an affair with some woman in the neighbourhood, there will be people who know of it and they will talk. Nothing like that can be kept secret here."

This was, of course, quite true, but before much could be assembled in the way of gossip, there was a puzzling setback to the entire investigation.

No less than three people were found who had been in a position to view the front door of the restaurant and they all swore that no one had come out at any time within the period between the shooting and the arrival of the police.

"And the back door?" said the disappointed Inspector Keroglu. Obviously, if no one had entered or left the building, then the murderer had to be Omar Demir and he had felt quite certain that the young waiter was not guilty.

"The back door was heavily barred from the inside when we arrived," said the sergeant. "The daughters and even that idiot of a waiter all say that it was always barred from the inside."

"He is not an idiot," said the inspector absently. "He is only a poor, simple boy who is now unemployed."

"He is an idiot because he did not have the sense to take the bar off the back door," said the sergeant. "Now, he is the only person who could possibly have killed Karayigit. He need not concern himself over being unemployed. He will have free board and lodging at government expense. Shall I arrest him and prepare the file for the prosecution?"

"Yes, I suppose we must," said the inspector reluctantly, "though I still find it hard to believe that he is the murderer. Make certain that there is no other entrance to the building. Perhaps the murderer was still hiding there when we arrived and only left after things had quietened down."

"That is not possible," said the sergeant. "I personally made a thorough search of the premises after you had returned to the office. There was no one in the building and there was no way that anyone could have left."

The inspector sighed. "Well, then it must be Demir," he said. "There was no one present except him and Karayigit and Karayigit certainly did not commit suicide."

There was no disputing this last statement. Even if the restaurant owner had shot himself through the head and managed in some way, possibly by holding the gun wrapped in a corner of the sheet, to avoid having his fingerprints on it, there would have been no conceivable reason for him doing such a thing.

Even more illogical, he would have had to shoot himself through the groin seven times before firing the fatal shot into his forehead. Suicide was completely out of the question.

However, murder by Omar Demir was, despite the sergeant's convictions, scarcely more logical than suicide.

To begin with, there was a total lack of motive. Kadir Karayigit's daughters knew where he kept his money and a check had shown that not a penny of it was missing, not even what had been taken in during the course of the lunch hour that day and which still lay openly in the cash drawer.

Demir had been taken into police custody immediately after the shooting and had remained in it until transferred to the station where he had been most thoroughly searched. He had had barely enough cash on him to buy two packs of cigarettes and no valuables of any kind at all.

He had since confessed several times, of course. The interrogators had been very persuasive. But, in every case, once the persuasion ceased, he retracted his confession and he invariably made a very good point which convinced the inspector, if no one else.

"Why would I shoot Karayigit and then run out into the street shouting for the police?" he demanded. "I am not mad. If I had killed him, I would have stolen everything and run out the back door. Do you think I like being questioned by the police?"

The question was so difficult to answer that, despite Demir's repeated confessions, the magistrate responsible for deciding whether he should be tried for the crime refused to issue the charge. As he knew how the confessions had been obtained he did not put very much faith in them, and there were too many other points which required clearing up.

The most important of all was the motive. It had turned out that a number of persons connected with the police had access to the gossip of the quarter and they were unanimous in what they said.

Kadir Karayigit had had no affair with any woman since

60

the death of his wife or before her death either, for that matter. He was, as a matter of fact, mildly famous for his astonishing chastity, particularly as there was no need for it now that he was a widower, and, had it not been for the obvious evidence of his virility in the form of three lovely daughters, there would have been speculation about his homosexuality.

For a time, the inspector thought that this apparent chastity might actually be the motive of the murder. The location of the seven bullets fired through the groin after death indicated a sexual motive and, although Omar Demir was not a very attractive man physically, he was young, and Kadir Karayigit might have found other uses for him than waiting on tables.

Such a sexual relationship would not have been startling or even unusual in Turkey and it would explain why Karayigit had not found it necessary to become involved with any of the local ladies.

Perhaps, reasoned the inspector, the young waiter had found his employer's attentions distasteful and had murdered him in order to free himself of them.

Demir, however, denied that any such relationship had existed and said that Kadir Karayigit might not have been the most generous employer in the world, but that all he wanted of his waiter was plenty of work and a modest appetite. If he had been providing other services of a more personal nature than waiting on tables and washing dishes, he would, he suggested, have been in better financial shape than he actually was.

This too appeared to be true. After all, Demir had not been a slave. Work was, of course, hard to find, but if he had had sufficient reasons for dissatisfaction with his job to murder his employer, he could have more easily and safely quit. This might have left him without a job, but, with Karayigit dead, he was out of a job anyway.

The investigation, therefore, hung at dead centre between two irreconcilable points.

Omar Demir had had no reason and probably no opportunity to murder Kadir Karayigit, but there had been no one else in the building to do it.

"Which can only mean one thing," said the inspector. "We are mistaken in our belief concerning one or both of these contradictory assumptions. Either Demir had a reason or he was not alone in the building."

"It would have to be that he had a reason of which we know nothing," said the sergeant. "The fact that no one entered or left the building immediately before or after the crime is dependent upon the testimony of disinterested parties, none of whom has any reason to conceal the truth."

"Assuming that they really are disinterested," said the inspector. "I think that we must take a closer look at these neighbours of Kadir Karayigit who happened to be watching the door of his restaurant so closely on the day that he was murdered. It was the period following lunch. Why weren't they sleeping?"

All the witnesses had good explanations as to why they had not been asleep at the time, and in all cases their statements could be verified. None of them had had any reason to watch the door of Karayigit's restaurant. It had merely happened that, from the place where they had been sitting, the restaurant door was in full view.

"If one of them is lying, then they are all lying," said the sergeant, "and that would mean that all of these people conspired in some way, if not to murder Karayigit, then at least to conceal the identity of the murderer from the police. I cannot believe this."

"Nor can I," said the inspector. "This is infuriating. Who reached the restaurant first following the shooting?"

"Our own men," said the sergeant. "Hassan and Mulazim. Do you want to talk to them?"

The inspector did, and the two police constables were summoned to his office. There, they repeated precisely what had appeared in their written report on the circumstances of the arrest of Omar Demir.

"When you arrived, Demir was standing outside the front door, according to your report," said the inspector. "Was there anyone in the restaurant itself or anyone near Demir?"

"No," said Mulazim, who was the senior of the two officers. "Everyone in the neighbourhood was gathered into

62

a crowd on the other side of the street, but they did not go near the restaurant because they were afraid."

"Of the murderer or of the police?" said the inspector.

"I do not know," said Mulazim. "Perhaps both. In any case, Demir was standing perhaps ten feet in front of the door and he seemed nervous. When we placed him under arrest, he began to cry."

"Did you enter the building and see the corpse?" said the inspector.

"No," said Mulazim. "Mrs Guenzel said that he was dead and that there was nothing we could do for him. She thought it best to wait for the rest of the police."

"Mrs Guenzel?" said the inspector. "You mean Karayigit's oldest daughter, the one who just got married? Where was she?"

"Inside the restaurant, sitting at the table next to the door," said Mulazim. "She was drinking wine and she looked upset."

"Fantastic!" said the inspector. "Ali, I would like to speak with Mr Demir immediately. Did he ever mention in any of his statements that Mrs Guenzel was in the restaurant at the time of the murder?"

"Never," said the sergeant, turning to the two police officers. "Did Demir see Mrs Guenzel sitting inside? Did he hear you speaking to her?"

"I don't know," said Mulazim. "Hassan was holding Demir when I went into the restaurant. I don't know whether Demir could see us talking or not."

"Mrs Guenzel was at the restaurant when we arrived," said the inspector. "I thought that she had been summoned after the shooting by the neighbours of someone. I did not realize that she had been there all the time. I am afraid that this solves our murder case."

"Afraid?" said the sergeant. "I do not understand. What does this mean?"

"I am afraid it means that Mrs Guenzel killed her own father," said the inspector. "It is the missing piece of information we were seeking. You recall that we agreed that we were either wrong about Demir having no motive or we were wrong about their being no one else present? Well, here

63

is the answer. Someone else was present. Mrs Guenzel, Karayigit's oldest daughter. No one remarked on her going in or out of the house because she was a member of the family and, up to a week ago, she was living there. It was natural that she would be going in and out of her own home. All the witnesses were thinking of a stranger."

Omar Demir immediately confirmed that Guel Sultan, the oldest of the three girls, had been at the restaurant on the day in question, although he did not know whether she had been there at the time of the murder or not. He had not seen her leave, but she could easily have done so when he was busy with the customers or in the kitchen.

"But Dr Degali said that the motive was sexual," said the sergeant. "What possible sexual motive could the girl have had to murder her father?"

"She was just married," said the inspector. "Six days after her marriage, her father was murdered. This is not a coincidence. I think that she may have been the person who pulled the trigger, but I think that someone else is responsible."

"Who?" said the sergeant, who was finding himself in considerably over his depth.

"Her husband and cousin, Fahri Guenzel," said the inspector. "I am afraid that he learned on his wedding night that his bride was not the virgin that he had expected. A father is responsible for the purity of his daughters until they are married and no doubt he felt that Karayigit had swindled him by passing off so to speak secondhand goods for new."

"I have heard of murders for such reasons," said the sergeant slowly. "It is possible, but why did Guenzel not murder him himself?"

"Because he would have been too easily found out," said the inspector. "People would have seen him entering or leaving the restaurant. His wife would not be noticed because she belonged there, and perhaps he demanded that she carry out the murder as a proof of her loyalty and her repentance."

"He was right, too," said the sergeant. "No one mentioned Mrs Guenzel because she was too obvious. What now?"

"Arrest both her and Guenzel," said the inspector.

64

"Question them separately and play off their statements, one against the other. It should not take too long to extract the truth."

The inspector's estimation was quite correct. Guel Sultan Guenzel had already confessed to the murder of her father before she even arrived at police headquarters.

Her confession was, however, substantially different from what the inspector had been expecting.

"He was a monster!" sobbed Guel, sitting curled up like a terrified small animal in the chair in front of the inspector's desk, and weeping torrents. "Death was too good for him! He should rot for a thousand eternities in hell!"

The inspector was bewildered.

"But everyone who knew your family described the relations of your father to his children as extremely warm," he said.

"Extremely warm! Much too warm!" shrieked Guel. "He ruined me! He took my virginity! I had already suspected it and then, when we found on our wedding night that I was not pure, I knew the truth. There was nothing I could do but kill him."

"Your husband demanded it of you?" said the inspector. "What was your father doing? Selling you to the customers?"

"Fahri knew nothing of what I was going to do," said Guel. "He suspects now of course, but I told him nothing before. Father did not sell me to the customers. It was worse than that. He took me himself!"

"You mean your father forced you to have sex with him?" said the inspector, horrified. "Why didn't you tell someone? Why didn't you go to the police?"

Guel had not gone to the police, she said, because she had not been sure and she had feared the disgrace if such a thing became known. Like many people, she had ignored reality because she was unwilling to face it. If nothing were done, perhaps it would go away.

In any case, she had never been conscious when her father had intercourse with her.

Shortly after the death of her mother, he had begun to make a practice of giving her a glass or two of strong, sweet wine after the evening meal. As she was only thirteen at the time, she had invariably become drunk and had passed out.

On the next morning, she had found herself undressed and in her bed, and she assumed that her father had put there. She had thought this only natural and it had not occurred to her that, like many girls of her age, she was physically fully developed. The thought that her father might be entertaining sexual feelings towards her never crossed her mind.

Then, however, a number of things had arisen which puzzled and alarmed her and, in the end, aroused her suspicions.

On the mornings following her excessive drinking of wine, she had experienced soreness and an irritation of the genital area and there had been a sort of discharge which had worried her greatly. Finally, on one or two occasions she had come to in the middle of the night and had found herself naked and not in her own bed, but in her father's.

She had demanded an explanation from him and he had told her that he too had drunk too much wine on the preceding evening and had passed out while trying to put her to bed.

"I think I have really known for a long time what he was doing," she told the inspector, "but I did not want it to be true so I shut my mind to it. It was only on my wedding night when we discovered that I was not a virgin that I was forced to accept the truth."

"There could be another explanation," said the inspector. "You did not lose your virginity to your father, but to one of the young men in the neighbourhood. When this could not be concealed from your husband, you decided to place the blame on your father and in order to convince your husband that you were telling the truth, you murdered him for something which he did not do."

Guel Sultan shook her head sadly. "It is not true," she said. "I wish it were true for I don't think I am the only one to suffer from our father's unnatural desires. You should have Tuerkim and Labdi examined by the doctor. I am afraid that you will find they are no more virgins than I."

They were not. An examination of the two girls showed that neither was a virgin and, confronted with their sister's statement, both admitted that they had undergone almost exactly the same treatment.

As each girl arrived at the age of thirteen, their father had begun to ply them with sweet, heavy wine after the evening meal and both reported awakening in the morning with sore and inflamed genitals and traces of some strange discharge.

Both had also had the experience of waking up during the night in their father's bed and Labdi, whose initiation had begun less than three months before the murder, said that when she had come to on one occasion, her father had been lying on top of her. He had said that he was doing it because the night was cool and he wanted to keep her warm, but the night had not been cool at all.

The inspector was now convinced that Guel Sultan was telling the truth, but he wanted to be certain that the court would also believe her and very extensive interrogation of the young men and boys in the neighbourhood was undertaken to determine whether the Karayigit girls were known to have engaged in sexual relations with any of the male residents of the quarter.

The results were conclusive. All three Karayigit girls enjoyed unblemished reputations. Their father was known as a strictly moral man who did not allow the women of his family the slightest contact with any male who was not a blood relative.

In September 1974 Guel Sultan was brought to trial, charged with premeditated murder. She was given a five-year suspended sentence and sent home to her husband who had remained loyal to her throughout the proceedings.

Her sisters now live with her, but the family has moved to another part of Turkey where nothing of their history is known.

FIVE

INTERNATIONAL YOUTH CONTACTS

As with practically every other place in the world enjoying
the five-day working week, Friday evening is a time for
rejoicing in the city of Pirmasens, West Germany. Many
people have collected their pay and the whole, long, glorious
weekend stretches ahead.

Washed but still wearing his work overalls, twenty-year-
old Gerhard Langdoll pushed through the door of the Café
Strecker, where he frequently stopped after work for a beer,
with a feeling of pleased anticipation. For no reason he was
convinced that the coming weekend was going to be exciting
and different.

And no sooner was he inside the door than there came
immediate confirmation, for there, in the far corner of the
taproom, sat two old friends whom he had not seen in years,
not, as a matter of fact, since he had left secondary school to
take his motor-mechanic's training while they went on to
university. They would not, of course, be finished yet. Like
himself, Peter Melchert and Achim Arnstädt were twenty
years old and few people graduate from a German university
at twenty.

"Peter! Achim!" yelled Gerhard in delight. Although the
three youths came from very different family circumstances
(Peter being the son of a high ranking police official and
Achim the son of an engineer), they had been close friends,
partly because of their common interest in motorcycles and
cross-country racing.

"Gerhard!" shouted Achim and Peter as one man, rising
to their feet and literally dragging him to the table. "My
God! You old sod! Where have you been?"

Gerhard had, of course, been right in Pirmasens and it was Peter and Achim who had been away at university. He noticed they had changed very little, although Peter, who had always been tall and athletically built, now stood well over six feet and Achim sported a rather straggly moustache.

So too, did Gerhard, although it was black and neatly trimmed. His hair was also a good deal shorter than his old friends', but then, he had always been a rather small, neat sort of person.

Beer was ordered and the renewing of old ties and associations began, but there was not too much said about what the three had been doing since they had last seen each other. Gerhard did not think that the others would be interested in his work at the garage and they apparently found their university studies equally boring for little was said of them.

And this was right and good, for who wanted to talk about jobs and studies when there was a whole weekend ahead? It was not long before the three friends had decided what they were going to do.

"We'll go to France!" roared Peter. "That's the place to have a good time!"

"France! France!" bellowed Achim, and Gerhard joined in.

"I'll have to go home and change first, though," he said, getting to his feet.

"To hell with that!" cried the others. "Come the way you are. We're not going to be there long."

Gerhard allowed himself to be persuaded. The French border lies only some five miles to the south of Pirmasens and the three had often taken trips there when they were still at school. It was going to be an exciting weekend, although, from the point of view of weather, it was scarcely ideal vacation time.

That Friday was, as a matter of fact, February 9, 1979, and this being the very heart of the central European winter, it was cloudy, grey, dank, chilly and sufficiently depressing that anyone with less high spirits than three twenty-year-old Germans would have been more inclined to suicide than weekend junkets.

The party set off at six o'clock in Achim's red Fiat and, after crossing the border at the unguarded frontier post of Schweix, arrived in the little French town of Bitche before the shops had even closed.

Peter and Achim, it seemed, had plenty of cash for they bought a dozen bottles of the best Burgundy that they could lay their hands on and, to Gerhard's astonishment, a twelve-gauge shotgun and a box of fifty shells loaded with buckshot.

"What do you want that for?" said Gerhard in wonder.

"Target practice," said Achim laconically.

And he was as good as his word. With Peter at the wheel and Gerhard in the back seat he blazed away out of the passenger side window with the shotgun at everything they passed – dogs, cats, chickens, the windows of houses and, where the road ran parallel to a canal, the passing barges.

The target practice made Gerhard a little uneasy, but the third bottle of the heavy red wine was already making the rounds and he was less inclined to caution than he would normally have been. In any case, Achim was not much of a marksman and so far he did not seem to have hit anything living although a few windows had been shot out.

What made Gerhard more uneasy was how far they were getting from Pirmasens. The Fiat was fast and Peter drove with his foot flat to the floorboards so that they were, by ten that evening, already a good many miles to the south.

"Look fellas," said Gerhard, "I don't want to break things up or anything, but I gotta be at work on Monday morning."

"You gotta be at work?" said Achim. "What about me? I gotta be back at the barracks. I only got a weekend pass."

It was the first intimation Gerhard had that Achim was not at the university any longer, but apparently performing his compulsory military service.

"Don't worry, we'll get you back in time for your job," whooped Peter. "God Almighty! It's not even Saturday yet."

It was getting close to it, however, and at a little after midnight, rendered drowsy more by wine than weariness, Peter pulled the car into a lay-by and they went to sleep.

The place was on the north-south highway running from Dijon to Lyon and less than ten miles away another, smaller party of travellers was spending the night in a youth hostel.

This smaller party consisted of a twenty-one-year-old engaged couple who were even more unfamiliar with France than were the three junketing Germans, for they came from a small community outside Sydney, Australia, and were making their first trip to Europe prior to their wedding.

As they did not have a great deal of money, they were spending their nights in youth hostels and dining off bread, sausage and fruit bought in the markets. They travelled mainly by hitch-hiking and, from the moment of their arrival in Europe, the weather had been beastly.

Melinda Park and David Harman were, nonetheless, having a wonderful time. By three o'clock in the afternoon of Saturday, February 10, 1979, they were standing at the side of Route Nationale 7, within sight of the village of Pirlat to the south of Donzère and less than fifty miles to the north of Avignon, with their thumbs out, when the red Fiat bearing Peter Melchert, Achim Arnstädt and Gerhard Langdoll came into sight, travelling south at high speed.

At the wheel was Arnstädt, who had taken over from Melchert, now dozing in the front seat. A much worried Gerhard Langdoll sat in the back, with the shotgun stored on the floor by his feet.

Langdoll had good reason to worry. Rather than turning back to Germany and his job in Pirmasens, the trio had been pushing steadily south and were now more than two hundred miles from home. Melchert and Arnstädt were already talking about reaching the Mediterranean and, perhaps, catching a ship at Marseilles. So far, there had been no discussion of where the ship might be going.

Secondly, although a fast driver himself, Langdoll was becoming very nervous about Achim's driving which was not only even faster than Melchert's, but more dangerous. Achim, it seemed, found it amusing to come roaring down the wrong side of the road at a hundred miles an hour, heading directly for some oncoming car and then, only at the last minute, swerving over into his own lane. Sooner or later, Langdoll thought, one of the terrified drivers would also swerve and in the same direction.

Finally, he had been learning a little more about his old friends and it seemed that their careers since he had last seen them had been nothing like he had imagined.

Achim, the engineer's son, had not gone on to university, but had been kicked out of school for not studying. He had worked briefly as a warehouse labourer and then enlisted in the army, serving first in the town of Schwarzenborn and now in Koblenz. He was still in the army, but he was not on any weekend pass. He had simply deserted.

Peter's career had been scarcely more distinguished. He had lasted a full year in college before being expelled for not studying and alcoholism and had gone into the border police where he had served two and a half years with so little distinction that he had been forced at the end of that time to change his profession to that of factory guard.

Peter and Achim had, it seemed, seen a great deal of each other, however, and there were a good many private references in their remarks which Gerhard did not understand.

Nor did he understand very well the two Australians who now climbed into the back seat of the red Fiat with him. Not having had the benefit of a liberal education, he spoke very little English and the Australians spoke nothing else.

Peter and Achim were hardly better off, but the bonds of sympathy within the age group were sufficient to overcome any difficulties with the language. It is, however, possible that Melinda Park and David Harman never realized that their new friends were not French.

In any case, the wine bottle made the rounds, there was laughter, singing, half-understood jokes and the red Fiat thundered steadily onwards towards the south and the shores of the Mediterranean. The five young people were getting on famously.

Gerhard particularly was finding his old friends' jokes side-splitting. Aware that the Australians could not understand what they were saying, they were making some remarkably ribald remarks and suggestions to the attractive Miss Park who was smiling and nodding agreement to propositions that would have made her hair stand on end if she had understood.

They were not, however, nor were the more practical suggestions that the Australians hand over whatever money they might have on them so that the trip could continue.

These last proposals Gerhard Langdoll found especially amusing as he did not think that a couple of foreign hitch-hikers would have any money to begin with or that they would be so stupid as to hand it over.

He was not, however, reckoning with the unusually persuasive nature of his old school friends.

Pleasant as the ride was, it did not last long and at a point approximately halfway between the towns of Donzère and Pierrelatte, the Fiat slowed and swung off Route Nationale 7 into a track bordered by thickets.

It was a lonely and desolate spot, made none the more cheerful by the grey, threatening skies and the lifeless vegetation.

From Lyon south, the highway had paralleled the Rhône river, an important commercial waterway, and there were many side canals used by the barge traffic. At this point, the road crossed a bridge over the canal leading from Donzère to Mondragon with the railway on its own bridge only some fifty yards to the west. Both bridges extended far enough to clear the tow path along the canal which, after cutting through the railway embankment, passed an old and shallow gravel pit overgrown with weeds, bushes and small trees. To the south and on the higher ground above the gravel pit was a small grove of mixed conifers and hardwoods and, still further to the west, a dirt road ran along the edge of the pit, ending near the grove. Beyond this road, the land fell away steeply to the Pierrelatte canal which made junction with the Donzère-Mondragon canal just to the west of the gravel pit by means of a lock. The entire area was covered with dead weeds and brush and none of the gravel pit was visible from the road or either of the canals.

Driving along the tow path, Peter brought the car to a stop at the entrance of the dirt track leading back along the western edge of the gravel pit.

"What are we going to do here?" asked Gerhard in wonder.

"Hunt rabbits," said Achim, reaching over the seat to bring out the shotgun.

It was an automatic which held six shells and he held it up

so that the two Australians could see him feed the six shells of buckshot into the magazine.

"Out," he said curtly in English, pointing the gun at Harman. "Get out of the car."

"Aw come on now, Achim," protested Gerhard. "You'll scare the life out of them. They don't realize that you're joking."

"I'm not," said Achim. "We're running short of money and, if we want to keep going, we need theirs."

Gerhard stared at him unbelievingly and then turned to Peter for support, but Peter had gone around to the trunk of the car and was now returning with a heavy hatchet in his hand. He was a big man with a none too friendly face and he did not look as if he was joking either.

For the first time, Gerhard Langdoll realized that his friends were deadly serious. They were going to rob the young Australians and it would be a marvel if it stopped at that, considering the remarks in German that they had been making about Miss Park's physical characteristics and hoped-for sexual abilities.

Melinda Park and David Harman had also grasped that the matter was becoming serious. They had got out of the car and were standing, tense and nervous, close together, their eyes on the menacing muzzle of the shotgun which they had just seen loaded.

"Give us your money, all your money," said Achim in broken heavily accented English.

The Australians did not reply and Harman shook his head stubbornly. They had had to save for a long time to assemble the money for the trip to Europe. They were not going to part with it so easily.

Peter Melchert took a step forward and lifted the hatchet. His face was contorted into a fearful frown and he towered like a giant over the now thoroughly frightened hitchhikers.

Hesitantly, David Harman reached into his pocket and brought out a hundred-French-franc bill. It was worth approximately twenty-five dollars.

Anstädt laughed savagely. "All!" he snarled. "All! Quick!"

"No!" cried Gerhard, pushing between the Australians and the shotgun. "Don't do this, Achim! Peter! You must be

74

mad! You'll go to jail. Here! Take my money. I've got all of my pay with me still. Take it all and let these people go."

He stretched out a hand towards the shotgun and found himself looking directly into the black muzzle. For an instant, he had the illusion that he could actually see the deadly cluster of buckshot awaiting its release in the breech and the hair on the back of his neck rose as he suddenly realized that his old schoolfriend was fully prepared to pull the trigger.

"Get the hell out of the way or I'll blow your goddam brains out!" growled Achim.

Langdoll stumbled backwards, shaking. Something terrible was about to take place, he knew, and there was nothing he could do to prevent it.

As if in a sort of nightmare, he saw the two young Australians, taking advantage of his confrontation with Anstadt, turn and run down into the gravel pit and disappear into the bushes. They were shedding their backpacks as they ran, obviously aware that what now counted was escaping with their lives.

Anstädt and Melchert, shotgun and hatchet in hand, ran after them, leaving Langdoll standing transfixed beside the Fiat.

A moment later came the crash of the twelve-gauge shotgun going off and, immediately following it, the voice of Melinda Park raised in a long wail of shock, sorrow and terror. She had just seen her fiance's head nearly blown off by a charge of buckshot fired from a range of little more than a yard.

As Langdoll watched, stiff with horror at the grisly tragedy which was playing itself out before his eyes, the girl appeared out of the bushes, running up the slope in the direction of the little grove to the south of the gravel pit.

Achim Anstädt ran after her, the shotgun held at the ready and murderous intent in his every movement.

And then at the last second, salvation hove into view in the form of a barge passing sedately down the Pierrelatte canal, less than fifty yards away. The barge captain was at the wheel and there were several people, including a woman, on deck

75

as they were approaching the lock where all hands would be needed.

From the height above the gravel pit, Melinda Park was clearly visible to the people on the barge and she began to jump up and down, waving her hands and calling out for help in English.

Behind her, with great presence of mind, Achim Anstädt held the shotgun behind his back out of sight and began to wave with the other hand and call out, too.

The people on the barge waved cheerfully back. Young people often waved to the passing barges. They were all so open and friendly nowadays.

The barge passed slowly out of sight in the direction of the lock.

Melinda Park, sobbing with fear and disappointment, had turned and run back towards the bushes into which she now disappeared, followed by Anstädt. An instant later, there came the sound that Gerhard Langdoll had been dreading, the murderous boom of the shotgun.

The sound smashed his nerves like a charge of buckshot fired into a crystal chandelier. With no conscious knowledge of what he was doing, he leaped into the Fiat, turned the key, backed into the tow path, swung around and went roaring back towards the road.

He was a good twenty miles to the north and screaming down the highway in the direction of Germany and home before he realized that he had marooned his two old friends in a French gravel pit with a couple of corpses.

At the same time, he realized that he had wet his pants.

During the early hours of the morning, the red Fiat crossed the border, again at Schweix as Langdoll had neither papers for the car nor even his own personal identity card with him, and regained Pirmasens.

The long drive had wearied the young car mechanic to the point where he no longer even had the strength for hysteria, but he was still in a state of psychological shock. He had liked the Australians, had thought of them as persons of his own generation and good, if only temporary, companions. It was impossible to believe that his own two best friends had murdered them in cold blood.

76

For a long time, Gerhard Langdoll sat slumped behind the wheel of the Fiat parked in front of his house, his tired mind trying to cope with conflicts that no mind could cope with and remain sane.

In the meantime, back at the gravel pit, Achim Anstädt and Peter Melchert had been indulging in a fit of rage and indignation. They had generously taken this low-class car mechanic along on a trip to France and he rewarded them by stealing their car.

Fortunately, Melinda Park and David Harman had not been long in Europe and had, therefore, not had the opportunity of spending much of their money. The bulk of their savings was still intact and it would be quite enough to pay train fares back to Pirmasens, not for Melinda and David, of course, but for Achim and Peter.

And, as a matter of fact, there was even enough left over for some refreshments so, leaving the shotgun and the hatchet lying beside the two bodies, the young Germans walked down the Route Nationale 7 to the nearest bistro where they had a few glasses of wine and some sandwiches and where they gradually recovered their tempers over the treacherous desertion by their old friend.

Calmed and comforted by the food and drink, they then returned to the gravel pit where they discovered that, despite a charge of buckshot in the back of the head, Melinda Park was still alive.

This was an unhoped for opportunity and they promptly stripped her naked, took care of their personal sexual needs, burned off her pubic hair with a cigarette lighter and inserted a few pebbles in her vagina.

Peter Melchert then took the shotgun by the barrel and smashed the girl's head to a pulp.

The clothing and backpacks of the victims were once again searched in the event that anything of value had been missed, the passports were hidden under a large stone and the shotgun and hatchet were wiped clean of fingerprints. After all, Peter's father was a police officer. Peter knew something about crime detection.

Not really all that much, however. The hatchet had been

stolen from a weekend house less than a month earlier on one of Peter and Achim's forays into France. It could be identified by the owner and both Peter and Achim had left their prints all over the weekend house.

These arrangements completed, the two young men set off up the Route Nationale 7, hitchhiking in the direction of Lyon where they decided to remain for a day or two before returning to Pirmasens to look for Anstadt's car and, perhaps, have a few violent words with their ex-old friend.

Neither thought that the murders would soon be discovered or that, even if they were, they could be traced to them.

Up until roughly two hours before they killed them, they had never even laid eyes on the victims and there had been no witnesses where they had picked them up in the car.

Melinda and David were foreigners, not registered anywhere in France. They had probably not even stayed at any hotels. Their relatives in Australia would not realize that they were missing for some considerable time and, even when they did, they would not know where they had been when they disappeared.

The old gravel pit was an isolated, out-of-the-way place which scarcely anyone would have any reason to visit, particularly at this time of year. By the time the bodies were found, they would be no more than skeletons. It would probably be impossible to identify them.

Achim and Peter were rather proud. On their very first excursion into murder, they had committed a perfect crime.

Curiously enough, it did not occur to either of them that Gerhard Langdoll might go to the police. Perhaps they thought that he was by now so ashamed of his cowardly betrayal of his friends that he could be happy to forget the whole business.

They did not, however, really know Gerhard Langdoll. He believed a crime was something to be reported to the police and, although he had not actually witnessed the killings, he had no doubt but that they had taken place.

After sitting slumped behind the wheel of the Fiat in front of his house for some considerable time, he had started the car again and had driven to police headquarters where he reported everything that he knew about the affair in detail.

It was a long report. The details, down to the very smallest, of that excursion to France were burned indelibly into his mind and it was doubtful whether he would ever forget them again as long as he lived.

The Pirmasens police were, at first, not completely convinced of the accuracy of Gerhard Langdoll's account, but, after having had him examined to see if he was under the influence of alcohol or drugs and finding that he was not, they began to check what they could immediately.

The red Fiat was indeed registered in the name of Achim Anstädt, but Anstädt had been disqualified for drunken driving at the end of January. A check with the army in Koblenz showed that Anstädt was absent without leave and presumed to have deserted as he had taken all of his personal possessions with him.

In the meantime, the French police had been contacted and they reported that no information concerning the murder of two foreigners had, as yet, been received. They were, however, still looking for the gravel pit which Langdoll had described.

This was not easily found as Langdoll had not been paying much attention to where they were at the time and could only say that it was south of Montélimar off Route Nationale 7. Although they had passed through Donzère, he had not caught the name of the town.

He did, however, remember that it was at a point just after where the road and the railway line parallel to it crossed a canal on bridges and, on the basis of this information, a French gendarmerie patrol from Donzère located the scene of the crimes.

It was unquestionably the scene. From the point where the red Fiat had parked, a pitiful trail of the belongings of the young Australians led back into the brush where the two bodies lay within fifteen feet of each other.

David Harman lay on his side, the back of his head blown off. He had been killed instantly.

Melinda Park lay sprawled on her back, naked and with her pubic hair burned away. Her head was smashed to a pulp by the stock of the shotgun which lay nearby. The hatchet had also been left there, but had, apparently, not been used at all for either of the murders.

The sole comforting detail revealed by the post-mortem was that, although she had lived for more than an hour following the charge of buckshot in her head, Melinda had not regained consciousness and had not known what was being done to her nor had she seen the giant figure of Melchert swinging high the shotgun before smashing it down on to her head.

Informed by the French police that Gerhard Langdoll's story was accurate in every appalling detail, the Pirmasens Department of Criminal Investigations immediately sent out a nation-wide arrest and hold order on Achim Anstädt and Peter Melchert, but without much expectation that it would produce any results.

Following such a savage crime, it seemed hardly likely that the murderers would return to Germany at all, but would probably continue on to Marseilles for the ship which they had talked about in Gerhard Langdoll's presence. The logical thing for them to do would be to get out of Europe altogether.

Two days later, Peter Melchert and Achim Anstädt calmly descended from the train in the main railway station of Pirmasens and were taken into custody by the amazed police officers doing the normal railway station beat.

Taken to police headquarters, the two men offered little resistance to interrogation and quickly confessed to the murders. They were not, however, prepared to go into much detail and neither would admit to the sexual assaults of Melinda.

Because he had been present at the time, Gerhard Langdoll was also charged with the murders of Melinda Park and David Harman, but promptly acquitted by the court at the time of the trial. As a matter of fact, had it not been for Langdoll the murders might never have been discovered at all.

Peter Melchert and Achim Anstädt were both found guilty of murder and sentenced to the maximum possible under Germany's lenient juvenile code – ten years' imprisonment.

With the customary time off for good behaviour and the usual rehabilitation programmes intended to reinstate them as useful members of society, they could expect to be free within four or five years. As was pointed out by the defence, keeping them in prison would only make real criminals out of them. The court should give young persons who, in juvenile exuberance, had strayed from the path of righteousness a second chance.

There was no mention of a second chance for Melinda Park and David Harman.

SIX

MARRIAGE CAN DAMAGE YOUR HEALTH

In Gela, on the southern coast of Sicily, the spring has already long since arrived by the beginning of March. Washed by the warm (if sadly polluted) waters of the Mediterranean, the white sandy beaches gleam through the traces of oil slicks, palm trees nod in the breeze blowing up from Africa, there are fruit, leaves, plants and flowers, flowers, flowers everywhere.

An ideal time and place for romance and, the Sicilians not being noted for their lack of temperament, there is a good deal of romance in Gela. There are wholesome, healthy courtships, engagements and, eventually, marriages where an intact hymen is a matter of family honour and an ill-considered slur can bring out the stilettos.

Sunday, March 5, 1973, was just such an ideal day for romance and handsome, twenty-three-year-old Orazio Drago led lovely, seventeen-year-old Angela Loggia to the altar. The bride wore purest white and she was entitled to it in every way.

To the left of the aisle sat the Loggias – Angela's seven brothers, the uncles, the cousins, the aunts and, of course, the joyfully weeping mother of the bride.

To the right of the aisle sat the Dragos, equally numerous, equally delighted. No one had the slightest objection to the wedding.

The ceremony at the church completed, the Loggia and Drago families assembled at the Loggia house for a mighty feast which went on until the early hours of the morning. Many toasts were drunk and there was general, if slightly drunken, rejoicing.

Sometime after midnight, Orazio and Angela slipped away to the bedroom on the second floor which they could now legally share. Their departure was noted, but not commented on. This might have been construed as lacking in respect and in Gela any lack of respect had to be dealt with.

In addition to respect there was also consideration, and it was, therefore, past noon when fifty-four-year-old Nunzia Loggia ascended to the bedroom on the second floor. To her astonishment, she found her son-in-law absent and her daughter sitting in the bed looking remarkably sulky.

"So?" said Mama Loggia, raising her eyebrows.

"*Niente*," said Angela. "Nothing. Nothing at all."

"What do you mean?" exclaimed her mother, turning pale with horror and hurriedly throwing back the sheets.

They were spotless.

Nunzia Loggia staggered back as if struck and her plump hand flew to her ample bosom.

"Jesus have mercy!" she gasped. "Angela! How could you . . .? When did you . . .?"

"Never!" cried Angela, bursting into tears. "Not before and not last night!"

"You mean, you did not . . .? That he did not . . .? Why? Why? Are you mad? How can you refuse your own husband?" Mama Loggia began to weep as well.

"I did not refuse!" snivelled Angela. "I did everything! I stripped myself naked before his eyes! I pressed my body on his! I smothered him with kisses! Nothing! Nothing! He could not!"

"Could not?" said Mama Loggia incredulously. "But, there is no such thing! Could not . . .?"

"Have you ever tried to thread a needle with boiled spaghetti?" said Angela sadly.

"Where is he?" screamed Mama Loggia, her grief and astonishment suddenly giving way to anger. "Where is this pervert? This degenerate! This homosexual who spurns the most beautiful woman in all Gela!"

The bridegroom, it turned out, had gone for a little walk to try and clear his head. It had not been an entirely satisfactory wedding night for him either. Now he was frightened and puzzled. Was he truly impotent?

Up until the time of his wedding, he had not been impotent, that was certain. Like many young men of his age, he had tried out his sexual equipment in one of the local houses of prostitution. Everything had worked perfectly, even though he had not found the woman particularly attractive.

Angela was a thousand times more desirable. She was young, beautiful, passionate and with a fully adequate, if theoretical, knowledge of how to go about things. He had been waiting for this night for over two years and now, when it had finally come, *niente!*

And this, undoubtedly, was precisely the problem. Orazio had waited too long, he had been too excited, he had had too strenuous a day and he had gone to bed too late with, perhaps, a little too much alcohol in his stomach. The result had been that he could not achieve an erection immediately and this had brought on embarrassment, doubt, fear and finally total incapacity.

A misfortune which has befallen many another man on his wedding night and at other times as well. A great deal of the male sex drive is in the head. If something goes wrong there, the rest of the mechanism is blocked and, unlike the female, the male cannot pretend.

Something had gone wrong with Orazio Drago's wedding night and doubts of his own virility were now deeply planted in his subconscious. It would be some little time before he would be able to take advantage of the rights offered him by the wedding ceremony.

Some little time, that is, if the matter went no further than between him and Angela. Unfortunately, it already had.

When Orazio Drago returned to the house of his parents-in-law, he found all seven of his wife's brothers solemnly waiting for him. Their faces were grave. They looked like a jury in a trial of some particularly heinous crime and, in their own minds, they were.

The charge was presented without delay.

"You do not like our sister, brother-in-law?" said Carlo who, at thirty-four, was the oldest of the brothers and the nominal head of the family since the death of the father several years earlier.

"Kill him!" said Rocco, who, at twenty, was the youngest

and most impetuous of the brothers. "Why waste time talking? Kill him!"

"Why do you want to kill me?" exclaimed Orazio, turning pale and beginning to tremble. "I love your sister. I have done nothing!"

"Precisely," said Carlo.

Orazio realized that Angela had discussed the fiasco of the wedding night with someone, possibly the whole family, and he also realized that he was in a difficult situation. Had the same thing happened in his own family, he would have unhesitatingly recommended death for the defiler of the family honour.

He, therefore, began to talk very fast and very earnestly.

"It was too late at night," he protested. "I was drunk. You must know yourself that, when you have drunk too much, sometimes it does not go. Normally, I am like a wild animal. Five times a night. Six! Seven! It is nothing for me! All of my family are very strong in this way. My father had nine children by two wives. My grandfather had seventeen children and used to go to the house when he was seventy-five. They charged him double because he wore out the girls. My uncle . . ."

"Our sister is not married to your uncle," said Carlo. "How do you feel today?"

"Perfect! Never better!" shouted Orazio. "Things will be different tonight, I can tell you."

"They may be very different for you by tonight," said Pietro who was thirty-two years old and second in command to Carlo. "Come."

The seven brothers rose up as one and, laying hands upon Orazio Drago, led him out of the house to two cars parked in the street in front.

"What are you doing?" cried Orazio nervously. "Where are we going?"

He did not, however, struggle or make any sudden movements. Several of the brothers were holding their right hands inside their jacket lapels and Orazio knew very well what they kept there.

"We are going to find out whether our sister is a wife or a widow," said Rocco, giving Orazio a dreadful smile and slipping his hand half out of his jacket so that the hilt of his stiletto was revealed.

Orazio was bundled into the back seat of one of the cars with a brother on either side. Two more slid into the front seat, the remaining three got into the second car and, with a howl of tortured rubber, the cars shot away in the direction of the less desirable residential section of Gela.

To Orazio's horror, he realized that they were heading for Aunt Rosa's Family Whorehouse, as it was called by the more facetious elements in the town.

Now, as has been previously noted, sexual potency in the male resides largely in the head and Orazio had already had a somewhat traumatic experience in that respect the night before. He was undoubtedly no less virile and no more sensitive than any other man of his age and background, but, even under the best of circumstances, it would have been difficult, if not impossible, for him to have performed the sex act in the presence of others. Many men cannot, a failing which has ruined many a plan for an evening of untrammelled group sex. However, if he was to win an acquittal from the grim, seven-member jury now hearing his case, it was obvious that he was going to have to perform and perform convincingly.

As the cars drew up in front of Aunt Rosa's sporting establishment, Orazio Drago began desperately to think of every dirty, obscene thing that he had ever heard, read, seen, thought or experienced in his life.

A quarter to one in the afternoon is not exactly the height of the rush hour in a Sicilian whorehouse, and Aunt Rosa was as surprised as the operator of a whorehouse is capable of being surprised to see eight young but gloomy-looking customers file into the front parlour.

Assuming that this represented some kind of a stupid bet, she scurried around, dragging the girls out of their beds and hustling them down for inspection and, hopefully, approval. Her efforts were, however, wasted.

"We require only one girl," said Carlo politely, but in a very businesslike manner. "Your best. Is Anna still here?"

"Anna is still here," said Aunt Rosa, "and she is still my best girl, but, if you think that all eight of you are . . ."

She paused, puffing indignantly like a pink mountain. Aunt Rosa always wore candy-pink silk dresses and, although she had been very beautiful when she was younger, she now weighed over twenty stones.

"Only one," said Carlo, holding out some money. She looked at the Loggias, some of whom she knew by sight although not by name. Orazio Drago had been at the house once, but it had been several years earlier and she did not remember him. It was, she decided, as she had thought – some kind of stupid bet such as men make when they have been drinking. The amount of money she was offered was very large. Aunt Rosa took it.

"Of course," she said graciously. "If the signori will step this way . . .? I will call Anna."

Anna Scolari was the accepted star of the whorehouse. Nineteen years old, beautiful and with a figure which was so perfect it appeared exaggerated, she enjoyed her work and took pride in it. Although she had only been with Aunt Rosa a little over a year, she was already famous throughout Gela. There was nothing about sex which she did not know.

This highly sophisticated knowledge was not going to be needed in this case. Following Carlo's curt, if not unfriendly, instructions, she stripped herself, lay down on the bed and opened her legs. Her pubic hair had been shaved into the shape of a heart.

"Proceed, brother-in-law," said Carlo softly. "Show us."

"I cannot!" gibbered Orazio. "I am modest! I have never done such a thing in front of others!"

"You have never done it in front of others or alone!" raged Rocco. "Pervert! Pansy!"

"Silence!" said Carlo. "Pietro! Giovanni! Help him."

The two brothers, standing on either side of Orazio, unbuckled his belt and stripped his trousers down around his ankles. A third brother stepped forward, drawing his stiletto, and Orazio shrieked in terror as the slim blade snaked in between his legs. However, all that happened was that the crotch of his underpants was cut away. Then, many hands reached out, Orazio Drago was lifted bodily into the air and deposited between the thighs of the lovely but by now more than a little apprehensive Anna.

"Begin," said Carlo.

Orazio could not, even if his life depended upon it, and, as a matter of fact, it did. If nothing else, the sharp, cold, double-edged stiletto passing between his legs had swept out of his mind every salacious thought that he had been cultivating so frantically.

For the moment, Orazio Drago was as pure in heart as the most ascetic of saints. His terrified penis had retreated so far into his body that his external anatomy was not much different from Anna's.

Nearly unconscious with fear, he lay limp on the body of the beautiful young girl, his bulging eyes staring into hers and his mouth slightly open as he gasped for breath.

Anna was hardly less frightened. She was not at all sure what was going on, but, whatever it was, it was not some good-natured bet.

The only thing that she had grasped clearly was that the young man lying on top of her had to perform the sex act and, this being her speciality, she did her best, thrusting up with her hips and raking her pointed fingernails over Orazio's naked buttocks.

There was no response. Paralyzed with fear, Orazio was as rigid as a block of wood, rigid that is in every place except the one which so desperately counted.

The seven brothers stood in a circle around the bed, staring down, their faces expressionless. There was total silence broken only by the wheezing sound of Orazio's breath whistling through his parted lips.

"*Basta*," said Rocco suddenly. "Enough!" He took a step forwards, his right hand came out of his jacket with a flash of bright steel and the eleven-inch, razor-sharp blade of the stiletto slid into the flesh of Orazio Drago's back, just below the shoulder blade and to the left of the spine, like a needle going into butter.

Orazio gave a deep, gasping groan. All the tension went out of his muscles. The hands that had been clutching the sheets went slack. His head tipped forward and, from between his trembling lips, a great gush of blood poured out over the face of the horrified girl beneath him.

With a jerk, Rocco wrenched the stiletto free, wiped the

blade on his victim's hair and returned it to the scabbard beneath his left armpit. Without another word, the brothers filed solemnly out of the room.

It was only after some fifteen minutes that Aunt Rosa decided to look in and see how Anna and the client were getting on. At first, she thought they were both dead, as Anna was covered with blood and motionless, but as it turned out she had only fainted.

Aunt Rosa was annoyed. "It's things like this that give a house a bad name," she said.

What she meant, of course, was if they were found out. Things that are not found out do not harm anyone.

With the exception, perhaps, of the police who are supposed to find out everything and a surprising amount of the time do. To begin with, however, they must be aware that there is something to find out and, in the case of Orazio Drago, this did not happen until the following day when Mrs Nunzia Loggia called to report her son-in-law missing.

Her report was routinely transferred to the Missing Persons Department who were mildly startled to learn that the missing man had only been married for two days before his disappearance.

"Perhaps he has gone home to visit his relatives?" suggested the sergeant in charge of the department.

"No, no," said Nunzia Loggia. "I have spoken with them. No one has seen him. I am afraid that something may have happened."

"Such as?" said the sergeant. "Was your son-in-law in any difficulty? Was he depressed?"

Nunzia Loggia hesitated. "Perhaps," she said. "There was a problem."

"Which was?" prompted the sergeant.

"He is a pervert," said Mrs Loggia, casting down her eyes in embarrassment. "He was unable to consummate the marriage. It may be that this depressed him."

The sergeant opened his mouth to say something, thought better of it and began hunting in his pockets for his cigarettes.

"Are you quite sure of this?" he asked, lighting the filter

end of the cigarette and then throwing it into the ashtray.

"Quite sure," said Mrs Loggia sadly. "My daughter is still a virgin."

The sergeant asked a few more routine questions, saw Mrs Loggia out with a promise to call immediately there was any news, and carried the missing persons report form directly to the office of Inspector Luigi Colletto in the Department of Criminal Investigations.

The inspector was a rather small, neat sort of man with large, brown eyes and a sad expression. As he listened to the sergeant's report, his expression became sadder still.

"You think he may have committed suicide?" he said when the sergeant had finished.

"I would if I were to discover such a thing on my wedding night," said the sergeant.

The inspector thought it over. "I do not believe that you find such things out only on your wedding night," he said finally. "If this man is a homosexual, he would have realized it long before. How old did you say he was?"

"Twenty-three," said the sergeant. "It is true. If he were a pervert, he would know it and not get married. But what then?"

"This may be worse than suicide," said the inspector, pursing his lips. "The report itself strikes me as bizarre. If he is a homosexual, why do they want him back?"

"Hmmmm, yes, I see," said the sergeant in some slight confusion. "That is . . . what do you mean?"

"Supposing your sister married a man who turned out to be a homosexual and could not consummate the marriage?" said the inspector.

The sergeant's black eyes flashed with rage and his index finger darted across his throat in a gesture not unknown in other parts of the world, but perhaps a little more seriously intended in Sicily than elsewhere.

Then, his features cleared and he relaxed. "I have no sister," he said with relief. "We are all brothers in my family."

"Nonetheless, I think you see my point," said the inspector.

"But, if the family of the girl killed him, why would they report him missing?" asked the sergeant.

"Because it would be very suspicious if they did not," replied the inspector. "Leave the report and, when you go out, ask Sergeant Angiari to step in here, will you?"

Sergeant Angiari was the inspector's assistant – a thoughtful-looking young man with a great deal of curly, black hair. He read the report and then looked questioningly at the inspector.

"I want you to look into it, Franco," said the inspector. "Find out if Drago is alive. That is all we need to know."

He did not issue any other instructions and he did not need to. The sergeant knew his business very well. Five hours later, he was back.

"It appears unlikely that Drago is alive," he said. "He went off with the seven Loggia brothers in two cars the day following the wedding and he has not been seen since. Several of the neighbours saw him leave."

"What time was it?" said the inspector.

"Shortly after noon," said the sergeant. "The Loggias, or at least some of them, returned after only an hour or so, but Drago was not with them."

"Strange," said the inspector thoughtfully, rubbing his chin and patting his pockets for his cigarettes. "Could they possibly have murdered him in the middle of the day like that and disposed of the body in only one hour's time? I doubt it."

"What then?" said the sergeant. "It does not take long to cut a man's throat and drop him into the Mediterranean."

"Of course not," agreed the inspector. "But few people want to do such things during the day. It is too easy to be seen."

"Perhaps they were wild with rage," suggested the sergeant.

"No," said the inspector. "If all of the brothers were present, then it was a family decision. The men of the family came together and said, 'What are we to do now about our new brother-in-law who is more interested in making love to us than to our sister?' and there were suggestions and something was decided."

"What decision could there be but death?" said the sergeant.

"Perhaps merely being driven out of town, soundly beaten

and told never to return," said the inspector. "After all, it was only an insult. He did not harm the girl. By the way, did you find out if he really was a homosexual?"

"No," said the sergeant. "Do you want me to?"

The inspector did and, after a little more investigating, the sergeant returned with the startling news that, if Orazio Drago had been a homosexual, then no one in Gela had known it.

"He is considered quite normal by everyone who knows him," said the sergeant. "Miss Loggia was his first serious engagement, but he has been out with other girls and I am told that he visited one of the houses at the time when the other young men of his age were doing so."

"Which house?" said the inspector.

"Aunt Rosa's," said the sergeant. "But she does not remember him. I have talked to her." He hesitated for an instant. "It is odd, but I had the impression that something was wrong with her. She is not a nervous woman, but she seemed nervous."

"Yes, odd," said the inspector absently. "I do not see what Aunt Rosa could have to do with this. What about the Dragos? Do they seem aware that Orazio is missing?"

"They think he is enjoying his honeymoon with his new wife," said the sergeant.

"Better that they should continue to think so," said the inspector. "We do not want a war here." He hesitated indecisively. "I really do not know what to do. If we expand the investigations, the fact that Drago is missing is going to become known. On the other hand, this may well be a murder and we will receive a great deal of criticism if we fail to investigate it."

"I still think there is something wrong with Aunt Rosa," said the sergeant. "Perhaps, it is only a hunch . . ."

"Well then, investigate Aunt Rosa," said the inspector. "That should be safe enough. And in the meantime, I will think about what else we can do."

The sergeant took this as an excuse for a somewhat more vigorous investigation that the inspector had probably had in mind, and had Aunt Rosa and all her girls brought to police headquarters where he began to grill them unmercifully.

Aunt Rosa was too well insulated to be troubled by grilling and confined her remarks to demands for legal counsel. The girls, however, all went to pieces, particularly Anna Scolari.

"It was awful!" she snivelled. "He bled all over my face! The sheets were ruined. I thought the knife had gone all the way through him and killed me too! I fainted."

Anna had not known the name of her unusual client, but her description of him and of his companions was enough to convince the sergeant that this was the place that the Loggias had come with their new brother-in-law. Obviously, they had wanted to test him and, just as obviously, he had failed the test.

The only question that remained was, where was the body?

Anna did not know. All that she could remember was Rocco stepping forward and drawing his stiletto. Over Orazio's shoulder, she had seen him raise the knife and then the man lying on top of her had groaned, gone limp and the blood had poured out of his mouth over her face.

The next thing she knew, she was in the bathtub and two of her colleagues were washing the blood from her face and body. She had promptly had hysterics and she had not asked what had happened to the body of her client. To begin with, curiosity is not a trait which is encouraged among the employees of Sicilian whorehouses and, secondly, she was only too happy to forget the matter entirely.

However, as she had been unconscious when the Loggias filed out of the room, she had assumed that they had taken him with them.

Confronted with this statement, Aunt Rosa said that this had indeed been the case. The Loggias had taken their victim with them and she had no idea what they had done with him.

"Do you not think it normal to report it when someone is stabbed to death in your whorehouse?" said the sergeant.

Aunt Rosa shrugged like a whale surfacing. "It is normal to stay alive," she said. "We had just had a demonstration that these were very serious people."

She had still not admitted that she had ever laid eyes on any of the Loggia brothers before or that she had any inkling as to who they were. Aunt Rosa was a prudent woman. Even if all the Loggia brothers went to jail, they would come out one day and, besides, there were a great many other Loggias who would not be in jail at all.

If Aunt Rosa was prudent, the inspector was determined. There was now no longer any question in his mind but that he was investigating a murder and, until it was solved and the guilty party brought to justice, the understandable fears of the brothel owner could not be taken into account.

There was, however, no hope of extracting anything from as solid a character as Aunt Rosa and so he concentrated on the girls, threatening them with charges of concealing information from the police and even aiding and abetting in the commission of murder.

It soon developed that only one or two of the girls actually knew anything. Anna had been unconscious when the body was taken away, and none of the other girls had been in the room when the blow was struck.

Under great pressure, Anna admitted that she would be able to recognize the man who had stabbed Drago if she saw him again and also said that she thought that he was the youngest of those present. He had had only the beginnings of a moustache while all the others had sported fully developed specimens.

This was sufficient evidence for the inspector to take Rocco Loggia into custody and ask for an indictment, but there was still one important element missing. The body of Orazio Drago.

It was pointless searching the area around Gela, because the best and most obvious hiding place for a corpse was the Mediterranean. If a body was taken out half a mile or so, had a pair of concrete blocks attached to it and was dropped over the side of a boat, the chances of it ever being found were almost zero.

The inspector, therefore, concentrated on the next best thing – witnesses who had seen his lifeless body being carried from the brothel. Every person living in the vicinity was interrogated and, the Loggias having been a rather large and conspicuous group to be leaving a whorehouse at that hour of the day, several persons were found who recalled seeing them. To the inspector's consternation, they all swore that the Loggias had been carrying no body nor anything in which a body could be concealed.

The inspector promptly ordered a thorough search of the brothel. If the body had not been taken away, then it must still be there.

But it was not. At this point, the inspector, in great exasperation, filed formal charges of aiding and abetting a murder, concealing evidence in the commission of a felony and obstructing justice against Aunt Rosa and three of her girls.

Even with this, Aunt Rosa did not crack, but two of the girls did.

"Aunt Rosa's afraid of being charged with concealing a crime," they said, "but, if she's already charged, what difference will it make? The Loggias didn't take Drago away. Aunt Rosa's friend Julio did. They carried him out in a laundry basket."

This was all that the inspector needed. Within an hour, he knew who Aunt Rosa's friend was and where to find him. An hour later, he had him in custody. Half an hour after that, he knew what had happened to Orazio Drago.

And by four o'clock that afternoon, he was chatting with the corpse.

For the corpse was alive and well and in the hospital at Licata, some twenty miles down the coast. He had been brought in by Aunt Rosa and her friend with a bad stab wound and internal bleeding, but not in any immediate danger of death.

Being conscious and not at all anxious to attract the attention of the Loggias, he had given his name as Alfredo Valpone and had solemnly stated that he had received his wound through falling on his own knife. As his story was corroborated by Aunt Rosa and Julio, the hospital accepted it, whether they believed it or not.

The cat now being out of the bag, charges against Aunt Rosa and her girls were dropped and Rocco Loggia was indicted on one charge of assault with a deadly weapon and one charge of attempted murder. He made no attempt to deny the charges and stated that what he had done was the least that a brother could do under the circumstances.

The court found that he could have done less, but also took into account his motives, sentencing him on September 7, 1973, to ten years' imprisonment.

And Angela Loggia and Orazio Drago lived happily ever after.

But not together.

SEVEN

A PERFECT MURDER, BUT THE WRONG VICTIM

In a way, it was a classic case and easily solved. A spouse is always the first suspect in an unexplained death of a married person and, in the murder of thirty-six-year-old Wilford Cahill, there had been the dual motives of sex and money.

Cahill, a vigorous, handsome man and one of the wealthiest farmers in South Africa's Cape Province, had been found dead in his bed on the morning of Sunday, August 13, 1978, by his very lovely, thirty-two-year-old wife Laura when he failed to appear for breakfast.

The Cahills did not share the same bed or even the same bedroom, but this was in no way remarkable. The mansion was enormous and married people of the Cahill's class did not huddle in together like the common herd, but had their own suites of rooms.

This, of course, explained why Wilford could have been dead in his own house for more than eight hours before anyone realized it, but it did not explain how he came to be dead in the first place.

Dr Ian Barton, the Cahill family doctor, who had been summoned by Wilford's now very rich widow, had examined him only weeks before his death and knew him to have been in perfect health. Despite his wealth, he had been obsessed with the functioning of his huge estate and had worked long, hard hours, mostly outdoors. Physically, it had, of course, been good for him.

And also financially, no doubt, but domestically . . .?

The doctor had heard certain rumours, certain scraps of gossip as, he supposed, had nearly everyone else in the area.

Large numbers of domestic employees are vital for the operation of such an estate and a great convenience, but it is almost impossible to retain any real privacy within the family. Servants talk.

Up until Wilford's sudden inexplicable death, the gossip had been nothing more than a bit of titillation in an otherwise quiet and mildly boring rural society, but now the rumours took on a decidedly ominous aspect.

It was with sincere regret that the doctor informed the widow that he could not issue the death certificate for her husband and that it would be necessary to notify the coroner's office in Cape Town.

He did not mention the police. Obviously, if the coroner's conclusions were the same as his own, the police would be called in automatically.

And so they were. Dr Peter Drysdale, the Cape Town coroner, came out to the Cahill farm, made a very brief examination of the corpse of Wilford Cahill and advised Laura Cahill that there would have to be a post-mortem. In the meantime, the body was not to be disturbed until the police had had a look at it.

To make certain that it was not, he remained at the farm until Inspector Brian Harrison and Detective-Sergeant Morton Bagley from the Cape Town Police Department of Criminal Investigations arrived and officially took over.

Asked by the inspector, a tall, lean man with a small, close-clipped moustache, if he had any idea as to the cause of Cahill's death, he said bluntly that he thought he had been poisoned.

The inspector did not like this at all and immediately sent the sergeant, a burly young man with a florid complexion and a short haircut, to summon reinforcements from headquarters.

In a very short time, the Cahill farm was swarming with investigators, the body of the farmer was on its way to the morgue in Cape Town where Dr Drysdale would begin the post-mortem immediately, even though it was a Sunday, and the widow and the couple's only child, eight-year-old Carol, were in tears.

Both had good reason. Carol was already a half-orphan

and, South Africa having the death penalty and no reservations about using it, it was beginning to look as if it would not be long before she was a full orphan.

Carol did not, of course, know this. Her tears were for her father whom she had loved very much and whose loss she regretted bitterly and sincerely.

As for her mother, her tears were also bitter and undoubtedly sincere, but whether they were for the loss of her late husband or for some other reason could not been said so easily.

The fact was, the investigators had already turned up a number of things guaranteed to make any widow weep.

To begin with, they had retrieved an empty beer bottle from the pedal-bin in the kitchen, which the police laboratory reported contained definite traces of strychnine. There was even enough of it to determine that it was of the type commonly used to poison rats in the farm's barns and graneries.

Secondly, a search of Laura Cahill's rooms had uncovered a bundle of highly compromising letters, either copies of ones she had sent or originals which had been sent to her by her lover.

The letters were undoubtedly to her lover and all began with "Beloved", "Sweetheart", "Dearest Darling" or some other suitable form of address and were signed with pet names, most of which were highly suggestive and some of which were downright obscene.

Unfortunately, there was no indication of the identity of the person to whom they had been addressed and Mrs Cahill was still protesting that they had not been addressed to anyone other than herself. They were, she said, a private fancy involving an imaginary lover who did not exist, had never existed and never could exist.

The police were not convinced and the questioning was continued, but, for the time being, without success.

"It really doesn't matter whether she gives us his name or not," remarked the inspector. "Unless they made all their contacts outside the district, the servants and the employees at the farm will not only know who the lover is, but how often they met, where it was and, probably, precisely what they did.

It would be impossible to keep something like that secret."

And, of course, he turned out to be quite right. Questioning of the Cahill employees promptly produced a copious collection of extremely damaging statements.

Buster Diggens, a forty-four-year-old mechanic responsible for the maintenance of the farm machinery, reported that he had accidentally come upon the mistress on several occasions when she had been in compromising situations with her lover.

Upon being questioned as to what he meant by compromising, it developed that he regarded anything short of actual penetration as uncompromising.

Asked why he had not reported Mrs Cahill's conduct to her husband, he replied that what Mrs Cahill did was none of his business. He was paid to repair the farm machinery. He repaired it.

Melanie N'gomo, the sixteen-year-old black maid who took care of making the beds and other housework at the main house, had had a better reason for not saying anything about her mistress's love affairs. Mrs Cahill, she said, would have scolded her if she had told people that she was having an affair with the farm manager.

For it was, of course, the farm manager, a charming, physically attractive man of thirty who had gone to work for the Cahills in May 1974.

Denis Hartson, who had a degree in farm management, had come down to Cape Province from Johannesburg and, being personable and highly qualified, had almost immediately found employment with Wilford Cahill.

This had been a great professional success, for the Cahill farm was one of the biggest in the province, and Hartson, who had arrived in the district a bachelor, had been equally successful in the affairs of the heart.

Within a week of his arrival, he had attended a local ball where he had been introduced to twenty-year-old Dorothy Ekquist, daughter of a well-to-do farmer and the acknowledged belle of the entire region.

A stunningly beautiful girl with shining curly gold-blonde hair, the soft, almost childish features of a juvenile movie star and a figure which made men stammer and shift about

100

nervously on their feet, Dorothy was quite rightly considered to be the catch of Cape Province.

Denis had caught her and so swiftly that by August of that same year they were married.

The couple had settled into the manager's cottage on the Cahill estate, an elegant little house a quarter of a mile from the main mansion. A year later, Dorothy had given birth to Cynthia who was now five years old and who looked very much like her mother.

All this made the inspector very sad. Here was an almost ideal arrangement, the husband successfully employed in his chosen field, a beautiful young wife, a pretty little daughter, a generous and friendly employer and a comfortable home. What more could a man ask?

The answer was obviously in this case his employer's wife.

And perhaps the estate as well. Laura Cahill was her husband's sole heir. The estate now belonged to her. If she were to remarry, ownership would or at least could pass to her new husband.

A severe temptation. Laura was beautiful. The estate was worth a fortune. Who could resist such a combination?

Apparently not Denis Hartson and, for this reason the inspector regarded him as the prime suspect in the case and not the widow, Laura Cahill.

"In fact," he told his assistant, "she had no real motive at all. She was already mistress of the estate and she was already having all the sex she wanted from Hartson. She stood to gain little or nothing from her husband's death. Hartson stood to gain everything."

"Yes," said the sergeant, "but he was already married."

"So was Mrs Cahill," said the inspector. "We know how he solved that problem. He would undoubtedly have applied the same solution to his own marriage."

"Well then, I'm glad that we got him before he carried out the second half of the operation," said the sergeant. "Dorothy Hartson is about as attractive a woman as I've ever seen."

"She should be available shortly," said the inspector. "A month or so after the trial she'll become the second beautiful widow in this district."

"You aren't planning to charge Mrs Cahill at all?" said the sergeant.

"Oh definitely," said the inspector. "Hartson was undoubtedly the instigator and he was probably the one who actually put the strychnine into Cahill's beer, but I doubt that he did it without Mrs Cahill's knowledge and approval. At worst, we should be able to charge her with conspiring to commit murder. We'll see what the questioning brings out."

One thing it did not bring out was a confession.

Arrested, brought to police headquarters in Cape Town, charged with the murder of Wilford Cahill and placed under separate interrogation, both Laura Cahill and Denis Hartson denied vigorously that they had had anything whatsoever to do with the crime.

Confronted with the statements of the employees of the estate, they both broke down quickly and admitted that they had been having an affair since September 1977 when Cynthia had come down with the measles and her mother had panicked, sending Denis out at ten o'clock in the evening to look for Dr Barton.

As there was no telephone in the Hartson cottage, he had gone to the main house where he had found Laura Cahill alone, her husband having gone off to an agricultural conference from which he was due to return the following day.

Sometime earlier, Laura Cahill had confided to Dorothy Hartson, who came to the main house once a week to supervise the cleaning, that she was a neglected wife who scarcely knew what sex was any more and she now told Dorothy's husband the same thing.

The difference was that she expected him to do something about it.

Wilford, she had said, was so busy with the farm that he always came home exhausted in the evening, drank two bottles of beer and went straight to bed.

And to sleep.

It was this part of the routine that troubled Laura Cahill, but the farm manager rose gallantly to the occasion. As an employee, he obviously did not work as hard as his employer and therefore had more free time and energy.

On that first night, he did not get back to the cottage until well after one o'clock in the morning. Dr Barton, he reported to his anxious wife, was nowhere to be found, but he had left a message for him to come and see Cynthia the following day.

Actually, he had left no such message, but on the following morning, he called the doctor who then came out immediately.

Dorothy had suspected nothing and, if Laura and Denis could be believed, neither had Wilford.

From that date on, Hartson had reported almost daily to the big house for sex duty during the afternoon. As proficient in the one field as the other, he had, it seemed, been found fully satisfactory by both his employers.

Considering that Laura Cahill and Denis Hartson acknowledged these circumstances which, admittedly, constituted an ample motive for the murder and, considering that hardly anyone else would have had access to the refrigerator in the kitchen of the main house where Wilford Cahill had kept his beer, it seemed probable to the inspector that the confessions to the crime would soon follow, but he was to be disappointed.

Neither Laura Cahill nor Denis Hartson would admit to the slightest involvement in the murder and both described themselves as totally mystified as to who might have wanted to kill Wilford Cahill.

With tears in their eyes and the most fervent expressions of sincerity, they swore that they never considered marriage, had never felt that Wilford stood in the way of their happiness, had never plotted his death, were in no way responsible for it.

"It was nothing but sexual attraction!" blubbered Denis. "I love Dorothy! I always will! I was just carried away. And besides, she was the boss's wife. What could I do?"

The inspector was of the opinion that he had done all that he could and, perhaps, a trifle too much, but on the other hand he was puzzled by the lack of confessions and the manner in which the statements of the suspects coincided.

"Normally," he told the sergeant, "when you have two suspects telling a prearranged story and you question them separately, you find that one or the other forgets part of what he or she is supposed to say and you can then play off the contradictions, one against the other, until you get the truth out of them.

"That's not the case with Cahill and Hartson. Their stories check to a hair, no matter how often we rephrase the questions."

"Seems funny to me too," said the sergeant. "You'd think that, if they went to all the trouble of making up a story like that between them, they'd have gone about the whole thing differently, killed him in some way that they could fake alibis for themselves or something. They should have realized that Barton wouldn't issue a death certificate in circumstances like that."

"They must have realized it," said the inspector. "These are both educated, intelligent people. It's impossible to believe that they would poison Cahill with something so obvious as strychnine and then simply toss the bottle with the dregs into the rubbish bin. No one but an ignorant savage would do that."

There was quite a long silence.

"A lot of the labour employed on the Cahill farm is pretty ignorant," said the sergeant finally. "I don't know about savage. It could be that . . ."

"One of them had a grudge against the boss," said the inspector, completing the unfinished sentence. "We're going to have to look into it. I want to solve the case, but I don't want the wrong people hanged."

The question of Wilford Cahill's relationship with his employees was looked into and rather thoroughly. Almost at once it became clear that the police were on the right track at last.

Cahill, a very hard worker himself and a man who took a strong interest in every aspect of his farm business, had not been easy to work for. Although he had been generous and reasonable with his general manager, he had expected a great deal from the other employees and even Buster Diggens, the farm mechanic, had not been spared extremely sharp language when Cahill had felt that he was not working as hard or as quickly as he would have desired.

Moreover, a check of Diggens' background showed that he had been discharged elsewhere on two occasions for carrying out physical attacks on his employers. A man with a violent temper and a reputation for holding a grudge indefinitely, he had access to the strychnine used for poisoning rats and mice around the farm, and it would not have been difficult for him to sneak into the kitchen of the main house without being seen.

And yet, the inspector hesitated over having him formally charged and questioned. The motive seemed weak and there was the question of why, if he was going to poison his employer, he had not done it before. He had worked for Cahill for nearly seven years and, by all accounts, their relationship had been stormier at the beginning than it was later on.

"Well, we know that neither Mrs Cahill nor Hartson saw him in the house on the day in question," said the sergeant, "or they'd have said so to save their own skins. If anyone did, it would have had to be the housemaid. She was in the main house all day."

"But probably upstairs," said the inspector. "He could have easily sneaked into the kitchen, put the strychnine into the beer and cleared out without her even knowing that he was in the house. He wouldn't have needed more than a couple of minutes."

"We'll see," said the sergeant. "I'll go and bring the girl in for a little questioning."

To everyone's surprise, Melanie N'gomo promptly confirmed that she had seen Buster Diggens entering the house on the afternoon of the day that someone had put strychnine into Wilford Cahill's beer.

"He looked real sneaky like he didn't want anybody to see him," she said. "I expect he killed Mr Wilford."

Buster Diggens was immediately arrested, charged with suspicion of murder and confronted with the statement of Melanie N'gomo.

Diggens' reply was that he had not been in the main house or anywhere near it at any time during the day or evening of August 12 and that he could prove it. Melanie N'gomo was simply trying to get him into trouble because he had caught her stealing a few months earlier and had tanned her bottom for her.

"Prove it then," said the inspector. "Prove you weren't near the house that day."

And Buster Diggens promptly did. He had been working with a group of other employees and two neighbouring farmers at the other end of the estate nearly five miles away the entire day, and had only started back to the farm at a time when Wilford Cahill was already drinking his poisoned beer.

Moreover, it was possible to show that he had not poisoned the beer at any time previous to the murder. The two bottles which Cahill had drunk on that evening were from a new case which he himself had brought back from town only the preceding day. The beer had been poisoned on the afternoon of the day that he drank it, or it had been poisoned already when he picked up the case in town.

For a moment, the inspector thought that his case was turning out not to be murder after all, but merely a tragic accident. Strychnine had somehow got into the beer at the shop and Cahill's death was not due to design but, at the most, to carelessness.

There was, however, the statement of Melanie N'gomo who had been very positive about Diggens sneaking into the house and who now refused to retract her statement, although it had been demonstrated that it was false.

Such obstinacy led the inspector to wonder whether there was not some more valid reason behind it other than simple unwillingness to admit to a falsehood.

"The girl had the run of the house including the kitchen," he told the sergeant. "We know that Diggens caught her stealing so it's not at all unlikely that Cahill did too and we also know that he could be hard on his employees if they didn't do things the way he wanted them to.

"He gave her a dressing down, maybe even beat her the way Diggens did, and she decided that she'd get even with him."

"And get Diggens hanged for the crime as well," said the sergeant.

"That I doubt," said the inspector. "This is a young, simple girl. I don't give her credit for being that subtle. She never mentioned seeing Diggens until we brought her in for questioning. I think it was just a spur of the moment thing. She wanted to name somebody so as to draw off suspicion from her and she was mad at Diggens anyway so she named him."

"He can thank his lucky stars that he happened to have an alibi," said the sergeant. "Otherwise that girl would have framed him like a picture. You think you'll get the truth out of her?"

"Probably not," said the inspector. "The fact is, we haven't got any physical evidence against her. We can't even prove she had trouble with Cahill, and the girl's as stubborn as a warthog. She won't even admit she lied about seeing Diggens that afternoon."

"Isn't that evidence?" said the sergeant. "The fact that she lied to the police?"

"It's evidence that she wanted to stick Diggens with the murder," said the inspector. "It's not evidence that she murdered him herself. I don't think we can charge her."

"We could charge Cahill and Hartson," said the sergeant. "Motive, opportunity, no alibis."

"Right," said the inspector. "I'm in the very peculiar position of being able to charge suspects who I now doubt very much are guilty and not being able to charge the suspect who I believe is."

"So what do we do?" the sergeant asked.

"We question the life out of Melanie N'gomo and, if that doesn't produce anything, we turn the whole thing over to the prosecutor's office," said the inspector. "It will be up to him to decide who goes on trial."

"I think I can guess in advance," said the sergeant.

So did the inspector and, as it turned out, both were right.

Melanie N'gomo proved to be less stubborn than the inspector had feared. She eventually admitted that she had lied about seeing Buster Diggens sneak into the main house on the afternoon in question, and confirmed what he had said about giving her a spanking for stealing, although she insisted that she had been falsely accused.

She also admitted that she knew of her employer's habit of drinking two bottles of beer every evening when he came

107

back to the house from his work, and she knew where the beer was kept in the refrigerator as it was one of her duties to put the two bottles there to cool every morning.

She had done so on the morning of the day that Cahill had been poisoned and she had not noticed anything unusual about the bottles – she had simply taken them from the fresh crate in the pantry.

She had also thrown the empty bottles in the rubbish bin that evening after Cahill had gone to bed and she explained a fact that had puzzled the investigators up to now. There had been no fingerprints other than Cahill's on the bottles because she had been wearing the rubber gloves which Mrs Cahill had given her to use when washing up.

She denied, however, that she had ever had any trouble with her employer and said that she really liked him better than her mistress who sometimes scolded.

Asked to open and reseal a beer bottle, she succeeded in getting it open easily enough but not in getting it shut again.

Given a cardboard box marked strychnine but actually containing cornflour and asked to taste it, she unhesitatingly did so and, in reply to questions as to whether she knew what strychnine was and where to obtain it, she said that she had heard that something which sounded like that was used to kill rats, but that she had never seen any.

Her manner was so childishly simple that the inspector was forced to the conclusion that either he was confronted with one of the most clever criminals and, at the same time, brilliant actresses that he had ever encountered, or that Melanie was telling the truth.

Faced with such a choice, there was only one possible answer, and Laura Cahill and Denis Hartson were turned over to the public prosecutor's office with a formal recommendation that they be charged with murder and conspiracy to commit murder.

A conviction on such charges was equivalent to the death sentence.

And a conviction was almost inevitable.

It was true that there was still no physical evidence connecting either Laura Cahill or Denis Hartson to the crime, and it was also true that neither had confessed or had even attempted to push the blame on to the other.

In fact, the only possible description of the reactions of the two former lovers to their charges was hysteria.

Nonetheless, the prosecutor's office felt that there was an adequate case against them. They had been lovers by their own admission. The immensely valuable Cahill estate had been at stake. Either could have put the strychnine into the beer bottle and resealed it without detection. Neither could offer any kind of an alibi.

And, above all, there were no other possible suspects.

Except one, and on the morning of September 1, Mrs Dorothy Hartson appeared at the office of Inspector Harrison to present evidence for which she had not been asked.

She did not present it at once, but began by asking the inspector what her husband's situation was in the case.

The inspector was unwilling to reply bluntly, but, upon being pressed, finally admitted that, short of a miracle, Denis Hartson had very little chance of celebrating his thirty-first birthday.

Dorothy Hartson nodded her head as if that was what she had been expecting to hear. The morning sun was coming in through the window of the office and it turned her blonde curls into a golden halo around her chubby young face.

"Dennis didn't kill Wilford Cahill," she said in a grave voice. "I did."

She then proceeded to tell the inspector how she had become suspicious of her husband when he had lied about not being able to find Dr Barton when Cynthia had the measles. The doctor had come the next day and she had mentioned that they had been unable to locate him the night before. The doctor had expressed surprise, saying that he had been at home all evening.

Less than a week later, she had gone to the main house on a Monday rather than Thursday as usual, and had heard the sounds of lovemaking from upstairs. Creeping up, she had opened the bedroom door a crack and had seen her husband and Laura Cahill naked and making love on the bed.

From that time on, she said, she had thought of nothing but revenge, but it was nearly a year later when she hit upon the plan of poisoning Wilford so that his wife would be hanged for the murder.

She had known, of course, of his beer-drinking habit in the evenings and had simply slipped into the kitchen that afternoon, poured the strychnine into one of the beer bottles and recapped it.

"No one saw me," she said. "It went off just the way I planned it. The only thing was, it didn't occur to me that Denis would be suspected. I love him even if he did have an affair with Laura Cahill. If he's executed, I'll have lost everything so I might as well be dead anyway."

Faced with this confession, the inspector had no choice but to withdraw the charges against Laura Cahill and Denis Hartson and ask for an indictment on a charge of premeditated murder against Dorothy Hartson who, despite the most intensive questioning, never changed her story in the slightest detail.

However, the inspector was not completely convinced for it had immediately occurred to him that Dorothy's confession was intended to save her husband from the gallows and that she could have made it as easily if he were guilty as if he were innocent.

Whatever the case, the young mother stuck to her confession and in February 1979 was brought to trial.

The doubts that had plagued the inspector appear to have arisen in the mind of the court as well for, although she was found guilty as charged, she was granted substantial extenuating circumstances and given the relatively light (for South Africa) sentence of twenty years' imprisonment.

Legally, she murdered Wilford Cahill in the hope of getting his wife hanged for it.

But did she?

EIGHT

PECULIAR MADNESS

Both the man and his son were dishevelled and streaked with dirt, their clothing stained and rumpled and their hair uncombed. Although it was nearly noon, it was obvious that neither had yet washed that morning.

Standing in the shady, paved patio of the luxurious villa, they presented a strange contrast to their surroundings, but neither seemed aware of it. Whatever had resulted in their untidy appearance, it had apparently been nothing to disturb their calm.

"We should like to speak to Sabine, if we may, Herr Doctor," said the man humbly. Like most Germans, he was inclined to regard a doctor's title with reverence.

"Of course, Herr Alexander," said Dr Walter Trenkler, tactfully concealing his surprise at his countryman's appearance. "If you will be so good as to wait a moment, I'll go and call her."

He went out of the patio and to the kitchen where fifteen-year-old Sabine Alexander was helping to prepare the family lunch.

"Your father and brother are here," he said. "They are waiting for you in the patio."

The girl inclined her head silently and followed him down the hall.

"Father," she said. "Frank." She walked forward, holding out her hands to her father and brother.

Dr Trenkler turned to leave the patio.

"Sabine dear," said Harald Alexander in a pleasant, conversational tone of voice. "We wanted you to know at

111

once. Frank and I have just finished killing your mother and your sisters."

Across the patio Dr Trenkler stopped dead in his tracks, one foot still raised in the air.

"Oh, that's wonderful, father," said Sabine. "Thank you for coming to tell me."

Dr Trenkler turned slowly and stiffly around. He had the feeling that he was caught in some kind of a nightmare, that what he was hearing could not be real, and for a moment he doubted his own sanity.

The three Alexanders were standing in the centre of the patio embracing one another. Sabine had rested her head on her father's chest and had wrapped her arm around her brother's neck. They made a pretty picture. All of the Alexanders were remarkably handsome.

A person of another nationality might have let the matter slide, might have pretended not to have heard what Harald Alexander had said or his daughter's response to it, but Trenkler was a German and Germans are a responsible people. He would not believe that Alexander and his son had actually killed Mrs Dagmar Alexander and her two daughters, the eighteen-year-old Marina and Sabine's twin sister, Petra. Something must be terribly wrong. The Alexanders had been involved in an accident of some kind and it had addled their brains.

But how then to explain Sabine's reaction?

It was true that the Alexanders were an abnormally close-knit family, withdrawn and lacking contact with almost everyone around them. The twins had lived in his house for months now, more as daughters than as maids, but they had always held themselves apart and had never become part of the family as he and his wife had wished. Frank, too, he had heard from the German consul, was completely un-approachable. The boy had been working for nearly a year as an apprentice in Consul Ahlers' shipping agency, but he had not even accepted the invitation to the firm's Christmas party which had taken place the week before.

And yet, the doctor knew that none of the family spoke Spanish and it would seem that a German family living here in Santa Cruz, the capital of the island of Tenerife in the

Spanish Canary Islands, would want to mix with people who spoke their language and knew their customs. As far as the doctor knew, the Alexanders mixed with no one.

All these thoughts passed very rapidly through his head as he crossed the patio. It did not occur to him to be afraid. Alexander was a well-built man of thirty-nine, but he was much smaller than the doctor and the sixteen-year-old Frank looked positively frail.

"You said . . .?" said the doctor.

"Ah, you heard?" said Alexander with a pleased look. "Of course. My wife and my other daughters. We have killed them. It was the hour of killing, you understand."

"The hour of killing . . .?" said Dr Trenkler uncertainly.

He was staring at the Alexanders and suddenly he saw that the stains on their hands and clothes were not those of normal dirt or earth, but brown, gummy streaks and splotches. As a doctor, he should have realized it before, but it had simply been too grotesque to accept. Now, however, he knew. Harald and Frank Alexander were smeared from head to foot with dried blood.

Slowly, cautiously, he raised his eyes to Harald's face. The man was looking directly at him over the top of his daughter's dark head and smiling. It was a pleasant, friendly smile – not in the least sinister.

It frightened Dr Trenkler more than if Alexander had snarled or roared at him.

"Wait . . . wait here . . .' he stammered, backing off. "Don't go away."

He turned and ran down the hall, heading for the telephone in his study. He was not so much afraid for himself but he was terrified for the safety of the girl, Sabine. To all appearances, her father and brother were utterly mad. They must not be allowed to take her away with them.

The Alexanders might speak no Spanish, but the doctor did and, a few moments later, he was pouring a flood of it into the shocked ears of the officer at the switchboard in police headquarters. Santa Cruz is a quiet place and even the suspicion of such crimes was unusual.

Suspicion was all it was so far, of course, but Dr Trenkler was well-known and respected and the police were taking no chances. Within a matter of minutes, the first police officer arrived at the house. He was followed by another and another until there were finally no less than ten uniformed and plain-clothes officers present in the patio.

The three Alexanders regarded this with interest but no apparent signs of alarm.

Almost the last of the police to arrive were the detectives of the murder squad, Detective-Inspector Juan Hernandez and his assistant, Detective-Sergeant Manuel Perera, both small, neat, dark-skinned men with large, rather melancholy brown eyes.

The inspector listened to Dr Trenkler's account of the matter and then approached Harald Alexander with the doctor at his elbow to serve as interpreter.

"Where are your wife and daughters, Mr Alexander?" said the inspector.

The doctor interpreted.

"Flat One-D, 37 Calle Jesus Nazareno," said Alexander promptly.

The inspector signalled to two of his men.

"Go to the flat and report back at once," he ordered.

The men disappeared.

The inspector turned back to Alexander.

"Dr Trenkler says that he heard you say that you had killed them," he said. "Is this true?"

Alexander shook his head.

"I only helped and furnished the music," he said regretfully. "It was the Prophet. The Prophet declared that the Hour of the Great Killing was at hand. Praise the Prophet!"

"Who is the Prophet?" said the inspector.

"Why, right there," said Alexander in mild astonishment, indicating his son with his head. "There is the Prophet."

The inspector did not have to wait for the doctor to interpret. He had understood the gesture very well.

"Manuel," he said to his assistant in a low voice, as if he feared that Alexander would be able to understand him. "Call the station and tell them to summon Dr Francisco. Explain the circumstances. These people are sick, very, very sick. They must be placed under observation."

114

The sergeant nodded and hurried off.

"Do you think he is telling the truth?" said Dr Trenkler in Spanish. "Is it possible that they have really murdered the women?"

The inspector shrugged. "We will know that when my men report from the flat," he said.

The men were, however, unable to enter the flat as the door was locked and no one answered the doorbell.

"We can easily force the door and go in," said one of the detectives speaking on the telephone to the inspector at Dr Trenkler's house, "but should we? Or do you want to obtain a warrant first?"

"I think in view of the circumstances, we are justified in entering by force if no one answers," said the inspector. "I am beginning to have a very bad feeling about all this. Force the door and report immediately on what you find. I will wait here at the telephone."

"Understood," said the detective. "We are calling from the phone box at the corner. It will take us a few minutes."

There was a wait of perhaps ten minutes while the inspector stood patiently by the telephone.

Suddenly, the phone rang and the voice of the detective came back on the line. It was very loud as if he were almost yelling into the receiver, and he was breathing in great gasps as if he had been running.

"You must come at once, sir!" he choked. "It is horrible! The blood! Their hearts hanging on the wall ... Mutilation ... The sex organs ... They are all dead! All dead!"

"Let no one approach the flat!" snapped the inspector, slamming down the telephone and shouting for his assistant as he ran for the street door.

Sergeant Perera appeared out of the patio looking startled.

The inspector was already climbing into his car behind the wheel.

"Come on!" he shouted. "It is as bad as the man said."

He threw the car into gear and the sergeant barely had time to scramble into the front seat next to him. While the inspector shot the car like a rocket through the heavy traffic, the siren screaming and the warning lights flashing, he issued a constant stream of orders.

"Contact Dr Francisco over the radio and tell him to come to 37 Calle Jesus Nazareno. Phone headquarters and tell them to send the entire laboratory staff. Call the emergency ambulance. Phone Dr Trenkler's house and tell Luis to take the Alexanders to headquarters and hold them in maximum security."

The sergeant complied, quickly, silently and efficiently. The Santa Cruz murder squad might not have a great deal of experience in dealing with mass murder, but they were ready for it.

What they were not ready for was the scene which met their eyes upon arrival at the modern block of flats in which the Alexanders had lived.

Lying on the floor of the living room were the bodies of two girls, later to be identified as Marina and Petra Alexander. Both had been savagely beaten about the head and face and were completely naked. The corpses were unbelievably mutilated. Their breasts had been cut off and were nailed to the wall above their heads. The sex organs had been slit and gashed and strips of skin with the pubic hair attached were nailed to the wall next to the severed breasts. The stomachs were slashed and the older girl was partially disembowelled.

Covering the floor of the room was a sea of torn clothing and ripped papers, including the Alexanders' passports, books, household utensils, shoes, broken dishes and food. All of these things, the walls and even the ceiling were so heavily smeared with blood that it looked as if it had been applied with a paint brush. Against one wall stood a small organ such as is sometimes used in chapels to accompany the hymns. The white keys were covered with bloody fingerprints.

In the bedroom beyond, the scene was even worse. Thirty-nine-year-old Dagmar Alexander had suffered all of the mutilations visited upon her daughters and, in addition, her heart had been cut out, tightly bound with cord and hung on the wall. She lay naked on the bed, an enormous bloody

116

wound between her wide-spread thighs where her sex organs had been.

The sergeant was not able to control his nausea and had to retire to the hall where he vomited violently and copiously, as had already done one of the detectives who had been the first to enter the apartment.

Detective-Inspector Hernandez did not vomit, but he was unable to speak for some time and his nostrils flared like those of a shying horse. Slowly and gingerly, so as not to disturb anything, he walked through the horrors of the flat and then came out into the hall where the detectives were waiting.

"You may tell the emergency ambulance that they are not needed, Manuel," he said softly. "They can do nothing for these poor people. Has Dr Francisco arrived yet?"

The doctor had not, but he appeared some fifteen minutes later, having only found out that he was to come to the Calle Jesus Nazareno upon his arrival at Dr Trenkler's house.

He was an elderly man, white-haired and white-moustached, and, under normal circumstances, very well controlled, but when he emerged from the Alexanders' flat, his hands were shaking and there were tears of compassion and horror on his cheeks.

"This is terrible!" he exclaimed. "Terrible! I have never heard of such a thing! What do you want of me, Juan? I am an old man. I cannot examine those bodies. It would make me ill."

"I am afraid you must, Diego," said the inspector gently. "You are our medical examiner and there must be a medical examination before we can proceed with the investigation. You will also have to perform post-mortems for the court when the trial is held."

"There will be no trial," said the doctor, shaking his head violently. "Anyone sufficiently insane to do what has been done in there can never be held responsible for his actions. A man like that must have spent most of his life in mental institutions and that is where he will be returned."

"We have every reason to believe that it was a sixteen-year-old boy," said the inspector. "The son and brother of the victims."

The doctor stared at him as if he doubted his sanity.

"How could any sixteen-year-old boy do such a thing?" he said. "Where would he have got the strength? How could he kill all three of these women without being over-powered by them? You don't mean the boy at Dr Trenkler's house, do you? He hasn't the strength to beat a mouse to death."

"That is the boy," said the inspector. "He may have had help from his father, although the father denies it."

"He definitely had help from his father or from someone," said the doctor with great conviction. "There is no indication that these poor women were tied or restrained in any way. It is beyond belief that they would simply sit there and allow the boy to beat them to death."

"Perhaps when you examine the bodies more closely, you will find that they were stabbed or shot or poisoned," suggested the inspector. "I agree with you that it is not possible to believe that they simply sat there and made no effort to defend themselves."

But this, it seemed, was exactly what Dagmar, Marina and Petra Alexander had done. The autopsy on the bodies showed no signs of poison, gunshot or stab wounds. The actual cause of death was repeated blows to the head with a wooden clothes hanger, according to the statements of Alexander and his son and also according to the findings of the police laboratory.

"In so far as it is possible to reconstruct the events," read the laboratory report, "all three women were beaten to death with the wooden clothes hanger found near the bed on the floor of the bedroom. This, and only this, bears traces of hair, blood and fragments of skin from the scalps of all three victims.

"The hammer, pincers, chisels, saw and other utensils found amidst the debris covering the floor were apparently used in the mutilation of the corpses and in attaching the various organs to the walls, but the hanger was the primary murder weapon.

"Since there is only one hanger, the victims must have been beaten to death successively and, considering the light weight of the implement, a considerable number of blows must have been required before the victim even lost consciousness.

"As the post-mortem report states that there are no indications of restraint on the bodies, and as no cords, ropes or other material suitable for tying was found in the flat, the conclusion must be that the victims submitted willingly to their fate.

"The laboratory has been unable to develop a theory to account for this.

"Fingerprints on the organ are entirely those of Harald Alexander. A complete palm print on the murder weapon, i.e. the hanger, is that of Frank Alexander. Prints found on other implements used in the mutilations are of both Harald and Frank Alexander.

"No drugs, stimulants or alcoholic beverages were found in the flat."

"Which," said the inspector, passing the report over to his assistant, "corresponds exactly with the Alexanders' statements. The only problem is that I find it impossible to believe. How can three women sit quietly while their son and brother beats them to death slowly, one after the other?"

"The only explanation possible is that they were as mad as the men are," said the sergeant. "You recall that the girl who survived is reported by Dr Trenkler as having received the news of her mother's and sisters' death without any signs of dismay. The whole family must be violently insane."

"Considering what has taken place, they must be," agreed the inspector. "However, it is a strange form of madness. No one who knew them suspected them of being insane and no one who had contact with them found their behaviour in any way out of the ordinary. They were merely somewhat reserved. The German consul and Dr Trenkler, who knew them best, both had the impression that they were a very close-knit family. As for the other tenants of the building in which they lived, they report that the Alexanders seldom went out, usually kept their curtains drawn and that someone played the organ most evenings, not very well, it seems."

"Very badly, as a matter of fact," said the sergeant. "One of the other tenants is a piano teacher. She says that the person playing it knew nothing at all about music and was apparently pressing the keys at random."

"I didn't see that statement," said the inspector. "There are so many." He sighed. "There will be a great many more I am afraid by the time we get the reports back from Germany and by the time the observation on Sabine is completed."

Sabine had been sent to a convent where she was under observation by the leading psychiatrists of the city. It had been necessary to restrain her physically when her father and brother had been taken to police headquarters as she had insisted on accompanying them.

The observations were not going well. Sabine Alexander was, it seemed, a remarkable person, completely normal in appearance and behaviour, but mentally living in a world which bore little resemblance to reality.

"She believes, for example," said Dr Francisco, reporting on the latest findings to Inspector Hernandez, "that our entire civilization is only temporary and that it will soon be replaced by a new order of which her brother is the prophet. He is, therefore, something more than human and yet, at the same time, there are definite sexual aspects in her attitude towards not only the brother, but her father as well."

"Incest," said the inspector, nodding. "Either real or imagined. Have you examined her physically?"

The doctor nodded. "Technically, she is not a virgin. However, she could have ruptured the hymen through means other than sexual intercourse. There is no certainty that there has been incest between her and either her brother or her father."

"Perhaps only within her mind," said the inspector. "What do you think of the statements by Alexander and the boy?"

Although they had been taken separately, they had corresponded closely, too closely, the inspector thought, to be the result of collusion between them. On the other hand, neither statement had been very long or very complex.

Frank Alexander had stated, "Father and I were sitting in the bedroom with Mother, and Marina and Petra were in the living room. It was approximately two o'clock in the afternoon on December 16, 1970.

"I saw that Mother was looking at me and I had the feeling that it was not permitted for her to look at me in this manner.

120

I therefore took the clothes hanger and struck her on the head. After I had struck her several times, she fell over and lost consciousness.

"Father had gone to the living room to play the organ and I also went there. First, I struck Marina on the head with the hanger, and after she had lost consciousness, I struck Petra.

"Father continued to play the organ and to praise Jesus, but when I began to remove the offending parts, he came to help me."

Asked why he had struck his mother and sisters on the head, Frank Alexander had replied that "the vessels were unclean" and that "the lust of women had to be punished." However, he would not elaborate on this statement.

Harald Alexander's statement had dovetailed neatly with that of his son.

"We were sitting in the bedroom," he told Inspector Hernandez. "The Prophet, his mother and I. It was perhaps two o'clock in the afternoon. Dagmar looked at the Prophet in an unclean way and he took up the clothes hanger which lay to hand and began to administer the just punishment.

"After a time, she fell over and lost consciousness. I knew then that the Great Hour of Killing had arrived and I went to the living room to play the organ.

"After a time, the Prophet came out of the bedroom and began to visit his punishment upon Marina and Petra.

"I continued to play the organ, but afterwards I went to help with the removal of the unclean parts. When this was completed, the Prophet went to meditate and I performed music suitable to such a solemn occasion on the organ.

"The Prophet then went away and I followed him, but losing our way, we wandered for many hours through the wilderness before arriving the following day at the house of the good Dr Trenkler where we wished to bring the glad news to Sabine."

Dr Francisco had been present when these statements were made and he had since listened to tape recordings of them. He was not, however, prepared to offer a definite opinion.

"I cannot say with certainty that these people are mad," he said. "It would seem that there were terrible emotional pressures within the family which eventually led to an explosion, but we do not know what these pressures were or even if the man and the boy are sincere in their statements. Do they really believe the boy to be a prophet of God? Or has this story been invented to conceal the real reasons for the murders, the guilt feelings arising from imagined or real incestuous relations within the family?"

"It is possible that the answers to these questions can be obtained through psychoanalysis, but I am not competent to conduct it or to evaluate the results."

"Perhaps this has already been done sometime in their past," said the inspector. "We have contacted the German police and asked them to investigate the background of the family. After all, they only arrived in Santa Cruz in January last year, so they had been here less than a year at the time of the murders. It would seem to me that, if they are actually insane, they were already insane when they came here and there may be some record of this. Perhaps they have all been released from a mental institution, but if that is so I cannot understand why the German authorities issued them passports."

The German authorities had issued passports, according to the report later received from the German police in Hamburg, because there was no record of mental illness in the Alexander family nor any other reason why such passports should not be issued.

Nor was there any such record in Dresden in East Germany which was where the Alexanders had come from. On such matters, the two Germanys cooperate and the Dresden police had furnished a full report for their colleagues in Hamburg.

From this, it could be determined that all of the Alexander family had been born in Dresden and that Harald Alexander had been trained as a stonemason, a trade which he had followed both in Dresden and later in Hamburg.

The only thing that was in any way exceptional about the life of any of the Alexanders was that Harald Alexander had taken care of a lay preacher up until such time as he died. The lay preacher's name was Georg Riehle and he was a wagon-maker by trade. An admirer of the German mystic, Jakob

Lorber, who had lived from 1800 to 1864, Riehle had attempted to found a sect and had been called the Prophet by his very modest number of disciples. In his will, he had left Harald Alexander an organ, his sole possession, as compensation for having cared for him until his death.

"There is a connection," said the inspector, "but I cannot see what it means. Alexander cared for the prophet Riehle and later he called his son the prophet. Also, this organ must be the one which he inherited. I wonder what the tenets of Riehle's faith were?"

"I think that would be very difficult to find out now," said Dr Francisco. He and the sergeant were sitting in the inspector's office and listening to a translation of the Hamburg police report. "Riehle is dead. The East Germans are officially atheists and I doubt that they have much patience with sects of any kind. Besides, as I understand it, Riehle was not successful in his attempt to found a sect. I have heard of Lorber, but I do not think he was very important either."

The Hamburg police obviously did not think so for, although they mentioned that there was still a Lorber Society in Hamburg, they merely observed that it was a peaceful, non-violent association devoted to the study of Lorber's writings and that Alexander had, in any case, not been a member. Georg Demeteriades, the director of the society, had been questioned and had reported that Alexander had apparently been interested, but nothing more.

Aside from the Lorber society, the Alexanders had had no more contact with outsiders in Hamburg than in Santa Cruz. With one exception. A psychotherapist named Dr Udo Derbolowsky. He had been questioned by the Hamburg police and his statement was included in the report.

"As a child in Dresden, I often played in the workshop of Georg Riehle, otherwise known as the prophet," read the doctor's statement. "He was a great man and I admired him very much. I do not believe, however, that he knew Harald Alexander or any of the members of his family at that time.

"I first met the Alexanders in spring 1963. They had just arrived from East Germany and Alexander came to see me.

He told me that Riehle was dead and that he had told him, Alexander, before his death that, if he ever came to West Germany, he should come and look me up. They had just come from the east and had been able to bring nothing with them except the organ which had belonged to Georg Riehle.

"I loaned Alexander two hundred marks which he repaid when he found work. Later on, I occasionally called on the family and brought them small presents and food. Only Alexander was working and it was not easy for them.

"I found them attractive, decent people, but rather strange. They had no contact with anyone in Hamburg and seemed to live in a world of their own. They were very anxious to please God and everything in their lives revolved around Jesus of Nazareth.

"Alexander often played Georg Riehle's organ, but having had no musical training whatsoever, the results were remarkable to say the least."

"Interesting that he says everything for the Alexanders revolved around Jesus of Nazareth," remarked the sergeant. "Their flat here was in a street named after him."

"Probably no coincidence," said the doctor. "But how could they come here in the first place if they had no money. The passage alone for six people would not be cheap."

"Mrs Alexander received a small inheritance from an aunt," said the inspector who had already heard the translation once. "Twenty thousand marks. Not a great deal, but enough to move to Tenerife. After they got here, the girls went to work as maids with Dr Trenkler and the boy was apprenticed to the German consul's shipping agency. Everyone reports the same thing – they had no contact with anyone. Even the twins, who lived with the Trenklers, held themselves completely apart from the family. Whenever possible, the Alexanders gathered in their flat and remained there with the curtains drawn. Usually Alexander played the organ in the evenings and afternoons."

"He didn't work?" said the doctor.

"No," said the inspector. "Only the boy and the twins."

"They must have been religious fanatics and the crimes are the result of this," said the sergeant.

"Religious fanatics undoubtedly," said the inspector, "but

124

I cannot see that this has any connection with the murders. Jesus of Nazareth is not a violent character. Quite the contrary. Nor, as far as I can determine, was there anything violent in the teachings of Lorber or Riehle. Besides, I do not think there is such a thing as a sect where the members murder each other. There have been sects where murder was committed, but always on outsiders or specially chosen victims."

"I agree," said the doctor. "I think that what we have here are two forces, the one obscuring the other. On the surface, they were a family of religious fanatics, strange perhaps, but not dangerous either to themselves or to others. Beneath this surface, however, there was something much more sinister, something which placed such stress on the unreal world in which they already lived that this hideous explosion of violence took place."

"You are referring, I suppose, to our previous theory of possible incest?" said the inspector.

The doctor nodded gravely. "But how will you ever be able to determine such a thing? I doubt very much whether any of the surviving members of the family would discuss it."

"Well, perhaps not," said the inspector, "but we have people who are not exactly lacking in training in interrogation. After all, accused criminals are seldom anxious to discuss their crimes either and yet we persuade them to in many cases. We shall see what we can do with extended interrogation."

"Does it matter?" said the sergeant. "There is no question of guilt. Alexander and his son both admit to the murders, although Alexander claims that it was his son who really carried them out. Why must the court know the motive behind them?"

"First, because in a murder case, particularly one as horrible as this, it is essential that all possible information be collected concerning the matter so that the court can reach a just and reasonable verdict," said the inspector, "and secondly the record must show that every effort was made to eliminate any possibility of trickery. Granted, in this case that seems almost impossible, but deliberately causing a murder to look like an act of madness is not an original idea."

"I have a suggestion," said the doctor. "The girl Sabine is now separated from her family and no longer under their influence. She was not actually involved in the murders and there is no reason to believe that she is pathologically insane. She undoubtedly knows the truth about her family and, if one of the younger nuns at the convent could . . ."

"Befriend her," concluded the inspector. "Yes, it might work. The only thing is, I do not know if any of the nuns would do it. They might regard it as a breach of confidence."

"You could point out that in no case whatsoever will there be any prosecution of the girl and also that it may be beneficial to her mental health," said the doctor. "Even if the girl is not insane now, the knowledge of such terrible things might very well make her so."

"That is true," said the inspector. "The child is going to have to make a very great adjustment in her life. Her entire family is dead or permanently confined, whether in prison or a mental institution, and, as we already know, she has no contact with anyone else. Whether it helps the investigation or not, every effort should be made to help her clear her mind and conscience."

Although up to now both Harald and Frank Alexander had been under continuous interrogation, the object had been to learn the exact sequence of events and, if possible, the motives leading up to them. The direction of this interrogation was now altered to concentrate on the Alexanders' family life and a trained psychiatrist from the mainland was brought over to assist.

At the same time, a young nun who had previously studied in Germany and who spoke good German was found to attempt to breach the wall of silence with which Sabine Alexander had surrounded herself.

Upon first being separated from her father and brother, she had threatened to run away, but as it became obvious that this would be impossible, she had lapsed into a state of almost complete withdrawal. She was not uncooperative and she did not resist anything done to her, but she did nothing on her own initiative and she did not reply to questioning.

It was to be months before she would respond in any way

to Sister Ursule with whom she now came to share a room at the nunnery and who had been carefully briefed by Dr Francisco concerning what was believed to be hidden in the girl's background.

Whatever was hidden, it was hidden very deep, deeper perhaps in the case of Sabine than in the case of Harald Alexander or his son. Although apparently convinced of the divine nature of her brother and accepting him fully as the prophet, she had had certain doubts about the arrangements within the family and, as these were in conflict with the concept of the divine brother who could do no wrong, the events which she considered to be abnormal had been pushed down into her subconscious to the point where she was no longer aware of them.

This was not the case with Harald or Frank. Both believed without question that Frank was the prophet and that he was infallible. His father was his adviser and could offer suggestions, but an order by the prophet was to be carried out without protest and without hesitation.

According to Harald Alexander, his part in the murders of his wife and daughters had been the result of such a direct order and this order had been accepted equally by the victims themselves.

"When your son began to strike his mother on the head with the hanger, did she not attempt to protect herself or, at least, escape?" asked the interrogator.

"Of course not," said Alexander. "She had been commanded to sit still. The commands of the prophet are to be obeyed."

"And your daughters, Marina and Petra, were they aware that Frank was killing their mother in the bedroom?"

"I do not know. It was, in any case, none of their business."

"Was Petra present when Frank began to strike her sister with the hanger?"

"Yes."

"What did she do?"

"What could she do? She had been commanded to wait her turn."

"Did you suggest to your son or in any other way influence him to kill his mother and sisters?"

"No."

"Why did he kill them?"

"Who can know the ways of the prophet?"

One person who could know the ways of the prophet was Detective-Inspector Hernandez and this by the simple expedient of asking him. Frank Alexander showed no hesitation about discussing his motives for the murders or, at least, the motives as he understood them. The true motive was apparently something different.

"Why did you kill your mother and your sisters, Frank?" asked the inspector, speaking through an interpreter.

"They were unclean."

"In what way?"

"They were filled with lust. They wished to come between me and my father."

"How do you know they were filled with lust? Did you have physical contact with them?"

"They came into my bed. They caused the great feeling and the weakness that follows. I no longer wanted to go to my father."

The questioning continued for a long time and the answers were collected and evaluated by the psychiatrist who had been brought into the case. More information was provided by Sister Ursule who had now gained the confidence of Sabine Alexander to some extent, and gradually a picture emerged. It was a composite picture in which much had to be deduced and in which much remained unclear. How accurate it is can never be known for, within the twisted, tormented minds of the surviving Alexanders, fantasy and reality are inextricably mingled.

It appeared, however, that up until 1964, the year after the family arrived in Hamburg, the Alexanders had been a normal, conventional and highly religious family. Although impressed by the personality of Georg Riehle, they had not necessarily accepted all of his views and they had not, it seemed, been convinced that he was the Prophet of a new religion. Basically, they were worshippers of Jesus of Nazareth.

During the course of 1964, however, when Frank was twelve years old, there had been a certain amount of experimentation in sex between him and his sisters. This was, in itself, not particularly abnormal. The family lived withdrawn even at that time and there were no other children with whom they could test their sexual urges as they approached and passed puberty.

Although the liberty sex wave was, by now, sweeping over Germany, the Alexanders took no part in the new freedom. At the same time, it was inevitable that all of them would be exposed to the pornography with which enterprising businessmen swiftly flooded the country.

Marina was fourteen at this time and the twins were eleven. All had matured early physically and all were extremely pretty. The effect on the adolescent Frank must have been overwhelming.

And not only on Frank. Sometime during that fateful year, Harald Alexander took up sexual relations with his children, at first, apparently, only with the girls, but then later a homosexual relationship with his own son. It was not long after this that he began referring to Frank as the prophet.

What role Mrs Dagmar Alexander played in this tangle of relationships is not clear. She could hardly have failed to know what was going on. The family quarters were not large enough for that. As to whether she had actually engaged in an incestuous relationship with her son, Harald Alexander appeared to believe that she had not, Sabine appeared to believe that she had and Frank was incoherent on the subject. It must be remembered, however, that according to the statements of both Harald and Frank, Dagmar was the first to be murdered. The murders of the girls were possibly triggered by and an extension of the murder of the mother.

"What we apparently have here," said the psychiatrist, "is a more or less average German family which became involved, in all probability through the contact with Georg Riehle, in a mild form of religious fanaticism. They were not members of a sect; they were the entire sect.

"There is nothing very startling in their religious beliefs which seem to have been generally primitive Christian. There was an emphasis on prayer, spartan living and, above all, moral purity.

"It was undoubtedly for this reason that the Alexanders left East Germany and came to the west. Although the communists are more strict morally than the West Germans, they are also officially atheists and do not approve of religious sects, Christian or otherwise.

"It is perhaps significant that, when the Alexanders moved to Tenerife, Harald Alexander told Dr Derbolowsky that they were doing so because they feared that the Russians would overrun West Germany and that they would once again find themselves living under a communist regime. He also told Dr Derbolowsky that they had chosen an island belonging to Spain because in Spain there was strict morality and the sexual licence and promiscuity becoming prevalent in Germany were not permitted.

"Although it seems contradictory that the Alexanders should seek a morally strict place to settle when they themselves were already at that time engaged in a complicated incestuous and homosexual relationship, in actual fact the conflict between their high moral standards and their sexual activities had been eliminated by the simple expedient of elevating Frank to the role of the prophet.

"Being the prophet he could do no wrong and he was above ordinary human standards of morality. At the same time, his orders had to be obeyed, so if he directed the family to engage in incest this carried the authority of a divine command.

"Whether Frank gave these directions on his own initiative or whether he did so in compliance with a suggestion by his adviser, Harald Alexander, is not clear, but he did give such directions and, in so doing, relieved the other members of the family of any responsibility for their acts.

"On the surface, all was well. The Alexanders formed a closed society, living by their own rules and cut off completely from the outside world. Subconsciously, however, all of them must have had grave doubts as to the correctness of their actions.

"It must be remembered that these people were quite sincerely religious and convinced of the value of sexual morality. Yet, they were living in a manner which profoundly

130

violated the most stringent of all sex taboos. The emotional strain must have been tremendous.

"And of all the family, the one who bore the greatest burden of guilt was Frank. Although, perhaps, originally convinced of his divine role as the prophet, as he grew older and came into greater contact with the outside world, doubts must have arisen. The conflict between reality and belief became ever stronger until it finally crushed him and swept away the entire family in a single explosion of ghastly violence.

"Probably since the time of the murders he no longer thinks of himself as the prophet subconsciously, but consciously he is unable to admit this for it would entail full realization of the enormity of his crimes.

"As realization would lead to final and irrevocable madness, his mind is protecting itself by refusing to recognize the truth.

"There is no question of Frank Alexander standing trial for the murders of his mother and sisters. He was undoubtedly, then as now, in no way whether legally or mentally responsible for his acts nor did he realize the consequences of them.

"It is recommended that he be sent for psychiatric treatment to a suitable institution for an indefinite period of time. At the present moment, no prognosis is possible."

The psychiatrist's report on Harald Alexander was different only in that Alexander apparently had lost none of his faith and still firmly believed in the divinity of his son. He too was judged not fit to stand trial.

Both Harald and Frank Alexander are now in institutions for the criminally insane where they are receiving psychiatric treatment. So far, neither has responded.

Sabine Alexander has been given permission to leave the convent, but has chosen, for the time being at least, to remain. Although now a grown woman, she has had very little contact with the outside world and has neither friends nor relatives to whom she can turn.

And so ends the strange history of the Alexanders. One in a convent, two in mental institutions and three dead.

These three deaths, where a mother and her two daughters

sat quietly, patiently and unprotestingly waiting for their son and brother to murder them while the husband and father played wild, discordant music on the organ, are and will undoubtedly remain among the least explicable murders of all time.

NINE

THE IMPOTENT GIANT

It was a crisp, autumn evening on November 15, 1969, when sixteen-year-old Sieglinde Huebner disappeared. A pretty, vivacious brunette, she had left her parents' home in the village of Kaltenbrunn shortly after seven to catch the bus to nearby Rossach where she was planning to attend a dance.

When Sieglinde had not returned by midnight, her father, Fritz Huebner, telephoned her best girlfriend from whom he learned that his daughter had not arrived at the dance at all.

He immediately dialled the number of the district police headquarters in Coburg, ten miles to the north.

By the time that he was connected with the desk sergeant on night duty he was already so alarmed that he had some difficulty in making himself understood.

There was a good reason.

Within the past year, two other pretty teenage girls had also disappeared.

When they had been found, their throats were cut.

Nor was that all. The girls had died neither easily nor quickly. They were found stripped naked, bound hand and foot with their own brassieres and stockings and their bodies covered with countless stab and slash wounds by means of which the sadist, who was to become known as the Beast of Oberfranken, had sated his lust.

And a strange lust it was, for despite the naked, nubile bodies, there had been no penetration of the sex organs.

The first murder had shocked the residents of the district. The second had roused them to a state approaching panic. Many parents refused to allow their teenage daughters out of

133

the house after dark and Fritz Huebner was now cursing himself for not having followed their example. He had thought that in a village as small as Kaltenbrunn and with the bus stop less than a block away there would be no danger.

The investigations of the police would later show that Sieglinde Huebner had never arrived at the bus stop at all that night.

If Inspector Karl Messing of the Criminal Investigations Branch of the Coburg District Police, who was now being summoned from his bed, had had the power to make such a decision, he would not have let a female of any age step foot outside her home unless accompanied by an able-bodied male. Unlike the relatives, the inspector had seen the bodies in the condition in which they were found. Hence his instructions that he be called regardless of the hour upon receipt of any report which might conceivably represent another attack by the Beast.

A tall, erect man with a hard, square-jawed face, the inspector was normally responsible for criminal investigations in all the many little communities surrounding Coburg, a medium-sized town a hundred miles to the north of Nuremberg, West Germany and a stone's throw from the communist East German border.

Now, however, he was relieved of all other duties and was concentrating exclusively on the Beast of Oberfranken (Oberfranken being the name of the district).

During the past year he and his assistant, Detective-Sergeant Peter Vogel, had followed up over a thousand leads and tips. Not one had led to anything at all.

There were only a few things which the inspector thought he knew about the Beast of Oberfranken. One was that he was at least twenty-five years old.

It could be assumed that the Beast was a local man, for all of the crimes attributed to him had taken place within a relatively small area and nothing similar had been reported anywhere else in Germany.

As for the weapon, the Beast had repeatedly thrust it so deep into the living flesh of his victims that it had been possible to take casts from the wounds. The weapon, said the

134

experts in the police laboratory, was a very sharp knife with a ten-inch serrated blade known as a "Cutting Devil". They were even able to say that it had been sharpened between attacks.

Finally, the Beast could not be much younger than twenty-five if it was accepted that it was he who had attacked nineteen-year-old Irmgard Feder, for that attack had taken place on Christmas Day 1959, nearly ten years earlier.

Irmgard was the only known survivor of one of the Beast's attacks and, according to her description, he could have been anywhere between fifteen and twenty-five at the time.

That Irmgard could not give a closer estimate of his age was excusable. When you are lying naked in the snow with your throat cut, you do not give a great deal of thought to the physical characteristics of your attacker.

The assault had taken place shortly after eight-thirty in the evening in the street of her home village of Freiberg, less than two miles from Kaltenbrunn where Sieglinde Huebner was now reported missing.

Irmgard had gone to a Christmas-Day movie in the little town of Staffelstein and had returned on the eight-thirty bus.

It was, of course, already dark and it was snowing, but Irmgard was not frightened. Her parents' house was only a few hundred yards from the bus stop and the street was lighted although, at this hour, deserted.

She had covered nearly half the distance when she was struck a violent blow over the head from behind. Her wool cap was knocked down over her eyes and she fell to the ground, stunned and surprised but not seriously hurt.

Pushing the cap back from her eyes, she saw in the light of the street-lamps what looked like a stocky boy or young man. He was gripping an umbrella and it was apparently this with which she had been struck.

As she stared in terror and amazement, he dropped the umbrella and produced a long knife.

"Strip!" said the man in a sort of strained whisper.

With something approaching wonder, Irmgard Feder realized that the man was about to rape her right in the middle of the street, within sight of her own home.

More indignant and angry than frightened, she obediently

began to unfasten her clothing. She had not forgotten the advice of her parents and her teachers – never to resist a rapist, particularly one armed with a knife.

Still lying on the snow-covered ground, she stripped down to her wool cap and socks, expecting at any moment to have the rapist fall upon her.

However, although she could hear him panting with excitement, he made no move, but simply stood over her fumbling with the front of his trousers.

This went on for what seemed a long time and then, abruptly, like a great, squat toad, he dropped on to her naked body with such force that it took her breath away.

Deliberately, she parted her legs to facilitate the entry. Irmgard had still not lose her presence of mind and the sooner that the ordeal was over the better.

It was to end differently from how she had expected.

Instead of the anticipated forcing of her vagina there was a searing pain in the side of her neck.

The man's hand swung upward again and the street-light gleamed dully on the long blade of the knife.

Nearly insane with sudden fear, and helpless under the weight of her assailant's body, Irmgard Feder realized that she was not going to be raped.

She was going to be murdered!

Six times the knife rose and fell, the sharp, saw-toothed blade plunging into the soft flesh of her throat and then, as suddenly as it had begun, it was over.

The weight on her body lifted and he was gone.

Flopping like a fish on the agonizing hook of pain in her throat and with her mouth filled with blood, Irmgard Feder rolled over on to her hands and knees and began crawling in the direction of her home. She left a trail of blood the whole way, but she still had the strength to hammer on the door with her fists before she lapsed into unconsciousness.

Thirty minutes later she was on her way to the emergency hospital in Coburg, the ambulance screaming its way over the snow-covered roads while the intern held the transfusion bottle high over his head.

An hour later, Inspector Messing was listening to a somewhat incoherent report over the telephone by the village constable of Freiberg who had gone to the scene following a call from Irmgard's parents. He could only say that it reminded him of a pig sticking.

The inspector found the comparison apt once he had seen the blood-stained clothing in the snow and the red trail leading off down the street, and he turned out most of the Criminal Investigations Department.

The effort was in vain for, although they went over the area square centimetre by square centimetre, they found nothing to indicate the identity of whom they still thought was a rapist who had met with resistance.

It was only seventy-two hours later that they learned that he had not been a rapist and that he had met with no resistance.

By this time Irmgard Feder was out of danger and even reasonably cheerful, although she had scars which she would carry to her grave. By some miracle, none of the main arteries had been severed.

It was a bit of carelessness which the Beast, although he was not as yet so known, would not repeat.

In any case, the oversight produced no complications. Irmgard Feder was not able to identify her assailant other than to say that it was no one that she knew and that he seemed short, plump and, possibly, quite young. She thought he had a round face, but the street-light had been at his back and she had not seen his features.

"What do you make of it, Guenther?" asked the inspector.

Dr Guenther Heinemann, the department's lean, silver-haired medical expert, who had been summoned to the inspector's office to listen to the tape recording of Irmgard Feder's statement, took off his gold-rimmed glasses and began polishing them absent-mindedly before giving his answer.

"An adolescent perhaps," he said. "Possibly an over-weight boy who has problems in his relations with the opposite sex. In some adolescents the sex drive is strong enough that, if no other outlet is available, they may resort to crimes such as rape."

"But he didn't rape her," said the inspector.

"He may not have known how," said the doctor. "Or

137

perhaps he found himself incapable. In any case, it's obvious that he was unbearably frustrated and he took out his frustration on the girl. Were you able to turn up any leads?"

"Not one," said the inspector. "I think that it's someone from the area because I can't imagine what a stranger would be doing in a place like Freiberg. He isn't from Freiberg itself, of course, or the girl would have recognized him. We weren't even able to determine how he left the scene. Unfortunately, the entire village had got there by the time we arrived and the snow was so thoroughly trampled that he could have ridden off on a camel without our being able to find the tracks."

"He took the weapon with him?" said the doctor. "I wouldn't have expected that."

"He apparently took it with him," said the inspector. "At least, we didn't find it. The hospital made some wax prints of the cuts and the lab says they think it was one of those all-purpose knives called a 'Cutting Devil'. Serrated, single-edged blade with a sharp point."

The doctor nodded. "You can buy them in any hardware shop," he said. "Probably got it out of his mother's kitchen."

The question to which the inspector really wanted an answer was whether the fat boy, as he thought of him, would do it again, but this the doctor could not tell him.

"I'm a doctor, not a fortune teller, Karl," he said. "It will probably depend upon just how abnormal he is."

He was not, it seemed, abnormal enough to repeat his crime for, although the Criminal Investigations Department spent the next few months on a state of alert, there were no further attacks on women reported.

A year later, the matter was regarded as a single, isolated incident which had, fortunately, not ended in murder and which would never happen again. By the time nine years had passed, everyone had forgotten about it.

Actually, it was not quite nine years for it was on December 19, 1968, six days before the anniversary of the Feder attack, that fourteen-year-old Nora Wenzl disappeared.

She was immediately reported missing by her parents, but it was assumed that she had merely run away from home.

138

Her missing report was placed in the file with those of the forty-one other missing girls and boys in the district.

Nora's parents did not accept this version of their daughter's disappearance and came to see the inspector personally. Nora was, they insisted, a hard-working apprentice in a hair-dressing salon in Staffelstein, a scant mile from Welsburg, the village where she lived with her parents.

The inspector promised to look into the matter, but he had no success. Neither he nor his men could find the slightest trace of Nora Wenzl.

Not until February 10, 1969, that is, when the body of a pretty, fourteen-year-old girl turned up in the locks on the river Main at Viereth, twenty-five miles to the south of Staffelstein.

The body was well preserved considering the length of time that it had been in the water, and the Wenzls had no difficulty in identifying their daughter although they were only allowed to view the face from the chin upwards.

The reason for this was that Nora had been found completely naked, her hands and feet still bound with the vestiges of her brassiere and stockings, her body covered with deep cuts and slashes and her throat cut from ear to ear. She had died a virgin.

The case aroused unpleasant connections in the mind of Inspector Messing, who had a long memory, and the first thing that he wanted to know from Dr Heinemann upon completion of the post-mortem was whether it had been possible to determine the instrument with which the cutting had been done.

"A 'Cutting Devil'," said the doctor. "And I think I know what you have in mind."

The doctor also had a long memory.

The technicians at the police laboratory did not have particularly long memories, but they kept excellent records. From them, they were able to determine that, beyond all reasonable doubt, the knife which had killed Nora Wenzl was the same one that had been plunged into the throat of Irmgard Feder.

It had, they said, been sharpened in the meantime, but

139

there was no mistaking it. They added, rather gruesomely, that there had been no difficulty in obtaining good casts of the blade as the murderer had thrust it in up to the hilt in several places.

"And, I'm afraid, slowly," said the doctor, wrinkling his brow in sincere distress. "The indications are that he tortured her for quite a long time before cutting her throat."

Sergeant Vogel cleared his throat brusquely. He was a man of almost frightening appearance – bushy-browed, completely bald and squat as a badger – but he was actually rather tender-hearted and his previous experience in police work had not prepared him for horrors such as this.

"We've had a circular to all stations on the telex for over seventy-two hours now," he said in a slightly husky voice, "and there's no report of anything similar anywhere else in Germany. Do you want to call Interpol?"

"Yes, to be on the safe side," said the inspector. "But he's not from some other country. He's from right here. The knife shows that it was that same fat boy who cut the Feder girl's throat. He's matured from an adolescent homicidal maniac to an adult one."

He had also become, if anything, even more skilled in covering his traces.

The only thing the police were able to learn was that Nora Wenzl had left Staffelstein at the usual time on the afternoon of December 19, 1968, and was presumed to have been going home. A belated search of the brush on either side of the road leading to Welsburg turned up the rusted remains of a bicycle which was of the same make as hers had been, but it was a common make and could have been abandoned by someone else.

"It was nine years between the two cases," remarked the sergeant comfortingly. "Maybe it will be another nine years before he strikes again."

The inspector was not comforted. He did not believe that it would be nine years before the Beast of Oberfranken struck again.

And he was quite right. The next interval was slightly over eight months.

On the evening of August 27, 1969, sixteen-year-old Helga

140

Luther, a pretty blonde who wore her hair long and her skirts short, set out to hitchhike from Coburg to her home village of Lichtenfels, fifteen miles away. She never arrived.

Upon receipt of the report, the police, who were by now highly sensitive to disappearances of pretty teenage girls, mounted an immediate and massive search operation.

Helga was found the following afternoon lying in a ditch. She was naked, her hands and feet were bound with her stockings and her brassiere, she was covered with knife wounds and her throat was cut through to the spine.

The murder weapon, said the police laboratory, was a "Cutting Devil", the same, in fact, with which Irmgard Feder had been stabbed and Nora Wenzl killed.

The victim, said Dr Heinemann, had not been raped prior to her death.

The investigations at the scene showed that Helga Luther had not been killed in the ditch, but in a field nearly half a mile distant where the clothing which she had worn still lay.

Both the clothing and the grass around it bore traces of the victim's blood and urine. According to the findings of the autopsy, she had been tortured for at least an hour before an end was put to her suffering.

Questioning of the dead girl's friends produced the information that she was thoroughly experienced in sexual matters and had had a streak of sadism in her nature. She had often boasted that she enjoyed nothing more than arousing a man to an almost unendurable pitch and then refusing or delaying his relief as long as possible.

Otherwise, the only information uncovered was that Helga had left the Mohrenkeller Tavern, a popular discotheque in Coburg, at approximately eleven-fifteen. She had said that she was hitchhiking home.

No one was ever found who admitted to having seen her after that time.

"Which means," said the inspector, "that she was probably picked up right here in Coburg."

An appeal to the general public for people travelling along the road between Coburg and Lichtenfels after eleven o'clock on the night of the murder had produced several motorists, none of whom had seen Helga Luther or anyone else hitchhiking on that evening.

All of these details had appeared in the local press and Fritz Huebner was well aware of them. He would have been even more terrified had he known all that the police knew.

Not only were periods between the crimes growing shorter; the time spent torturing the victim was growing longer.

If Sieglinde Huebner was in the hands of the Beast of Oberfranken, it was almost unthinkable what she was undergoing now.

The inspector did everything that he could. The entire Criminal Investigations Department was called out, the off-duty members of the uniformed branch were brought in, volunteers from the fire department and members of civic organizations were organized into search parties and for the rest of the night the search went on.

No trace of Sieglinde Huebner was found.

"I don't think that there's a square foot between Rossach and Kaltenbrunn that hasn't been gone over," said Sergeant Vogel, reporting to a grim, red-eyed inspector as the autumn sun began to climb above the tree-lined horizon. "She just isn't there."

"Then there's only one thing we can pray for," said the inspector. "Let's hope she's run off with some young man."

"Do we wait to see?" said the sergeant.

"I want every man in the department to report to me in Kaltenbrunn within an hour," said the inspector. "She disappeared in Kaltenbrunn and we're going to check out every resident."

The inspector already knew that Sieglinde had not caught the bus for Rossach. The bus driver had been one of the volunteers helping in the search and, like all drivers on local runs, he knew practically every one of his passengers by sight.

Sieglinde, he was certain, had not got on the bus in Kaltenbrunn that evening. As a matter of fact, no one had.

If this were true, then the inspector knew something important. Either the Beast of Oberfranken was a resident of Kaltenbrunn or there had been a stranger in the village that evening.

By ten o'clock that morning, the inspector was sitting in Kaltenbrunn's Gehrlicher Tavern and drinking black coffee and was reasonably certain that there had been no stranger. No one had seen one and the residents of small, European villages have remarkably sharp eyes for any strangers in their midst.

This left a possible suspect group of approximately thirty men above the age of twenty. None lived alone. All claimed to have spent the evening with their families or in the tavern.

"However, one of them didn't," said the inspector. "I'm practically certain of it and I'm certain of something else. There are people in this village who suspect the identity of the murderer."

"Then why don't they come forward?" said the sergeant. "We haven't had a single tip."

"They're probably not sure," said the inspector. "And in a place of this size, you don't go around accusing people of murder unless you're damn sure."

"So what do we do?" said the sergeant. "We've already interviewed every person in Kaltenbrunn."

"We're going to spread a false rumour," said the inspector. "We're going to let the people here think that someone has given us a tip and that we're going to make an arrest shortly. That should loosen a lot of tongues."

As a matter of fact, it only loosened one, but that was enough. A woman, who requested and was guaranteed anonymity, volunteered the information that she had seen Sieglinde Huebner getting into a grey Audi 60 on the evening of November 15.

"She undoubtedly knows that there's only one such car here in Kaltenbrunn," said the inspector, "which was why she was unwilling to make a statement before. It's the same as a direct accusation."

"You don't think there's a possibility that she's merely working off a grudge?" said the sergeant.

The inspector shrugged. "There's always the possibility," he said. "So we're going to go about it cautiously. Have you got the report of Wittmann's interview there?"

Manfred Wittmann had been one of the men previously questioned. A twenty-six-year-old worker in an asphalt plant in nearby Grossheirath, he lived with his parents in Kaltenbrunn and drove a grey Audi 60.

Wittmann, who was unmarried, weighed well over fifteen stone and stood a bare five feet six inches tall. He was popular in Kaltenbrunn, where he was assistant chief of the volunteer fire department and the founder of the table tennis club, of which Fritz Huebner was a charter member.

Most evenings Wittmann could be found at the Gehrlicher Tavern which served as a sort of social club for the men of the village and, according to his statement to the police, that was where he had been on the evening of November 15.

There was no question but that he had been at the tavern at some time during the evening, but it had not been possible to establish the exact time. In such a place there were continual comings and goings and no one kept close track of the time or who was present.

However, in concentrating the investigations on Wittmann, information concerning certain peculiarities in his background was brought to light which might or might not prove significant.

According to a statement made by one of Wittmann's friends, the stocky, round-faced man was afraid of women.

Some five years earlier, he and Wittmann had gone out together and, in the course of the evening, had picked up two girls.

The girls had taken them to their flat in another town and had immediately got down to business, stripping to the skin and making it clear that they were sexually available.

The friend had promptly followed suit, but Wittmann had turned brick red and had refused to undress. When the girls had attempted to undress him, he had thrown them violently off and had fled the flat.

The friend had found the incident comical, but Inspector Messing did not.

He was on the point of ordering that Wittmann be taken into custody when new information was received which excluded him as the murderer of Nora Wenzl.

Wittmann had been doing his military service at the time at a base a good hundred miles distant.

However, further checking placed Wittmann back on the

suspect list and even improved the likelihood that he was, indeed, the Beast of Oberfranken.

At the time when Nora Wenzl had been killed, Manfred Wittmann was home on leave in Kaltenbrunn.

"I think we have enough evidence now to make the arrest," said the inspector. "There isn't enough for a trial and, probably, not enough for a charge, but we'll have to get the rest out of Wittmann."

This did not turn out to be as difficult as the inspector had feared. A routine physical examination by Dr Heinemann revealed that Wittmann was no more developed genitally than an average ten-year-old boy, and this completely broke the fat man's spirit.

"It was me that cut the Feber girl that time in Freiberg," he said. "I didn't want to hurt her. I just wanted to have sex. But then, when she was lying there all naked, I couldn't. I just couldn't, you understand?"

The inspector understood. He had already been advised by the doctor that Wittmann was probably incapable of achieving an erection.

"And Nora Wenzl?" he prompted.

"I knew her," said Wittmann. "She used to cut my hair. That day, I saw her pushing her bike up a hill on the road to Welsburg. I drove past her, parked the car and came back. I had to do something. I had to get relief. I didn't want to kill her, but then, after it was over, I felt relieved and better."

"Helga Luther?" said the inspector.

"She was no good," said Wittmann. "I was in the Mohrenkeller that night and I heard her say she was hitchhiking home so I followed her out and offered her a ride. She got in the car and said that, since I was going to do something for her, she would do something for me and she pulled up her dress and took her pants down and she wanted me to touch her and I was like I was crazy because I couldn't do it."

The inspector drew a deep breath. "Where is Sieglinde Huebner?" he said.

"I'll take you to her," said Manfred Wittmann.

The body of the young girl lay in a pool in the forest some five miles from Kaltenbrunn. She was naked, her hands and feet were bound with her brassiere and stockings, her body was covered with countless deep knife wounds and her throat was cut.

A year later, Manfred Wittmann was brought to trial, repeated his confessions in detail and was sentenced to life imprisonment.

The details of the confessions were so horrible that much of the trial was excluded to the public. However, perhaps the most horrifying statement of all was Wittmann's reply to Inspector Messing when he asked, shortly after the discovery of the body of Sieglinde Huebner, what he had done with the knife.

"Why, it's in my drawer at the shop," said Manfred Wittmann. "I use it to cut up my bread and sausage for lunch."

TEN

GIVE THE POOR KIDS A RIDE

Driving down the Route Nationale 6 on that magnificent, high-summer day of July 15, 1972, the heart of forty-one-year-old Leon Millau rose up in his well-padded chest and nearly strangled him from pure joy.

It was a Saturday and he was setting off on that most beloved of French institutions, his summer holiday.

The unmarried forester had left his home town of Jarny in the Lorraine early that morning in his old Peugeot, heading south for the sunny hills and valleys of the Provence. Despite the fact that it was the second day of a holiday weekend, he had made such good time that he was now passing through the lovely countryside of Burgundy, approximately halfway between the cities of Macon and Lyons.

All the way down, he had been passing hitchhikers, some boys, some girls. Millau stopped for none. He did not dislike young people, but he was cautious and thought that some of these young travellers would be in need of money and, although he did not have a great deal with him, they would have no way of knowing that.

Not that he wasn't occasionally tempted. It was the era of the mini-skirt and some of them were so short as to be little more than wide belts. The wearers were in many cases attractive and as they attempted to persuade the drivers to stop they gave reason to believe that they were not totally unapproachable.

Millau stoutly resisted all temptations and, when he finally picked a side road to turn off, set up his little camp stove and prepare his lunch, it was at a point where no hitchhikers were in sight.

Like his own Lorraine, the area was heavily forested in places and the road he had chosen was one of the logging roads used by the local foresters in their work of tending, thinning, harvesting and replanting the trees. Forests in most parts of Europe are practically farmed.

The logging road went straight in for a hundred yards, made a turn to the right, a turn to the left, another right and then opened into a small glade some thirty yards across.

The glade was covered with relatively short, green grass with a number of wild flowers in it and was surrounded by old beeches, oaks and a few ashes. The early afternoon sun was streaming down like liquid gold gushing from a blast furnace.

It was the perfect place to have lunch, but, to his disappointment, he saw that someone had arrived before him.

Parked in the grass just off the road was a green Fiat 850 with a Lyons licence plate, and lying in the grass beyond it, on his back and apparently taking a nap in the sun, was the driver.

Unwilling to intrude and preferring to take his lunch alone, Millau drove on pas the Fiat, made a U-turn and started back towards the road.

As he did so, however, a large black bird, which he recognized as a raven, suddenly swept down across the glade and, to his amazement, landed on the sleeping man's face.

Millau yelled a warning, stopped the car, started to open the door and then stopped.

Although the bird was pecking at his face, the sleeper had not moved and Millau's forester's eye had caught something else. As the bird had lighted, a fine, black cloud had risen up around it and immediately subsided again.

Millau had seen that cloud often enough over the body of a dead deer or other animal. It was a cloud of feeding insects.

The man was dead and had obviously been dead for some time. The body was beginning to decompose in the hot July sun and it had attracted the bird and the insects.

For a moment, Millau contemplated getting out and trying to shoo the feeders away, but then he realized that he would have to leave to notify the authorities and that they would merely come back as soon as he was gone.

Throwing the car into gear, he drove as fast as the road would allow back to the main highway and turned south. He had come from the north and he knew that it was a good five miles in that direction to the nearest community.

As it turned out, he was only about a mile from the edge of the city of Villefranche-sur-Saône. He drove to the police station in the town centre and made his report in person to the officer on duty.

A large, blond, blue-eyed sergeant from the Department of Criminal Investigations was summoned and, having listened to what Millau had to say, asked him to accompany him to the scene of the discovery.

Upon their arrival, they found nothing changed except that the raven had been joined by two others and, while Millau waved a branch to keep off the insects, the sergeant covered the body with a plastic sheet and called headquarters over the police car radio, informing his superior, Inspector Denis Truffaut, that the report of a corpse was correct and that, in his opinion, the man had been stabbed or shot.

Half an hour later, the inspector arrived – a stocky, broad-shouldered man who wore his blue-black hair in a crew cut. He was accompanied by the Villefranche coroner and half a dozen detectives and specialists from the police laboratories. The entire area was immediately staked off and one of the detectives was assigned to drive Leon Millau back to his car so that he could be on his way.

In the meantime, Detective-Sergeant Pierre Moissonneur, the officer who had come out with Millau, had been going through the Fiat and had found the car's registration papers which indicated that the owner of the car was a Mr Jean-Michel Ray, aged twenty-five and a resident of Lyons.

Although the dead man appeared to be about this age, the identification was not complete until the specialists, going through the pockets of his clothing, produced a personal identification card bearing the man's thumbprint and picture.

The dead man was indeed Jean-Michel Ray, married, the father of a one-year-old boy and a salesman for an iron manufacturer.

Apart from the identification card and a few personal papers, there was nothing of value in Ray's pockets or in the car at all, indicating that he had been robbed.

Robbed or not, he had definitely been murdered and, according to coroner Dr Marcel Desmoines, by at least two people.

"The stab wounds are not identical," he said. "Both knives were single-edge and very long, eight or ten inches, I should judge, but one was broader at the base and it made a wider cut. There are seven or eight stab wounds, divided between two knives, and he has a few cuts on the right hand and on both forearms where he tried to protect himself. Time of death was about twenty-four hours ago."

"On Bastille Day then," remarked the inspector. "I don't know if that makes it harder or easier."

"It may be easier to trace his movements and those of the murderers," suggested the sergeant. "Everything was closed yesterday. Have you any theory yet?"

"Only that if robbery was the motive, he must have picked up a stranger in his car and probably a couple of women," said the inspector.

"Women?" said the inspector uncertainly. "Isn't this a pretty savage sort of killing for a couple of women?"

"It's a pretty savage sort of killing for any sex," said the inspector, "but I can't imagine the fellow driving back in here off the road with a couple of men."

"They could have forced him," said the doctor.

"Yes, but would he have picked up two men in the first place?" said the inspector. "There are not many people foolhardy enough to do that."

"It's true that you never see two men hitchhiking together," said the sergeant. "Two girls or a man and a girl, yes, but never two men. I suppose that it's because they wouldn't get a ride that way."

"The only other possibility is that the robbery is faked in order to throw off the investigation," said the inspector, "but I doubt that. Such a thing would indicate a sophisticated, carefully planned murder by someone having a personal motive, and this man wasn't old enough or rich enough to make him a likely candidate. We'll have to have the Lyons police check out his private circumstances, but I would be surprised if they found anything."

He was not going to be surprised. The Lyons police reported that Jean-Michel Ray had been exactly what his papers had said he was, a young man with an average job, married less than two years and with no known enemies or any reason to have any.

The post-mortem had not produced anything very significant either. Ray had been stabbed eleven times, five times with one of what the doctor estimated to be two butcher knives and six times with the other. Four of the stab wounds were in the back, but none had been immediately fatal. Ray had actually died of loss of blood at approximately four o'clock in the afternoon on July 14, after a death struggle which could have lasted up to an hour.

The only conclusion that the doctor was able to reach was that the murderesses were totally inexperienced and had only a rudimentary idea of where the vital organs in the human body lay. Despite the many stab wounds not one vital organ had been touched.

The specialists from the Villefranche police laboratory had also discovered confirmation of the theory that the crime was the work of two women in the form of a hair-clip which was recovered from the grass near the body.

It was taken to Lyons to be shown to the victim's wife, as it was possible that it had been in Ray's pocket or lying in the car, but, as the inspector had hoped, Mrs Ray promptly asserted that it was not hers and that she had never owned such a hair-clip.

There was, of course, also the possibility that the hair-clip had been dropped in the grass by someone else prior to the murder and had no connection with it, but the laboratory was able to establish the fact that it could not have been lying in the grass for more than two days, making it highly improbable that it was there coincidentally.

"I think that we can safely assume that it belongs to one of the murderesses," said the inspector. "In any case, it's the only clue we have so we'll follow it up."

"If we can," said the sergeant. "It's a cheap hair-clip, not exactly an uncommon item. However, it does have the

151

manufacturer's name on it so we may be able to learn over what area the things are distributed."

"This sort of thing sometimes has a smaller area of distribution than you'd think," said the inspector. "In any case, we're not going to work solely on that. We'll keep pushing for witnesses who may have seen Ray picking up his passengers, or his car with them in it. Route Nationale 6 isn't all that heavily congested on a Friday afternoon, even on a holiday."

"Something else has occurred to me, too," said the sergeant. "What about if we try to find out where they bought the knives? It's possible that they were bought not long before the crime and a couple of women coming in to buy butcher knives like that might be remembered. They probably didn't look like two housewives."

"A brilliant idea, Pierre," said the inspector. "Work on it. It's not at all unlikely that the knives were bought expressly for the job and, perhaps, even the same day."

The investigation now fanned out in all possible directions, the specialists of the police laboratory attempting to trace the origin of the hair-clip, the sergeant directing a squad of detectives canvassing hardware shops in the towns to the north of the point where the murder had taken place, as it was known that Ray had been headed south towards Lyons, and the inspector arranging for appeals in the press, radio and television requesting anyone passing along Route Nationale 6 on the afternoon of Friday, July 14 between the hours of one and six to report to the police.

The inspector had the most success immediately and a surprising number of people reported in. Traffic along the Route Nationale 6 had been heavier on that Bastille Day than he had expected.

There had also, it seemed, been a large number of hitchhikers along the road, all young and mostly single, but with a few boy and girl or girl and girl combinations.

It was the couples that interested the inspector, particularly the boy and girl couples who he now thought more likely suspects. However, all of these appeared to have got rides with one or other of the people reporting in and, as they had all been picked up to the north of the place where Ray had been killed and taken all the way into Lyons, they were eliminated as suspects.

With the all-girl couples he had rather more luck. All of these appeared to have got rides and all had eventually been taken on in to Lyons, but one couple, described as extremely young girls, showed an ominous pattern in their hitchhiking.

They had had three rides to the north of the point where Ray had been killed and, although they had asked the driver upon getting into the car if he was going all the way to Lyons, they had asked to be let out after only a mile or so.

Finally, this same couple had had a ride just to the south of the point where Ray had been murdered less than an hour after the murder had taken place and had then gone on all the way into Lyons.

All four drivers were brought to police headquarters for questioning and all told much the same story with the exception of the last, the only case where the girls had not asked to be let out after only a mile or two.

The first of the other three was an enormously broad, muscled driver of a brewery truck and he stated that he had picked up two young girls just outside Macon. Aside from asking him if he was going on into Lyons, they had not exchanged so much as a word with him or with each other and, after less than a mile, they had abruptly asked to be let out. They had been less provocatively dressed and looked promiscuous, but they had not made any sexual overtures towards him.

They had towards the driver of the second car who had picked them up at the spot where the truck driver had let them out. The girls, he said, were wearing very short miniskirts which they had let ride up when they sat down. One, at least, had not been wearing underwear.

The other girl, the older of the two he thought, had sat next to him and had attempted to touch his genital area. Both had spoken in a suggestive manner, saying that they were short of money and were anxious to earn some, making it clear that they did not care how.

The driver, an accountant, had not responded – not, as he bluntly told the inspector, because he had any moral reservations, but because the whole business struck him as suspicious and dangerous. He had told the girls flatly that he was not interested in sex with them, but if they would keep their hands to themselves, he would give them a ride into Lyons. Shortly after this remark, they had asked to be let down.

The third driver, who had picked the two girls up a short distance down the road from where they had been let out by the accountant, had also been the subject of sexual overtures, but had not even realized it. A totally unworldly man in his mid-fifties who was in charge of an animal shelter in a small town to the south of Lyons, he had taken the two for children, although if the descriptions of the truck driver and the accountant were accurate, they were very precocious children indeed.

Actually, the animal shelter director's description was not much different and, from what he told the inspector, it was obvious that the girls had been trying to sell him sex or at least lead him to believe that they were sexually available.

They had asked him to drive back into one of the side roads such as the one where Ray had been murdered for, as they said, a little privacy and rest.

The driver had naïvely replied that they could lie down in the back seat and rest. He was in a hurry to get back to his animal shelter as one of the dogs was due to have her puppies shortly and he did not want her to be alone at the time.

A little later, the girls asked to be let out. The point was less than four miles to the north of the forest glade where Jean-Michel Ray had met his death.

"I think we've got them," said the inspector. "There are just too many coincidences. Here are their descriptions – if they bought the knives in Macon, you should be able to find out where. God knows, they were a striking enough couple to be buying butcher knives."

Both were pretty and extremely well-developed physically, but both also gave the impression of being dirty and unkempt. The older of the two girls, a brunette, had had slightly curly hair and a round, full face. The other, a dark blonde, had straight hair. Both had worn their hair down to well below their shoulders.

They had been dressed in mini-skirts and, apparently,

154

little else and had carried large tote bags of beaded canvas or something similar.

According to all of the drivers with whom they had spoken, their language had been slangy and full of stylish obscenities. The truck driver said that he thought they had some sort of secret sign language between themselves for he had seen them making odd hand gestures shortly before they asked to be let out.

The estimates of their ages varied from twelve and fourteen by the naïve animal shelter director to sixteen and eighteen by the suspicious accountant, though both girls had been over five feet tall.

The word which was used to describe them by all the people interviewed, even the animal shelter man, was "hippies". Unfortunately, this was a term being generally applied to any young person with an unconventional manner of dressing or hairstyle. The sergeant made several false starts, tracing reports of hippies buying knives which turned out to be young housewives or daughters of respectable families who were following fashion.

Finally, however, he hit upon nineteen-year-old Gabriele Argoud, a clerk in a hardware store in Macon.

Questioned as to whether a pair of girls had bought butcher knives at any time shortly before Bastille Day, she said that two girls had bought two butcher knives on July 13 and she gave a description of them which coincided exactly with those given by the drivers who had picked up the two hitchhikers.

She remembered the girls very well, she said, because although they were younger than herself, they had frightened her.

After buying the knives they had requested that she sharpen them although they were already very sharp.

"Sharper!" they had said. "Get them sharper! We want them like razors!"

The knives had cost about a pound and she had the impression that that was all the money the two girls had, for they had priced them carefully before buying and she had not seen any more money in the older girl's purse when she had opened it to pay for the knives.

Asked why she had been frightened by her customers, Miss Argoud replied that she could not imagine what use two such young girls were going to make of such very sharp butcher knives and that this had made her nervous.

"Why didn't you report it to the police?" said the inspector. "Or at least to the owner of the store? I think you could imagine very well what those girls intended to do with the knives."

Gabriele Argoud was unable to answer these questions, but she did provide the police with one useful clue. The younger girl had called the older one Micheline.

If the knowledge of such a common first name as Micheline was a slim reward for all of the investigation work in Macon, the information concerning the knives which had been purchased on the day before the murder was not.

There were other identical knives in stock in the hardware store and, taken to the police laboratory in Villefranche, they were found to match precisely the casts made of Jean-Michel Ray's wounds.

There was now little doubt but that these two girls who had bought the butcher knives in the hardware store in Macon and who had, on the following day, been picked up by five drivers on the Route Nationale 6, were the murderesses of the young salesman.

Four of the drivers had escaped, the truck driver presumably because the girls had thought him too tough to handle, and the others because they had refused the sexual overtures intended to get them off the main road and into a secluded spot where the girls could carry out their deadly plans.

The fifth driver, Jean-Michel Ray, had succumbed to temptation and it had cost him his life.

The question was, of course, who and where these two girls were.

It was not an easy question to answer. So far, all the police had were five relatively good descriptions, the first name of the older of the two and the fact that both were undoubtedly French.

The logical place to look was in reports of runaway girls but by now there were so many of these that a complete

156

search would have taken years. Worse yet, not all parents reported when their children ran away, some apparently being happy to see them go.

Without knowledge of the district from which the girls had come, tracing them from a missing report was almost impossible and there was no way of knowing where in France their homes were.

What was known, however, was where they had been on the night of July 13, for they had bought the knives in Macon that afternoon and had caught a ride with the truck driver just south of Macon on the following day.

Micheline and her friend had, therefore, spent the night of July 13 in Macon and probably in some place which cost little or nothing as they had had, according to Gabriele Argoud, scarcely any money.

Considering the impression that they had made on all of the drivers other than the man from the animal shelter, it seemed more than likely that they would have attempted to exchange their bodies for a night's shelter and, perhaps, dinner thrown in, but this was going to be hard to trace because the girls were obviously minors and any man who had spent the night with them would be afraid of admitting it to the police.

Nonetheless, Macon is a town with a population of only forty thousand, and there is not much that goes on there that cannot be traced if necessary. To find out if a couple of teenage female hippies had been trying to pick up men on the evening before Bastille Day, all that was needed was to ask the local prostitutes who, of course, had a keen financial interest in any such undertakings.

It seemed that two such teenagers had been trying to pick up men, but that they had not had any luck, the potential customers being, perhaps, thrown off by their youth. They had last been seen going in the direction of the local youth hostel where it was possible to sleep for little or nothing.

However, people spending the night at the youth hostel must register, and here the police finally learned the true names and ages of the suspects.

They were Micheline Brique, aged eighteen, and Jocelyne Chamand, sixteen.

There was no indication as to where they had come from, but the police soon found out.

Both girls had been in constant trouble with the juvenile authorities since the ages of eleven and twelve and, their families being unable to control them, they had been placed in an institution for delinquent girls.

It was in this institution that they had met and joined forces.

Whether in a deliberately planned escape or accidentally, both had managed to contract venereal disease in the all-female establishment and had consequently been transferred to a hospital for treatment. The hospital not having the security arrangements of the institution, it had been easy for them to escape. This they had done on July 11, taking with them what money they could find in the belongings of the other patients.

It had not been a large sum and presumably they had been broke and in need of money within two days. The last pound had been spent on the means of obtaining it – the butcher knives.

Armed now not only with the suspects' names, ages and descriptions, but even their pictures and fingerprints from the juvenile court, the police had little difficulty in taking the two girls into custody.

When arrested, they were still carrying the two butchers' knives with substantial traces of Jean-Michel Ray's blood on them.

Neither girl attempted to deny her part in the murder, both saying that they had planned to kill a driver in order to rob him and that Ray was the first suitable candidate.

The truck driver they had thought too big and tough and the others had not taken the bait.

They had not actually had sex with Ray and they did not know whether he had expected it from them. Arriving at the glade in the forest, there had been practically no conversation. Micheline had dropped her hair-clip deliberately and as Ray bent to pick it up for her, Jocelyne had stabbed him in the back.

Ray had swung around to defend himself and had been stabbed by Micheline in her turn. The two had then

158

continued to stab him until he fell to the ground. He had not died immediately and they had stood watching him for what they estimated to be half an hour or forty-five minutes while he bled to death. He had been conscious and moaning with pain most of the time, they said.

They had then taken his money, a sum of about five pounds, and had gone back to the highway to get a ride into Lyons.

Both girls recounted this story with no sign of emotion, as if it were the most natural thing in the world. They had needed money. They had killed Ray to get it.

They appeared to be under the impression that, being minors, the worst that could happen to them was that they would be sent back to the institution for delinquent girls and, had they been in Germany, they would have been right.

However, this was France, where even a teenager can be sentenced to the guillotine if the crime warrants.

The question was whether the girls were legally responsible for their acts or whether they were mentally and emotionally incapable of distinguishing between right and wrong, and here the psychologists who kept them under observation until the time of their trial were divided in their opinions.

On the one hand, their entire background showed an almost total lack of all normal moral values, and some psychologists maintained that murder would have appeared to them a logical and acceptable means of obtaining money.

Other psychologists were of the opinion that money was only a secondary consideration in the murder. Despite their extreme youth, Micheline Brique and Jocelyne Chamand were so sated with sex that they could stimulate themselves only through the most savage violence.

Evidence for this theory was the fact that they had let Ray die slowly while watching him, and both girls eventually admitted that they had engaged in mutual sexual gratification during his death agonies.

The court presumably found these conflicting opinions confusing enough to give some reason for doubt because, instead of sending the two young murderesses to the guillotine, they sentenced them to thirty years' imprisonment each.

ELEVEN

DADDY'S GIRL

It was a tragic choice because it was based on a false belief. If lovely forty-one-year-old Hilda Miller really did have cancer of the liver, she might have been justified in taking her own life, but, as a matter of fact, she did not.

What she did have was nothing more than an attack of kidney stones which, on October 15, 1979, led to her hospitalization in Victoria Hospital.

There she responded so well to treatment that she was soon able to return to the comfortable flat in the residential section of Melbourne, Australia, which she had shared for the past fifteen years with her common-law husband, forty-year-old Arthur Houdson, and her daughter from her first marriage, Charlotte.

Charlotte's father, Steven Miller, who would be forty-four now if he was still alive, had deserted his family when Charlotte was three. All subsequent efforts to locate him had failed, which was why Hilda's marriage to Arthur remained a common-law one. Legally, she was still married to Steven.

Charlotte was now eighteen, although she looked younger, a softer, even prettier version of her mother, and she did not miss her father at all. As far as she was concerned, Arthur Houdson was her father and she was devoted to him.

It had been a happy little family living in the apartment in Russel Street. Hilda and Arthur worked in the same import-export firm; in fact, they had met there. They were well paid. There were no financial or other problems. Charlotte was a good girl who had never given her mother or stepfather the slightest cause for concern.

The kidney-stone attack changed all that. Although Hilda had recovered completely from a physical point of view, the psychological shock resulting from her fear of cancer and her conviction that her family and even her doctor were concealing the truth from her, produced psychosomatic symptoms as severe as if she really did have the disease which she so dreaded.

Hilda returned home from the hospital in a state of profound depression, kept to her bed and suffered such nervous crises that John Fuller, her doctor, was forced to prescribe ever-increasing amounts of tranquillizers and barbiturates to ease the psychosomatic pain of the cancer which did not exist but which was killing her as surely as if it did.

In the end it did, and on the morning of Thursday, January 10, 1980, Charlotte called Dr Fuller in a state of complete hysteria to report that her mother was unconscious and that she could not rouse her.

Dr Fuller came at once, but he could not rouse Hilda either for she was already dead and had been for several hours at least.

How she had died was obvious. On the table next to her bed was a glass stained with orange juice and two empty tubes of the barbiturates which the doctor had himself prescribed. Each had contained twenty-five tablets, but they were now both empty.

It was, so to speak, psychosomatic suicide and the doctor could do nothing more than treat the violent weeping daughter for hysteria and shock and call the police. Hilda Miller had not died of natural causes and the death certificate would have to be issued by the Melbourne coroner.

Not long thereafter, Coroner Peter Macvay, a tall grave man going a little grey at the temples, arrived together with a detective-sergeant from the Melbourne Department of Criminal Investigations and carried out an examination of the corpse.

He agreed with Dr Fuller's diagnosis of suicide due to the ingestion of a massive dose of barbiturates, and thought that death had probably taken place as early as midnight. There would, of course, have to be a post-mortem.

While the doctor was proceeding with his examination, Sergeant Dirk Ralston, an amiable young man with a flat, square face which gave him an air of a cheerful bulldog, put on a pair of smooth, plastic gloves and collected the glass and empty tubes from the bedside table, placing them in plastic sacks for transport to the police laboratory.

The whole matter was routine and it was handled as such. In a city the size of Melbourne, suicides are not uncommon enough to startle either the coroner or the police.

The operations at the scene being concluded, the body of Mrs Miller was taken to an ambulance which transported it to the police morgue where Dr Macvay eventually carried out the post-mortem, reporting, as had been anticipated, that Hilda Miller had died as the result of the ingestion of fifty sleeping tablets dissolved in orange juice on the evening of January 9, 1980.

The death certificate was issued with the explanation that Mrs Miller had taken her own life in the false belief that she was suffering from incurable cancer. The post-mortem had shown no indications of cancer in the body.

Following the post-mortem, the body was turned over to the dead woman's common-law husband and daughter for burial, and the funeral took place very shortly afterwards. Apart from Charlotte, Arthur Houdson and sixty-six-year-old Mrs Mary Parks, Hilda's mother, there were no mourners and, of course, no publicity.

In the meantime, the police laboratory had completed the examination of the empty glass with the traces of orange juice and the two tubes which had contained the fatal tablets prescribed by Dr Fuller.

The resulting laboratory report was included in the file which the sergeant had set up describing the circumstances of the case, and this file eventually landed on the desk of the sergeant's superior, Inspector Thomas Hunt.

Inspector Hunt, a very large man who tended to look as if his suits were a size too small for him and who wore his hair short without sideburns, was not pleased.

"You've made a bit of a mess of this, Dirk," he said. "How'd you come to wipe the prints off the evidence?"

"I didn't wipe anything," said the sergeant indignantly. "Why would I do such a stupid thing?"

"Unintentional, I suppose," said the inspector shrugging. "Hard to believe that the woman wiped them off herself. Suicides aren't usually that concerned about where they leave their prints. Was there a towel or a cloth lying with the glass and the empty tubes?"

"Nothing," said the sergeant wonderingly. "Let me see that lab report, will you?"

He had not actually bothered to read it himself, assuming that the glass and the tubes would bear the fingerprints of Hilda Miller, but he now saw that the laboratory reported no prints of any kind and concluded that the items had been wiped clean after use.

"I don't know," he said, handing the file back to the inspector. "I certainly didn't wipe the things. Used gloves and put them straight into the sacks. They must have been wiped before we got there."

"But with what, if there was no cloth on the bedside table?" said the inspector.

"A sheet, I suppose," said the sergeant. "There were sheets on the bed."

"Sounds damn funny to me," said the inspector. "Here's a woman who's so out of her mind with depression and fear at having cancer that she deliberately kills herself, but she stops long enough to clean up the stuff on her bedside table with the sheet. I can't buy that."

"Certainly doesn't sound likely," agreed the sergeant. "I'll go to see her doctor. He was the first one to examine the body. Maybe he wiped the stuff, although I can't see why he'd do such a thing."

Neither could Dr Fuller.

"Of course not," he said emphatically. "I examined Mrs Miller only enough to ascertain that there was nothing I could do. I suspected immediately that it was suicide and I wouldn't have dreamed of touching anything in the room that I didn't have to, let alone wiping the glass and the tubes with a sheet."

"Apparently it was the girl," said the sergeant, reporting back to the inspector. "I talked to her and she said that she was in such a state that she's not sure what she did. She might have wiped the things without knowing it. She thinks that she had a dish towel in her hands when she went into the bedroom to wake her mother up. She's been doing all the cooking and housework ever since Mrs Miller came home from the hospital."

"I suppose it's possible," said the inspector. "Must have been an awful shock for a young girl like that. She's gone to live with her grandmother?"

"Oh no," said the sergeant. "She's still living in the flat in Russel Street."

The inspector jerked his head up in surprise.

"That's unusual," he said. "Her mother committed suicide in that flat. There wouldn't be many daughters who'd want to continue to live there alone after that."

"She's not alone," said the sergeant. "Her stepfather is still living there, too."

"Common-law stepfather," corrected the inspector absent-mindedly. "If there is such a thing."

He fell silent, apparently lost in thought and, after a time, got to his feet and walked to the window where he stood staring out at the street below, his hands clasped behind his back.

"How old is this Houdson?" he demanded suddenly, turning around to face the sergeant.

"Forty," said the sergeant. "You don't think that he . . .? the girl . . .?"

"I think a man of forty sharing a flat with an extremely attractive eighteen-year-old girl who is not a blood relative is exposed to more temptation than I would care to undergo," said the inspector. "I'm afraid we're going to have to take a little closer look at all this. If there is something between Houdson and his common-law stepdaughter, then that was a mighty convenient suicide."

"Any suggestions as to how I'm to go about that?" asked the sergeant. "These people are living in the same flat and have done so for years. They could be holding non-stop orgies seven nights a week and nobody would be any the wiser. I can't hide under the bed to see what they're up to."

"No, there's no way of knowing what goes on in the flat,"

164

said the inspector, "but you can talk to people who know them, see what they're like, what people think. You might begin by seeing if the girl has any boyfriends of her own age."

Charlotte Miller, it seemed, did. Not serious boyfriends, not steady boyfriends, but . . .

"Pretty close ones," said the sergeant. "The girl is not a virgin, if the boys I talked to can be believed."

"What kind of gossip did you pick up?" asked the inspector.

"Nasty," said the sergeant. "The neighbours think that Charlotte and her 'stepfather' are sleeping together. Nothing concrete, but they think that she acts more like a wife than a daughter. Pretty general impression."

"And probably a right one," said the inspector. "People have a feeling for that sort of thing. Well, on to the next step."

"Which is?" said the sergeant.

"To find out where Arthur Houdson was on the evening that his common-law wife so conveniently killed herself with sleeping pills and left him saddled with that beautiful eighteen-year-old daughter who is not a virgin," said the inspector.

"You think he did it?" said the sergeant.

"If I was paid to think, I wouldn't be a police officer," said the inspector. "Let's say it's at least possible."

Somewhat to the surprise of both the inspector and the sergeant, it transpired that Arthur Houdson had not been home at all on the night of his wife's death or, for that matter, even in Melbourne. That morning he had gone on company business to the town of Geelong, some fifty miles to the south-west, and had only returned the day after Hilda had been discovered dead in her bed.

"Or at least that's where he's supposed to have been," said the sergeant. "He was driving and Geelong is near enough for him to have come back during the evening if he had a good reason to."

"He did have a good reason to," said the inspector, who had in the meantime had a look at Charlotte Miller, although she did not know it.

"However, I've checked in Geelong," continued the

sergeant, "and he definitely was there and there's no evidence that he didn't stay. I've also done some more checking on Houdson himself. He has a very good reputation. Hard worker. Good father. Faithful as a collie dog to his common-law wife. No hint that he's ever even looked at another woman."

"You're conclusion then is that he didn't do it?" said the inspector. "What about his relationship with his step-daughter?"

"I don't know," said the sergeant. "Maybe there is one, but I don't see that it's any of our business. After all, they're not really related. It's not incest. Even if they decided to get married, there'd be nothing illegal in it."

"Definitely not," said the inspector, "unless we charge Arthur Houdson with aiding and abetting his wife's suicide. That isn't what interests me. What I want to know is did Houdson kill his common-law wife with sleeping pills in order to have a clear field with the daughter? If they actually were having an affair, he had an immensely strong motive. A man of forty having a sexual relationship with a beautiful eighteen-year-old could be expected to go all to pieces, regardless of how faithful he had been in the past. It's the old search for lost youth that gets so many people in trouble around that age."

"I doubt whether we can show that they were having an affair unless one of them decides to come in and tell us," said the sergeant. "There wouldn't be any witnesses and there'd be no point in them writing letters to each other when they were living in the same flat. With luck, we might be able to show that Houdson was in Melbourne on the night of the murder, but that's about all."

"There's something else that puzzles me," said the inspector. "How did he manage to give Mrs Miller the sleeping pills without the daughter suspecting anything? Even if she didn't notice anything at the time, she would surely have had some suspicions later on. Was she really attached to her mother?"

"Very much so," said the sergeant. "Everybody who knew them said that the girl was extremely fond of her mother and did everything she could for her. They were very close."

166

"Well, then she must suspect nothing," said the inspector, "or she wouldn't be still living with the man who may very well have murdered her mother. It's a strange set-up."

The sergeant thought so too.

There were only two possibilities and neither of them seemed very logical.

Either Arthur Houdson had been enjoying, as the neighbours believed, an affair with the daughter of his common-law wife and, having decided to get Hilda out of the way, had sneaked back from Geelong to kill her with the sleeping tablets, or Hilda had actually killed herself, either because she believed that she had cancer or, just possibly, because she had learned of the relationship between her common-law husband and her daughter.

In the case of the first alternative, it was difficult to see how Houdson could have given Hilda the sleeping tablets without being suspected of it by Charlotte.

In the second case, it was hard to accept that the suicide victim herself had wiped clean the instruments of her destruction, or that her daughter had done it unconsciously and with no memory of the act.

"The fact is," said the inspector, "wiping the glass and the pill containers was a deliberate act, not something that anyone would do absent-mindedly. The daughter coming into the bedroom and finding her mother unconscious or dead would have been concerned with reviving her or, at least, with summoning help. She would scarcely have stopped to wipe things and tidy up. No, the sole reason for wiping those things was to remove the fingerprints, and that, in my mind, means that Hilda Miller did not commit suicide, but was the victim of a deliberate murder."

"Unless," said the sergeant, "she wanted us to think exactly that. Supposing she learned that Arthur and Charlotte were making love in the living room while she was lying sick in bed? She might have decided to revenge herself by committing suicide and making it look like murder. I think I've heard of a case like that somewhere."

"So have I," said the inspector, "but I believe it was a fictional mystery story. People don't think so deviously in real life. Still, it's a valid point. Mrs Miller might have been

167

trying to frame Houdson because he had seduced her daughter. Any idea on how you can confirm or eliminate the theory?"

"None in the world," said the sergeant.

In fact, the case was extremely difficult to investigate. Hilda, Arthur and Charlotte had formed a tight, self-sufficient little family group to which no one had been admitted on such intimate terms that any information on the relationships within the group might leak out.

On the face of it, it had been a typical nuclear family, father, mother, one child. That the father was not married to the mother and also not the real father of the child was not an unusual aberration. With a record of fifteen years endurance, the unit was more stable than a good many legally constituted ones.

As for the neighbours' opinions that Arthur and Charlotte had been involved in something other than a parent-child relationship, it was just that – opinion. No one had the slightest real evidence of any such relationship, and it was hard to see how anyone could.

And yet, the matter stuck in the inspector's mind and troubled him. As an old experienced police investigator, the fact that there had been no fingerprints where fingerprints should have been rang an alarm bell in his subconscious, and the added aspect of a possible strong motive brought his suspicions to the surface. He would have produced a full-fledged investigation if only he had been able to find anything concrete to investigate.

So far, the only investigation that had been undertaken was by the sergeant, and it had not been entirely official. No charges had been brought. No murder file had been opened. Officially, the death of Mrs Hilda Miller was classified as suicide.

Both Charlotte and Arthur Houdson had been questioned, but only in connection with Hilda Miller's state of depression prior to her death, and Charlotte had made a brief statement concerning the discovery of the body.

Both had said that Hilda had been convinced she had cancer ever since her hospitalization for kidney stones and that she had been extremely depressed, had usually remained the entire day in bed and had sometimes refused to eat.

She had said repeatedly that she could see no point in waiting to die slowly of cancer and that it would be better to get it over with quickly and painlessly before the suffering became intense.

Although these statements could not be confirmed by Mrs Miller herself and might, therefore, have been suspect if it was to be assumed that the woman's death had not been suicide, they were fully supported by Dr Fuller who had said very much the same thing in a later statement to the police.

He had, as a matter of fact, not been at all surprised when his patient committed suicide, and had more or less expected to find something of that nature when he received the telephone call from Charlotte on the morning of January 10.

Asked why he had not had Mrs Miller committed to a psychiatric hospital if he thought she was a danger to herself, he pointed out that this could only have been done at the request of the next of kin or of the patient herself.

Mrs Miller, he said, would never have consented to such a thing and neither would her mother, Mrs Mary Parks, who was legally her next of kin. Charlotte, being a minor, could have no say in the matter and Arthur Houdson was no legal relation to the woman at all.

In addition, as Charlotte was continually home with her mother and was aware of her state of mind, he had felt that she was in as good or better hands than she would have been in a hospital.

Again, when checked, everything was logical, reasonable, in accordance with the theory of suicide. Hilda Miller had not been physically ill. She could easily have left her bed and taken the barbiturates from the medicine cabinet in the bathroom after her daughter was asleep. Arthur Houdson was not present, but in Geelong. Perhaps that was the reason she had chosen that particular night to kill herself . . . there would be no one to interfere . . .

The inspector gave up. Although he still had a funny feeling about the case, there was nothing more that he could do which might shed any further light on the true circumstances. If Arthur Houdson had murdered his common-law wife in order to replace her with her daughter, he had got away with it.

Conversely, the sergeant continued to poke about the case, a little like a child poking at a dead snake with a stick. Though he had started out with the idea that the inspector's suspicions had no basis and were merely the result of being a criminal investigator for too many years, he had gradually swung around to the opposite position.

This was not because of anything that had turned up during the course of his investigations.

Everything he had learned about Arthur Houdson tended to confirm that he was a respectable, conscientious man who had been sincerely devoted to his common-law wife and stepdaughter. He had often expressed regret that it was not possible to legalize their relationship and there was no reason to doubt that he had meant it.

The gossip by the neighbours concerning his relationship to Charlotte had no real foundation and was, probably, more the result of jealousy than anything else. Houdson was an attractive, well-kept man. Charlotte was young and beautiful. There were always people who would think that others had things a little too good.

The only interesting point which the sergeant had found out in all his investigations was that Houdson had not really had to go to Geelong on that day. He had volunteered. Had he been setting up an alibi?

It seemed hardly probable. Even assuming that he had gone to Geelong, had come back during the night and managed to enter the flat without waking Charlotte, how could he have persuaded Hilda to drink the orange juice containing the barbiturates?

It would have been late. He would, presumably, have had to wake her up and what possible excuse could he have given for being home when he should have been in Geelong, and for offering her a glass of orange juice in the middle of the night?

It was not completely certain when Hilda had drunk the orange juice, but the autopsy report had stated that it was not earlier than eleven o'clock at night.

Perhaps the reason that the sergeant continued with his

170

suspicious sniffing about was that he had now been keeping Arthur Houdson under observation for some little time and he was beginning to notice a change in the man's behaviour.

"There's something bothering him," he told the inspector. "He's got something on his conscience and it's worrying him so much that his appearance is changing. I've never seen a man look so haggard."

"Probably simple exhaustion," said the inspector. "Is he still living with his common-law stepdaughter?"

"Yes," said the sergeant, "and they're almost certainly living together as man and wife, but it's not simply that she's too much for him. It's something deeper. What's more, it's progressive. Houdson looks worse all the time."

"Well, maybe he's going to come in and confess that he murdered Mrs Miller one of these days," said the inspector. "It wouldn't be so unusual. More people get guilty consciences and confess when they don't have to than you'd think and, from everything we've learned about Houdson, he's basically an honest, highly principled type. Or do you think that we should bring him in and try to interrogate the truth out of him?"

"I don't think so," said the sergeant. "If it didn't work, it would scare him so badly that he probably never would work up the courage to come clean. I have the feeling that if we wait long enough, he'll crack all by himself."

"We'll wait then," said the inspector, "and let's hope that it won't be long."

It was not long. On the Monday morning following that conversation in the inspector's office, Arthur Houdson appeared at police headquarters and asked to see Sergeant Ralston who had taken his statement at the time of Hilda Miller's suicide and whom he knew by name.

He was taken into the inspector's office, seated in a chair, given a cup of coffee and a cigarette and not questioned as to the purpose of his visit. He was more likely to come to the point if left to do so in his own good time.

Houdson had identified himself and stated that he had something to say in connection with the death of Hilda Miller, but had then fallen silent.

Suddenly he raised his head, displaying to the inspector a

face almost unrecognizably contorted with emotion.

"Can you believe," he said in a hoarse, agonized voice, "that a sweet, lovely, eighteen-year-old girl would deliberately murder her mother?"

The inspector could, of course, believe far worse. His profession had taught him to. He inquired what reason Houdson had for his belief. He did not mention the name of Charlotte.

Houdson, according to his statement, had good reason. Charlotte had proposed the murder a good week before she had carried it out.

"It began while Hilda was in hospital," he said. "Charlotte was taking care of the flat and doing the cooking, and in the evening we watched television together. I was of course aware that she was a physiclaly mature and very attractive girl, but I did not think of her in a sexual manner. After all, I had looked upon her as my daughter since she was three.

"Then one evening I came home and she had prepared a festive dinner with wine and candles. She was also dressed very suggestively and, when we had finished dinner, she led me to the sofa and said that there was not going to be any television that evening. She had thought of a better kind of entertainment.

"She literally seduced me. I knew what I was doing was wrong and that it would lead to trouble later on. I wanted to be faithful to Hilda and I felt like I was committing incest, but put yourself in my place. How many men do you think would have been able to resist?"

"Very few," said the inspector.

Privately, he was horrified at Houdson's account because he did not believe it. He thought that the man had murdered his common-law wife and was now trying to throw the blame on to the woman's daughter in order to save himself. He had undoubtedly come to the conclusion that he was under suspicion.

"I was not," said Houdson, "and I regret it bitterly for, had I resisted, I think Hilda would still be alive. However, after that evening, it was too late. Our relationship continued, even after Hilda had come home from the hospital. After she had taken her sleeping pills and gone to sleep, Charlotte and

I made love in the living room or her bedroom."

"And then?" said the inspector, when Houdson showed no sign of continuing.

"And then," said Houdson, "one evening, just a week before Hilda died, Charlotte suggested to me that I kill her. She was jealous and looked upon her mother as a rival. She said that she wanted to die anyway, and why shouldn't I help her?

"I was horrified and told her to put such ideas out of her head. I loved Hilda, I said, and I would never abandon her. I think that when I said that, I sealed her fate.

"After Hilda's death, I asked Charlotte directly if she had had anything to do with it, but she refused to answer.

"I can't stand it any more. I know that she killed Hilda and it gives me no peace!"

By the time that Houdson had finished his account, the inspector was no longer so certain that he was lying and he ordered that Charlotte Miller be brought to police headquarters for questioning.

There she was confronted with a tape recording of Houdson's statement and, after only hesitating briefly, she confessed.

"She was my rival for Arthur's love," she said. "I regret nothing."

Charlotte is obviously an unusual sort of girl and she is currently being held under psychiatric observation. Whether she will come to trial for her matricide depends upon the results of the observations.

Whatever those results, she can only be tried as a juvenile, for that is what she is.

TWELVE

LIFE ON THE FARM AIN'T WHAT IT USED TO BE

Six-fifteen on a Sunday morning in November is not a popular time with G.P.s for making house calls, and the weather on November 5, 1972, was particularly dismal.

It was, of course, still pitch dark, but even if the sun had been up, it could not have been seen for the skies were heavily overcast with intermittent drizzle and gusts of bitterly cold wind.

Although not particularly pleased about going out into it, Dr Harald Nussbaum did not find the weather unusual, having lived in it all his life, and in any case he had no choice.

In West Germany, a doctor who refuses to come for what is described as an urgent call can be prosecuted, and this was West Germany.

But only just. Dr Nussbaum's practice was in the little town of Albbruck and a mile and a half away, on the other side of the Rhine river, was Switzerland.

The telephone call which he had just received was not, however, from Albbruck, but from the village of Rotzel, some three miles to the north, and according to the caller it was extremely urgent.

Or not urgent at all, depending upon the point of view. What the caller had said was that he had come home from work and had found his wife dead.

Dr Nussbaum was inclined to think that he was mistaken. Ingrid Kasper was only thirty-four years old and, like a good many farm wives, she was solidly built. She had been his patient throughout the fourteen years of her marriage to Karl Kasper, five years her senior, and he had attended her at

174

the births of Rolf, now thirteen, Erika, eleven, Stefan, nine, and the youngest, Gabi, who was only six. There was not much about Ingrid Kasper's physical condition that Dr Nussbaum did not know and there was nothing in it which might cause her to die suddenly.

Groaning slightly, the doctor hurried into his clothes, got out the car and set off for Rotzel. Karl Kasper had said that his wife was lying dead in bed, and the only thing the doctor could think of was that she might have committed suicide.

The idea was driven from his head the moment he saw the body. Mrs Ingrid Kasper was definitely dead and, if it was suicide, it was the strangest looking one that he had ever seen.

The woman lay face-down on the bed, her arms raised and stretched out on either side of her head and her legs slightly parted. She was wearing a very short baby-doll nightdress with no bottom and there was an angry red spot of swollen flesh on her left buttock as if she had been burned by something. There were similar red spots on her wrists.

The body was already cold and there was no sign of either respiration or heartbeat. Dr Nussbaum did not turn it over, but left it in the position in which he had found it, drew the anxiously waiting husband out of the bedroom and sealed the door with surgical tape from his bag.

"Have you called the police yet, Karl?" he asked. "Where are the children?"

"With their grandparents," said Kasper. He was a square-built man of medium height with his hair trimmed high at the sides of his head so that he looked exactly like what he was, a south German farmer. "You mean she's been murdered?"

He sounded awe-struck and incredulous at the same time.

"It's not a natural death, Karl," said the doctor. "I can't issue a death certificate."

"Where'll I call?" said Kasper uncertainly. "We ain't got no police here in Rotzel, just the constable. He can't do nothing."

"You'll have to call Waldshut," said the doctor. "This falls inside their jurisdiction. Tell them that the coroner will have to come down."

Waldshut was the district administrative centre, but with a

population of under twenty-five thousand it was not a very large place either. At this hour on a Sunday morning, there was no one on duty in the Department of Criminal Investigations.

It was, therefore, nearly eight o'clock before the investigations team of Inspector Otto Beissel and Detective-Sergeant Hans Hossmann arrived in Rotzel, bringing with them the Waldshut coroner, Dr Rudolf Sieg.

While the doctor went in to make his examination of the corpse, the officers took down Karl Kasper's statement on the tape recorder which the sergeant had brought along for the purpose.

It was a short statement. Although Kasper owned the small farm on which the family lived in Rotzel, he had had to go heavily into debt to buy it and, during the months when there was not much farming to do, worked at the paper factory in Albbruck where he drove a fork lift.

He was usually on the night shift and this last night he had gone to work at nine in the evening, coming home at six in the morning, as usual. He had found his wife on the bed. He had immediately called Dr Nussbaum, the family doctor.

Having heard this statement, the inspector, a tall, thin man with a long, somewhat sad face, went into the bedroom where Dr Sieg was still carrying out his examination of the body with Dr Nussbaum standing by in case he could be of any help.

"Well, whatever it was, it wasn't a natural death," said the coroner, who was short, stocky, white-haired and red-faced. "It looks to me as if she's been electrocuted."

"Electrocuted!" said the inspector. "My God! How is such a thing possible? Are you sure? You don't mean somebody deliberately electrocuted her?"

"I don't see how she could have done it herself," said the doctor. "And I don't see how anyone else could have done it accidentally."

"Who are these people?" said the inspector, looking at Dr Nussbaum. "Do you know them?"

"Very well," said the doctor. "I'm their family doctor and have been for the past fifteen years or so. They're poor farmers. Karl's father was an even poorer farmer who never

176

owned his own land and Karl's biggest ambition was to be able to buy a farm. He bought this one and he's kept it through sheer hard work. It still isn't paid for though, and won't be for a long time."

"And his relationship with his wife?" said the inspector.

"Good, I would say," said the doctor. "They have four fine children. I've always had the impression that they didn't have much money, but that they were happy. They've been married close to fifteen years."

"Enemies? Feuds with the neighbours?" said the inspector.

"None to my knowledge," said the doctor. "And I'm the family doctor to most of the people here in Rotzel. I've never heard anyone say anything against them."

"Then if this is a murder, it's the most mysterious one I've ever heard of," said the inspector.

"I'm afraid it is," said Dr Sieg. "The woman's been dead for seven or eight hours now – let's say she was killed somewhere between eleven o'clock and midnight. I'm almost sure it was electrocution. There'll have to be a post-mortem."

"Couldn't it be accidental?" said the inspector. "A defect in the wiring . . .? came into contact with the bed springs . . .? or . . .?"

He had got down on all fours to peer beneath the bed while he was talking and he suddenly reached under it and drew out a light cardboard box.

"Rubber gloves?" he muttered. "In the bedroom . . .?"

"The only thing I can suggest is some kind of a complete madman who broke into the house while the husband was at work and killed her for perverted sexual reasons," said the doctor. "However, there's no sign that she put up a struggle of any kind. Maybe I'll find something when I perform the post-mortem."

But Dr Sieg did not. There was not the slightest mark on Ingrid Kasper's body to indicate that she had tried to defend herself or that she had been restrained from doing so by any bonds.

On the contrary, the indications were that the woman had died in a state of sexual excitement bordering on frenzy. However, if there had been any male sharing this excitement, he had left no trace of it.

As the doctor had suspected, the cause of death had been electrocution, apparently a direct charge from the house circuits which, in Germany, are 220 volts. Two of the terminals had been wrapped around her wrists and one had been applied to the left buttock.

"It is completely out of the question that Mrs Kasper took her own life in this manner," read the post-mortem report, "and it is equally out of the question that her death was the result of an accident. In either the one case or the other, the wires, terminals and plug for the electrical outlet in the bedroom would have been present. They were not and it must, therefore, be assumed that they were removed by her murderer. The coroner's office is unable to suggest an explanation for Mrs Kasper's failure to defend herself."

"She didn't defend herself because she thought her lover was merely going to give her some kicks," said Sergeant Hossmann, a frail-looking young man with long, blond hair and horn-rimmed glasses. "He probably didn't mean to kill her either. Just got carried away and hit her with too heavy a charge."

The Kasper house had, by now, been very thoroughly gone over and the investigators had developed a theory that Ingrid Kasper had been carrying on an illicit affair with some, as yet, unidentified man while her husband was on night shift.

The theory was logical, as a man who worked as hard and as long hours as Kasper did would understandably not have a great deal of energy left over for sex, and Mrs Kasper, it seemed, had been more than casually interested in the activity.

The search of the house had turned up a veritable library of sex literature and pornography. There was hardly a drawer or cupboard that did not have a stock of books, magazines and pictures stashed away.

Nor had the sexual activity been purely vicarious. Also found throughout the house was a fantastic collection of the sex aids which are widely advertised in German magazines and newspapers. Vibrators in all shapes and sizes, contraceptives with rubber devil's heads on the end and textured surfaces, artificial male and female sex organs, even whips and bondage equipment – there was very little that had been left out and, in some of the literature, there were suggestions and instructions for sexual stimulation through the use of electricity.

Shown this vast collection, Karl Kasper had been dumbfounded. His wife, he said, must have bought all these things mail-order from the housekeeping money. He had often wondered why she was continually running short.

It also explained other things such as why Ingrid had sent the children to spend the night with her parents in Donaueschingen so frequently, and why she had habitually slept as she had been found, in a short, black-lace baby-doll nightdress with no bottom.

She had had other provocative pieces of clothing too – frilly, black-lace crotchless knickers and transparent blouses. None of it, said Kasper, had done him much good. When you work all day on the farm and all night in the paper factory, about all the sex you have is for the purpose of breeding children to help on the farm.

It was, therefore, comparatively clear what had happened, and it had probably been more of an accident than a murder. The fact that Mrs Kasper had not tried to defend herself showed that.

A healthy, possibly somewhat oversexed woman, she must have found her hard-working husband's performance in bed inadequate. As a matter of fact, he had hardly been in bed at all during the winter months.

Consequently, she had taken a lover who had come around while her husband was on the night shift and the children at their grandparents, and they had joyfully celebrated veritable orgies, equipped with all the finest that the mail-order houses could supply.

In the inspector's opinion, this had probably been going on for years. The pornography and sex aids had certainly not been bought all at one time, and much of it showed evidence of hard usage.

However, sex is like most good things – too much of it results in the partners becoming jaded and a stronger stimulus is required. To judge by the equipment and the state it was in, Mrs Kasper and her lover must have been very jaded indeed.

They had, therefore, begun experiments with electrical sex stimulation and, on the night in question, something had gone wrong.

The lover, presumably wearing the rubber gloves from the package which the inspector had found beneath the bed, had attached Mrs Kasper's wrists to the ground terminals of the electrical equipment - and was, perhaps, attempting to stimulate her buttocks with the live wire. Either there was a defect in the equipment or too good a contact had been made. In any case, Mrs Kasper had received the full 220 volts and it had killed her.

Terrified, the lover had removed the tell-tale equipment and had fled, taking it with him.

There was only one fault in this theory. The Kaspers were farmers, but in Europe, the farmhouses and barns are concentrated in the village with the fields outside. In such a small, tightly-packed community, everybody knows everything. Yet nobody had known that Ingrid Kasper had a lover.

"It's not possible," said the inspector. "I come from a village like that. If any woman there even shook hands with another man, it would be all over the place within half an hour. There is no way that anyone could hide such a thing."

But apparently Mrs Ingrid Kasper had, for as the investigation continued, a Miss Erika Jung came forward and testified that she had witnessed Ingrid Kasper having intercourse with a "foreigner" in the courtyard of a tavern on Kasper's last birthday. She was unable to identify the foreigner, but she thought that he might have been an Italian.

The twenty-nine-year-old Miss Jung was not a resident of Rotzel, but lived in Albbruck which was where the alleged incident between Ingrid Kasper and the foreigner had taken place.

A check of other persons who had been present at the birthday party in the tavern revealed that Miss Jung was not the only person who had witnessed the sexual activities in the courtyard, but it also revealed something else.

Apparently Erika Jung was Karl Kasper's mistress and he

180

had at times referred to her as his fiancée.

The case seemed to be taking on a classic form. Kasper had learned of his wife's infidelities and had gone looking for another candidate for her job. He had found her in the form of Erika Jung, a very attractive young woman whom he had contacted by running an advertisement in the newspaper, but his wife had refused the divorce.

Faced with this dilemma, he had solved it by murdering the unwanted wife.

Karl Kasper was, it seemed, more interested in sex than he had intimated to the police.

Given these circumstances, the inspector was inclined to place Kasper under arrest and charge him with the murder, but this he could not do for the simple reason that Kasper had an iron-clad alibi for the time of his wife's death. He had been at the paper factory in Albbruck and had evidence of it. Kasper had punched in at nine o'clock that evening and had punched out at six the following morning, precisely as he always did. His wife had been murdered at nearly midnight, give or take half an hour in either direction.

Nonetheless, the inspector continued his investigation of the farmer-factory worker and, at the same time, spared no effort to identify and locate the "foreigner" with whom Ingrid Kasper had been having intercourse so publicly a scant two months before her death.

With the identification, at least, he was successful. The person in question was a thirty-two-year-old Italian construction worker named Luigi Antoninni. A man with a strong constitution, he was reported to have been seen engaged in intercourse with two other women in the courtyard of the same tavern on the same day. One of the women had been another member of the group celebrating Karl Kasper's birthday.

However, Antoninni was no longer in Albbruck, and presumably not even in Germany. Perhaps significantly, he had disappeared at just about the time of Ingrid Kasper's murder and had not been seen since.

"There could be two explanations for his sudden departure," said the inspector. "Either he murdered Mrs Kasper, probably accidentally, or he learned that she had been murdered and cleared off because he was afraid of being suspected. Check with the construction company and see if he left without collecting all the pay due to him."

The sergeant checked and Luigi Antoninni had indeed left a small amount of his last pay still uncollected. He had also left his lodgings without informing the landlady and without waiting until the end of the week.

Neither the construction company nor the landlady were able to say precisely on what day Antoninni had left Albbruck. He was one of the countless thousands of foreign construction workers in Germany. No one had paid much attention to him.

A check with the office which handled the registration of foreigners living and working in the district showed that Antoninni had listed Bari, Italy as his place of origin and a request was sent to the police there, asking their help in locating him.

Otherwise, nothing had been learned about the suspect, other than that he was, apparently, fond of the ladies and had had considerable success with them.

A good deal more was being found out about Karl Kasper, much of it surprising and little of it good. Although Kasper was supposed to be so poor that he was hovering on the verge of bankruptcy and his wife had had to buy the family provisions on credit at the local grocery store, he had made a loan or a gift of over £500 to his new mistress, Erika Jung, the transaction being on record at his bank where he had written the cheque.

Questioned about the cheque, Miss Jung said that it had been intended as an investment in her business, but she was unable to say what her business was. It is not possible to open a business of any kind in Germany without a licence, and she had none.

The inspector responded by hinting that he might consider bringing a charge of unlicensed prostitution against her. It is also illegal to practise prostitution in Germany without a licence and, as the inspector pointed out, her so-called fiancé had been a married man who, under the law, could not also be engaged to someone else.

Erika Jung replied that she had never been on intimate

terms with Karl Kasper nor had she ever told anyone that they were engaged or going to be married. If Kasper had said that, it was his business, and if he claimed that he had been having intercourse with her, he was lying, possibly to impress his friends. She herself, said Miss Jung, did not engage in sexual intercourse with men to whom she was not married.

Whether pertinent to the investigation or not, the inspector did not think that he was going to need any further testimony from Erika Jung as so much evidence concerning Karl Kasper was coming in that it was beginning to look as if he could be charged even with a watertight alibi for the time of the crime.

Kasper, it seemed, was nothing at all like the person his casual acquaintances and neighbours had made of him, nor anything like the impression he had first made on the police.

It was true that he was a very hard worker, dividing his time between the farm and the paper factory and, apparently, scarcely sleeping at all.

It was also true that he had very heavy debts incurred in buying the farm.

But it was not true that he was practically penniless. In addition to the generous loan or gift made to Erika Jung, he had been frequently seen at the roulette tables in Baden-Baden and Konstanz, dressed to the teeth, drinking champagne and carelessly placing rather sizeable bets.

With his farmer's haircut, his farmer's manners and his farmer's vocabulary, he had been conspicuous.

Furthermore, the sex literature and toys had been ordered from the mail-order houses by Kasper and not his wife, for the order forms were filled out in his handwriting.

However, they had not been exclusively for his use, for included among the other items was a very large artificial penis and, when Dr Nussbaum was questioned concerning his knowledge of the conditions inside the family, he stated, somewhat reluctantly, that Mrs Kasper had come to him complaining of pains in the lower part of the abdomen and had admitted that she and her husband had been using this as a sex stimulant.

The doctor had found that the pains were not from the use

of this instrument, but rather a result of her four pregnancies.

Apparently coming to the conclusion that he might as well tell everything that he knew, he added that Kasper had sent his wife to him shortly after the episode with the Italian in the tavern in Albbruck with a request that he examine her for possible symptoms of venereal disease. Foreigners, he had said, were notoriously dirty and she might have picked up something.

Mrs Kasper had confessed to the doctor that she had had intercourse with someone in the tavern courtyard on her husband's birthday, but she did not know whether it was a foreigner or not. She had, she said, been very drunk and, while she remembered having intercourse with someone, she could not be certain exactly who it was.

Dr Nussbaum had not pressed her, considering the matter none of his business. She had not had a venereal infection.

By now, the inspector was convinced that Kasper's alibi was false, and although he could still see no way of breaking it, he concentrated on uncovering proof that the man had had not only a motive for murdering his wife, but also the knowledge of electricity to carry out the murder.

This evidence was obtained from an unexpected source. Although Kasper butchered his own pigs, the carcasses had to be inspected by the official veterinary inspector and pass through the district slaughterhouse.

The police had already picked up gossip from the village that Kasper was in the habit of killing his pigs not with an axe or a stock-bolt gun, a device which fires a bolt into the animal's brain, but with a new invention consisting of a pair of large metal tongs connected to a source of electricity. The tongs were placed on either side of the animal's head, the switch activated and the charge of electricity passing through its brain killed it instantly and, allegedly, painlessly.

This gossip was confirmed by the veterinary inspector and the employees at the slaughterhouse. Kasper's pigs, they said, had not had a mark on them, although they had been as dead as any others.

Even more significantly, the veterinary inspector reported that Kasper had told him that he was using such a device and that he had made it himself after having seen an article about it in a magazine.

Ingrid Kasper had not been killed by metal tongs placed on either side of her head, but the principle was the same – a charge of electricity passing through the body.

Despite the alibi, the inspector was very close to asking for Karl Kasper to be charged with premeditated murder. The only thing that was lacking was a really sound motive.

He had thought that he had found one in Erika Jung, but although Kasper had apparently sometimes introduced the girl as his "fiancée", it had been in a joking manner and no one had taken it seriously.

Moreover, Miss Jung denied that they had ever contemplated marriage or engaged in sex. They were merely good friends.

This statement might have been contested, particularly as it could be shown that Kasper had turned over more than £500 to his good friend, but there was also the fact that Kasper had sent his wife to be examined for symptoms of venereal disease, something which he, logically, would hardly have done if he was not intending to have intercourse with her.

The motive was necessary, although by this time enough was known about the working conditions on the night shift at the paper factory for the inspector to think that it would be possible, if not to disprove Kasper's alibi, to show that he could have been absent long enough to commit the crime.

The rolls of paper which he transported with his fork lift were needed at the machines at specific, predictable times. It would have been possible to be absent for as long as an hour without interrupting the work and for much of his shift he was alone in the warehouse.

In the end, it was a suggestion from the sergeant which produced the missing element.

"I don't think there was any sex motive to this murder," he remarked. "Kasper wasn't jealous of his wife and he wasn't crazy about Miss Jung. If he killed her at all, it was an accident while they were stimulating each other with electricity, or it was for some other reason."

"Next to sex, the most common motive for murder is

money," said the inspector thoughtfully.

For a moment, the two men sat looking at each other silently and then exclaimed, both at the same time, "Insurance!"

It was true. No one had thought of checking to see whether the late Mrs Kasper had been insured, but it turned out that she had been, and for nearly £25,000. The premiums were ruinous and, on his income, Kasper could not have continued to pay them for very long.

Of course, he had not had to. Ingrid Kasper had died exactly six months after the life insurance contract had been signed.

It was no wonder that Kasper had been prepared to make £500 gifts to his lady friends and to play for high stakes at the casinos. He was expecting to come into money.

Kasper denied this and he denied all knowledge of the death of his wife. He admitted to all the other things which the police could prove, the fact that he had killed his pigs with electricity and that he knew how to construct such devices, the fact that he had frequented the casinos, the fact that it was possible for him to leave the factory during the night shift and come home without being found out. He even admitted that he had sometimes come home for an hour with his wife, but he denied that he had been home on that particular evening.

A search of his car, however, turned up a home-made device of electrical cords, terminals and plugs, and the experts from the police laboratory stated that it was this which had killed Mrs Kasper.

They were not able to say whether it had been deliberate or accidental. The device was intended for stimulating the genital organs of both parties and it would have been possible to get hold of the wrong cord with fatal results.

In the end, that was what Kasper said had happened. He and his wife had been engaged in sex play and she had accidentally come into contact with the wrong terminal or, rather, too many terminals at the same time. He had been frightened and had tried to cover up his part in the crime.

There was, of course, no way to verify the accuracy of Karl Kasper's statements, but the post-mortem report had stated

186

that Ingrid Kasper appeared to have been highly sexually aroused at the time of her death and the jury, apparently, decided to give him the benefit of the doubt.

On October 5, 1973, he was found guilty of unpremeditated murder and sentenced to twelve years' imprisonment.

THIRTEEN

THE LIBERATION OF PENNY POTTERTON

Penny Potterton was fifteen years old when her father died.
The chief accountant for a large transport firm, he was not a
native of Glasgow, but had been transferred there in 1963
from the small Scottish village where Penny had been born.
Penny was three years old at the time.

The death of the husband and father naturally drew Penny
and her mother, Sally Potterton, into a still closer
relationship and, despite the loss, the warmth and security of
the family and the home were sustained.

There were no financial problems. The accountant had
left his family well provided for and Sally had been working
as a registered nurse ever since their arrival in Glasgow. An
intelligent woman of considerable ability, by now she had
become the right hand of a prominent local surgeon.

Penny had inherited her parents' intelligence and she did
well at school. A pretty, well-built and vivacious girl, she was
popular with her schoolmates and could perhaps have
enjoyed a more active social life had she not preferred to
spend much of her time at home with her mother.

At least, until shortly after her sixteenth birthday. At this
point, there was a change in Penny's life.

From the point of view of some of the girls with whom she
had begun to associate, it was about time. The year was 1966
and liberation was in full swing, to the accompaniment of a
veritable deluge of publicity by the media who were
proclaiming the joys of independence of youth for reasons of
their own that were not unconnected with their commercial
interests.

188

Penny began to wear a good deal more make-up than Sally liked to see, dressed sexily and her language became trendily obscene.

To Sally's reproaches, she replied that this was the age of enlightenment, that youth knew best what was good for it, that older people (such as Sally) were out of touch with the times, that young girls had to be free to live their own lives, that the old morality was dead as the dodo, etc., etc., all of which she had, of course, either read herself or been quoted by her new friends.

A nearly classic case for the time and place and, like so many other parents, there was little that Sally could do about it. Nor could she do much about Penny's choice of boyfriend.

Maurice Searle was barely twenty-one, but he was well-versed in the art of living in a modern society. Although given to petty theft and various rather simple confidence tricks, he had never been convicted of anything or even faced charges, and he had never worked a day in his life.

As he told Penny, "Why should I be so daft as to work for thirty-five pounds a week when I can get forty-five for not working?"

It was a legitimate question and Penny could see that Maurice was obviously much more in tune with the times than, say, her mother.

When Penny was seventeen, she moved out. As Maurice said, it was high time that she separated herself from the "old bag" who was nothing but a bad influence on her and who knew nothing about life as it should be lived.

Sally Potterton came down to the curb to see her daughter off. It was April 10, 1978, and Penny was leaving home to go and begin her new life with Maurice who was impatiently revving his motorbike. He was not a man who believed in wasting time in sentimental partings.

Penny was taking only one small suitcase with her because there was no more room on the bike and, in any case, she would not be wearing dresses and old-fashioned things like that any more.

Sally was not very happy, and after looking rather thoughtfully at Maurice for quite some time, she said that she had done a little checking on him and that, according to what she had learned, he was no good.

Maurice responded with a sneer.

"If," said Sally, choosing her words carefully and speaking with great deliberation, "anything happens to Penny, I shall hold you personally responsible for it. I cannot stop her from going with you, but remember, if anything unfortunate happens to Penny, you will suffer the consequences."

Maurice found this declaration so amusing that he nearly fell off his motorbike laughing.

"Oh Mother!" cried Penny, humiliated by this demonstration of gaucherie. She quickly climbed on to the bike behind Maurice and was whisked away.

"I hope you brought some money with you," said Maurice.

It was the last that Sally was to see of her daughter for over a year and, although no news is generally deemed to be good news, she was very much inclined to doubt that it was in this case.

In the meantime, Penny was learning the meaning of freedom as practised in a progressive society.

She had, of course, moved into Maurice's not exactly luxury quarters in an abandoned building in the Gorbals which, although it offered neither running water, a bathroom, electricity nor heating of any kind, was unquestionably cheap as he was squatting.

At the moment, the heating did not matter very much as it was spring and the weather was getting steadily warmer. As for bathing, it was not considered the thing to do in the circles which Maurice frequented.

For the essential things – food, drugs, alcohol, tobacco and petrol for the motorbike – there was money enough from Maurice's unemployment benefit, his petty thefts and, of course, her own savings which she had brought with her, but which did not last long.

And finally, there was love, passionate, free love, uninhibited and modern, untrammelled by the stuffy conventions of the past, but, as Penny secretly and naively thought, eventually leading to marriage and just such a home and family as she had been raised in herself, warm,

190

secure, permanent. Her education in modern morality was still far from complete.

Maurice was working on it however and, a little over a month after Penny had joined her destiny to his, he announced that they were going to a party where she would meet all his friends.

Penny was delighted. Such an obviously clever and superior person as Maurice would naturally have equally, or nearly equally, clever and superior friends. She was looking forward to a close relationship with them.

As it turned out, the relationship was going to be rather closer than she had anticipated.

The party was held in the cellar of another abandoned building in the Gorbals, and there were a dozen or so girls and young men roughly the same age as Maurice and herself. Nothing being more rigid than the conventions of the unconventional, they all looked and dressed very much alike.

Upon entering, each guest was given a large glass of neat whisky. There were flashing strobe lights, thundering loudspeakers hammering out the latest rock hits, and dirty mattresses scattered artistically about the floor for sitting or lying on.

Penny thought it was all wonderful. She was, however, a little startled to note that some of the guests had removed their clothing and were engaging in sexual intercourse on the mattresses although the party had barely begun.

She was even more startled when a large mass of black hair and strange vestments, which she rightly judged to be one of the male members of the party, came up to her and without so much as a word of greeting, began laying hands on the more private parts of her anatomy.

"I'm with Maurice!" squeaked Penny. "I'm Maurice's girl!"

She looked frantically around for Maurice, but he seemed to have disappeared.

Her new friend removed one of his hands from her body, took her by the wrist and led her around the corner of a projecting wall.

Maurice was lying on top of a red-haired girl on a mattress

and was making love. The girl was completely naked, but Maurice had not bothered to remove anything but his trousers. For some reason or other, he looked less superior than Penny usually found him.

Obviously the common practice among Maurice's friends was to exchange partners at their parties and, although she had certain misgivings, particularly as her new partner smelled as though he had been sleeping in a fish market, peer pressure was strong. This was the brave new world and the thing to do was to live in it.

During that night, she lived rather thoroughly in the new world, and by morning had developed meaningful relationships with practically all of Maurice's friends, at least the male ones.

There would have been even more meaningful relationships, but by the time some of the guests got around to her, alcohol, weak constitutions and the exertions of the evening had left them incapable of such.

Penny was not in much better shape herself and was beginning to show a tendency to fall asleep even at the most exciting moments, when she saw looming out of the alternating glare and darkness a figure which seemed familiar.

"We've already . . . ," she said faintly, hoping that he was not returning for a second meaningful relationship. She had had about as many as she could comfortably tolerate for that night.

However, the young man had something quite different in mind.

"Your old lady's a nurse, ain't she?" he sneered. "Then you ought to know how to use this."

"This" was a hypodermic syringe filled with a transparent liquid and he was holding it out to her as if he expected her to take it.

Penny was puzzled. She did, of course, know how to use a hypodermic syringe, but as her only experience with drugs so far had been with marijuana which she had smoked with Maurice, it simply did not occur to her that what she was looking at was a heroin injection.

"You want me to give you an injection?" she said, taking

the syringe hesitantly. "Whatever for? What kind of injection is it?"

The young man stared at her, open-mouthed, in sincere astonishment. Some of the little twelve- or thirteen-year-olds who ran away from home to live the free, modern life were as naïve, but this was, by his standards, a grown woman and not even a very young one.

"You're putting me on!" he said hoarsely. "You don't stick it into me. You stick it into yourself."

Someone, she could not see who, stepped up beside her and circled her arm with something tight and smooth. Dully, she realized what was being done. They were raising a vein for the injection.

She also realized what the injection was now. She had not known that Maurice and his friends were using hard drugs, but, well, it was the new style, wasn't it? And a lot of people were saying that the government was going to have to legalize drugs, weren't they? It was probably all right.

Hesitantly, she took the syringe which was still being held out to her.

She did not feel the prick of the needle as it slid into the distended vein of her left arm.

The next day she did not feel very good, and she said so to Maurice when they woke up in the middle of the afternoon on the pile of cushions and rags which served as their bed.

"I don't think I want any more of that stuff," she said. "I didn't like it very much."

"You'll develop a taste for it," said Maurice. "You can take my word for it."

Penny could take his word for it. Maurice had been hooked on heroin and anything else he could get for some time, and the only reason that he had not initiated Penny into the delights of hard drugs before was that he had estimated that their income was not enough to support two habits.

Now, although it was probable that they would have two habits to support after all, he was still not too upset over it. He was a reasonable man and it had occurred to him that pretty, young girls addicted to drugs usually find a way to pay for it and sometimes even have a little something left over for their friends. It could be that Penny would eventually become a paying proposition.

As a matter of fact, Penny did become a useful source of income. As he had anticipated, she soon developed a taste which quickly escalated into a raging addiction and, at this point, Penny was prepared to do anything, literally anything, to satisfy that addiction.

She did do anything and with anyone and so often that, as Maurice had hoped, there was often a little something left over for him. The Penny Potterton project was turning out rather well and he did not regret all the effort he had gone to in providing for her education.

Things were, therefore, in complete order with the Searle-Potterton partnership and they continued to remain so for over a year, but, of course, even in the most modern alliances, things do sometimes go wrong and, on the evening of July 29, 1979, things went wrong for Penny and Maurice.

It was, of course, all Penny's fault. Although Maurice had given her the most careful instruction concerning the theory and practice of birth control, she had managed in some way or other to get herself pregnant and, on that fateful evening, she announced the fact to her companion who, as she later told her mother, she expected would make an offer of marriage.

Despite her sixteen months of intense experience in modern living, Penny was still shockingly naïve.

Instead of expressing delight at his impending fatherhood, Maurice flew into a fearful rage, blacked one of her eyes, loosened her two front teeth and gave her a terribly sore stomach by trampling around on it, possibly with the thought that this form of home remedy might bring on an abortion.

It did not and Maurice continued the treatment by throwing her bodily out into the street. He was, he said, sick and tired of her stupidity and, anyway, she was getting old.

Maurice had beaten her up often enough before, but he had never actually thrown her out and Penny was forced to the conclusion that he did not, perhaps, love her any more.

And, though it might seem fickle to some, she was inclined

to think that she did not love him any more either.

Penny went home to mother. At that moment, the bourgeois life seemed oddly attractive. When Sally Potterton opened her door in response to the doorbell at eleven o'clock that night, she did not recognize her own daughter immediately and thought that she was being confronted by a beggar.

However, when the beggar flung herself weeping on to her mother's chest, Sally realized that her only child had come home.

Not in very good shape. In addition to the various bruises and contusions which her late friend had inflicted upon her, she was covered with a liberal and highly fragrant coating of dirt, and she had dyed her naturally blonde hair pitch black.

Sally immediately rushed her to the bathroom, cut away what few clothes she was wearing, dropped them into the dustbin and Penny into a hot tub.

To her horror, she saw that her daughter's arms and legs were as sewn with needle-marks as if she had been serving as a target for the local darts club, but she said nothing, assuming that Penny might have something to say about it.

Penny did. She talked for most of the rest of the night, lying in a clean nightgown in her old bed, in her old room and with her mother sitting beside her, holding her hand.

She told her mother absolutely everything that had happened to her since she had ridden away with Maurice on his motorbike that April morning nearly a year and a half ago. She did not make an effort to make it sound particularly exciting which was just as well because Sally would not have found it so in any case.

"Well, the main thing is, you're back home now," said her mother. "We'll talk some more this evening, but now I've got to go to work. Try to get some rest and make yourself a good breakfast when you get up."

She leaned over, kissed her daughter on the forehead and went off to the hospital.

When she came home, Penny was gone and there was a note from her lying on the kitchen table. It was short and terrible.

"Dearest Mother," wrote Penny. "I have destroyed my own life. There is no way that I can ever make things right again. I am so disgusted with this body that I do not want to live in it any more. Do not grieve for me. It is better this way."

The note was signed simply "Penny".

Sally called the police instantly, described something of the circumstances and read the note over the telephone.

"You must find her at once," she said desperately. "I'm a nurse. This is a genuine suicide note. She's planning to kill herself."

The police agreed that the note was genuine, but, try as they would, they could not find Penny.

It was the following morning when a barge captain spotted her body floating in the river Clyde between two barges. She was wearing her nicest dress.

Sally went down to the police morgue for the official identification of the corpse. She had sat up all night waiting for news and she looked haggard, but she did not cry. Her sorrow was too great for that.

There were some people from the social welfare and youth offices present, and there was a certain amount of rather loose talk about the failure of parents to understand the problems of young people and how things like this would not be allowed to happen in a truly liberal society.

Sally did not say anything other than the responses necessary for the purposes of the official identification and, when it was finished, she left. There were a good many things to attend to – first of all the funeral, of course, and then certain other things which she had in mind. They would require a little preparation, but not too much.

The funeral was very quiet. Other than Sally, there were no mourners and there was no publicity. Neither Maurice nor any of Penny's new friends came, one reason being that none of them knew that she was dead.

Following the funeral, Sally went home to continue with her preparations, and that evening she took the bus and went across town to wait in the shadows near a comfortable, well-maintained house not a great deal different from her own.

The house was occupied by the parents of Maurice Searle, a couple as conventional and respectable as she was.

196

Sally did not know where Maurice Searle was living, but Penny had told her that he sometimes went to visit his parents as it was possible to obtain food, tobacco and small amounts of money from them. Although a firm believer in the independence of youth, he was not a man to exaggerate and the money and the food came in handy.

She kept her vigil for four days until Sunday night, August 5, 1979, when Maurice finally appeared. Sally saw him as he arrived and entered the house, but remained hidden in the shadows, waiting patiently.

After a time, Maurice emerged and started down the street. Sally stepped up behind him and pressed the muzzle of the German army pistol which her husband had brought back from the war into the small of his back.

"If you move or cry out," she said firmly, "I shall shoot you through the spine. You will be a cripple for the rest of your life."

"What do you want?" said Maurice hoarsely. Although he had no reason for having a guilty conscience, he had recognized the voice of Penny's mother immediately.

"I want you to come with me to see Penny," said Sally. "She is very ill and she wants to see you."

"Oh well, of course, of course," said Maurice, sweating slightly. "Be glad to. You didn't need to stick a gun in my back."

It was a remark that would have made Maurice even more nervous than he was, had he known where he would have to go to see Penny.

He did not, however, and he went along with Sally or, rather, in front of Sally. After his initial fright, he was gradually recovering his self-assurance. No doubt there would be a tearful scene. He would promise anything and everything and then, the minute he got out of the house, he'd go straight to the police and bring charges against the old bag for kidnapping or assault with a deadly weapon. He knew what assault with a deadly weapon was. He'd nearly been charged with it himself once.

At the house, Sally herded him into Penny's old room, the gun very much in evidence.

"Where's Penny?" said Maurice. He was beginning to feel

197

a little nervous again and he did not like the way in which Sally was holding the gun. She gave the impression that she not only knew how to use it, but was ready to do so at a moment's notice.

"She'll be with you shortly," said Sally. "Lie down on the bed."

Staring with fascination at the round black muzzle of the Luger, Maurice obeyed, and an instant later felt the familiar prick of an expertly administered injection. Sally had had even more practice with a needle than he.

The nature of the injection was, however, different and it put Maurice out like a light. He did not even have time to wonder what was happening to him.

When he came to, he was still lying on Penny's bed and his arms and legs were bound firmly to the bedposts.

Sally Potterton was sitting quietly in a chair beside the bed, patiently waiting for him to wake up.

"You crazy or something?" demanded Maurice. "Let me off here!"

Sally did not reply, but got up and began to busy herself with some tubes and other equipment which were standing on a table next to the wall.

Presently, she came over and inserted a needle into his arm, taping it in place, and attached a clear plastic tube which she ran to a large glass jar standing on the floor beside the bed.

Maurice could not, however, see the jar from the bed and, noticing this, she brought over the little table and stood the jar on that.

There was a clamp on the clear plastic tube and Sally now opened this slightly. A thin column of rich, red blood pushed through the tube and began to drip into the jar.

Sally looked at it critically and then adjusted the clamp so that it did not drip quite so rapidly.

"You remember," she said in an almost conversational tone, "that I told you when Penny went away with you that, if anything happened to her, I would hold you personally responsible?"

"I didn't do nothing to her!" said Maurice hoarsely. His eyes were fixed on the red drops falling into the jar and he

198

was within a hairs' breadth of fainting from sheer terror.

"Penny is dead," said Sally, "but it may be that you are truly sorry so I am going to give you a chance to apologize to her personally."

"How can I apologize if she's dead?" said Maurice. "Take that thing out of my arm!"

He had never had a blood transfusion and he did not recognize the equipment which Sally had borrowed from the hospital, but he grasped very well what it was doing to him. Before his very eyes, the blood was draining slowly out of his body, drop by drop.

"Why, by going where she is," said Sally pleasantly. "That is where we are both going, you and I, but it is you who will be going first."

She settled herself comfortably in the chair beside the bed, clasped her hands in her lap, and sat looking expectantly at Maurice with an expression almost of release on her face.

"Beg," she said softly. "Why don't you beg? Maybe I'll change my mind."

Maurice begged. Not very hard and not very eloquently at first as he could not really believe that Sally was going to sit quietly there and watch the blood drain slowly out of his body. He thought that she was trying to frighten him and that, after a little time, she would get up and turn off the horrible little tap through which his life was leaking away.

However, as the minutes and then the hours passed and the level of the dark red fluid which was the most precious and most vital part of his essential being rose steadily in the jar, conviction dawned and his pleas were wondrous in their sincerity. There was nothing that his mind, now darting terrified and hyperactive like a caged ferret, did not bring up as a good and cogent reason why his life should be spared. His youth, his regrets over what had happened, his resolve to change his way of life, his repentance, the sorrow that his parents would feel, the suggestion that Penny had loved him too much to wish his death, all were paraded before the nodding, gently smiling executioner and all failed.

She was a cruel executioner, and sometimes she pretended to be impressed by his arguments. Occasionally, she laid her fingers on the little clamp which meant life or death to

Maurice Searle, but she never closed it, and the relentless soft rain of the fat red drops continued.

Sometime early in the morning of August 6, 1979, as the sunrise of a new summer day neared, Maurice Searle's pleadings died away to a barely audible mixture of whimpers and mindless croakings. He knew now at last that he was going to die.

As darkness swept over him, he felt Sally lay her fingers on the side of his throat, searching for the pulse.

As it fluttered, hesitated and finally stopped, she leaned forward and spat in the face of the corpse.

She then threw the clamp on the transfusion tube wide open and went to the telephone where she dialled the number of the police.

While the tape recorder at police headquarters silently recorded her message and while the duty officer on the communications desk strove frantically to trace the source of the call, she gave a clear, detailed account of what she had done and why she had done it.

Finally, when she was completely finished, she gave her name, her address and the name of her victim.

"You can come now," she told the appalled duty officer. "I shall be dead by the time you get here."

And she was.

FOURTEEN

PLANNED MOTHERHOOD

Among the many small countries which make up what was once known as the Balkans, one of the more famous is the former kingdom of Bosnia, a pleasant enough place on the shores of the Adriatic with the normal complement of vast forests, sinister mountains and picturesquely ruined castles to be expected in that part of the world.

Bosnia's principal claim to fame lies in the fact that it contains the city of Sarajevo where Archduke Ferdinand was assassinated on June 28, 1914, bringing on World War I.

One of the things that followed was the disappearance of Bosnia as an independent country – and it was incorporated into Yugoslavia as a district, and a rather odd one even for that country, as it lies well to the south and includes a large number of human vestiges of the countless invasions, occupations and resettlements to which it has been subjected over the centuries.

Some of the villages are inhabited by orientals, the region having once been a part of the Turkish empire, and although the communist government in Belgrade is serenely confident that its citizens have long since discarded the drug of religion, the villagers are inclined to believe themselves Mohammedans.

This difference of opinion troubles no one in Yugoslavia and certainly not the residents of the villages of Bosnia who have other problems to occupy their attention.

The most conspicuous of these problems is simply how to make a living. Needless to say, there are not many opportunities for gainful employment in a tiny village buried in the middle of an endless expanse of forest, and in order to support their families most of the men of these villages have to leave home.

Many of the villages are therefore peopled almost exclusively by women, children and the aged, and one such village is Jusic – Muslim, isolated, miserably poor and renowned for nothing whatsoever.

Jusic is home to seven families (all related more or less distantly by blood or marriage), thirty-seven cows, one somewhat haggard bull, one hundred and forty-two goats, an indeterminate number of chickens and a shifting population of cats. There are no dogs or pigs. Muslims are not fond of either.

There are also very few men, but among them on the morning of January 28, 1970, was one who, being only twenty-two years old and sound of mind and body, should have been in West Germany earning good money on the construction projects to send back to Jusic as did all other able-bodied males.

As a matter of fact, Emin Ibrahimovic was due to leave for Germany the following week, his papers having been arranged by the members of his family already there, but at the moment he was still in Jusic and busy looking for his sister.

As he already knew that she was nowhere in the village itself, he was looking in the forest near the Kamenjacka river, an area not far from the village which sometimes served as a sort of picnic ground, although not at this time of year.

It was here that he found her, lying on the ground in a little clearing, her skirts up over her head, dead and disembowelled.

The ground around her looked as if someone had been butchering a pig, although no one in Jusic ever butchered pigs.

The men of Jusic are not an emotional lot and since the entire region including the village itself is shot full of blood feuds, some running back for three and four generations, he was not unaccustomed to the sight of violent death, but this was unusual.

The family may have had enemies who had come to the conclusion that too much time had passed without any Ibrahimovics being killed, but the women folk were, by custom, exempt. Even if someone had violated custom, why would they have bothered to disembowel a young married woman of twenty-four who was expecting her second child?

Sadly but stoically, Emin turned the corpse over and found in the back of the head and at the nape of the neck the bullet holes which he had been expecting. Having had some experience in the effects of bullets on flesh, he judged them correctly to be nine millimetre. This meant nothing because there were, undoubtedly, more nine-millimetre-calibre pistols and rifles in Jusic than there were inhabitants.

There had been the barest possibility that Alija Hasanovic had had her belly ripped out by a wild animal of some kind, but the bullet holes proved that the animal had not been wild after all and Emin Abrahimovic arranged her sister's clothing, picked her up in his arms and carried her stolidly back the half mile to Jusic, running over in his mind while he was doing so all the Ibrahimovic family's enemies and deciding which ones he would kill first. There was, of course, also the possibility that it was an enemy of Georgi Hasanovic, Alija's husband who was now working in Germany, but that was something that would have to be discussed with Georgi himself.

The other residents of Jusic were saddened and enraged by the discovery of the murder, but one of the women immediately made a suggestion which had not occurred to Emin.

Alija had been within less than a week of giving birth to her second child, she said, and now it had been cut out of her belly. The intestines had not been brought out as in a true disembowelment – only the womb had been sliced open and, as he could see for himself, the baby had been removed.

"Alija was unfaithful to her husband," said one mother of five. "The child was not his so he cut it out of her body."

"You are mad," said Emin. "Georgi Hasanovic is in Germany. You know that as well as I do."

"Not all of his relatives are," said another woman.

"That's not true," said Emin. "You're all jealous because

203

Alija was the most beautiful girl in Jusic and she made the best marriage."

"Shefka Hodzic is as beautiful," said another woman, "and Marko Hodzic is a better husband than Georgi Hasanovic."

"But Shefka has been married as long as Alija and she has no children," said the mother of five.

"She will give birth this week," said the woman who had described Shefka Hodzic as beautiful and who happened to be her sister. "It will be a fine boy, better than the one that Alija had last year."

"But only one," said the mother of five. "It is not much for being married so long."

"In the name of Allah, what do you want?" cried Shefka Hodzic's sister. "The men are never here. Only the Christians have virgin births."

"We are not discussing births, virgin or otherwise," interrupted Emin. "We are trying to find out who has killed my sister so that I may kill him without delay. For each moment that he lives, I suffer."

"Then you may suffer for a long time," said one of the village elders who, together with his colleagues, had been examining the corpse of the dead woman. "No one from Jusic did this."

"No one?" said Emin doubtfully. Being totally uneducated and having no access to the benefits of a liberal, free press, he did not even know that he was supposed to despise his elders and he held them, as did everyone in Jusic, in some respect.

"No one," said the old man. "First, there is no active blood debt against the Hasanovics or the Ibrahimovics at the moment. Second, we do not kill women in Jusic. The death of a woman does nothing to settle a blood debt. Third, no one in Jusic has any use for an unborn baby and whoever did this took the child with him."

"Then who?" said Emin, the hair standing up on the back of his neck in anticipation of the answer.

"A magician, a sorcerer," said the old man, covering his white-bearded mouth with his hand as if to muffle the evil influence. "He needed an unborn child for his business."

There was a nervous muttering in the little crowd of

204

villagers gathered around the body on the rough table, and some of the women drew the corners of their shawls up over their faces. The women of Jusic do not normally go veiled.

Emin Ibrahimovic thought the matter over for a few minutes in silence.

"Then I am going to the police in Tuzla," he announced. "I don't know what to do about a sorcerer, but I know that the police don't like it when people are killed and they have no ways of dealing with such matters. Perhaps they will be able to find out who this sorcerer is, and then I can kill him."

"The police will not let you," said the mother of five. "When Emin Brojic killed Hasim Murakovic, the police came and put him in jail for two years, although Hasim also had his gun and Emin did not even shoot him in the back."

"And then when he got out of jail, Ali Murakovic cut his throat in his own house and did not get sent to jail at all," said another woman. "The police do not always act in the same manner."

"That was because Alija told the police that she was present when Brojic killed Hasim Murakovic and she said that Murakovic fired first."

"She only said that because Emin Brojic was our father and Alija was Shefka's best friend," said the sister of Shefka. "They did not take Ali because Hasim was his father and no one saw him cut our father's throat."

"I care nothing about all this," said Emin Ibrahimovic. "I am going to Tuzla." And he did.

Tuzla is nearly thirty miles from Jusic and less than ten thousand people live there, but because it is the largest community in the region, it is the district capital and has not only a police force, but even a Department of Criminal Investigations.

The cases with which this department is confronted are usually very different from those with which similar departments in other parts of the world have to cope, and Inspector Alef Nadovic, a compactly-built man with straight, black hair and a heavy, black, drooping moustache, was not startled when Emin Ibrahimovic appeared in his office with the report that his sister had been murdered and disembowelled by a sorcerer and that he wanted something done about it.

It was the morning of January 29 because, having no transport, Emin had taken so long in walking the thirty miles to Tuzla that he had arrived in the middle of the night and had had to wait until the offices of the Department of Criminal Investigations opened. He had, however, spent the time profitably in walking around Tuzla, a place which he had only visited once before, and looking at the sights.

"When did this happen?" asked the inspector, pressing the button which would summon his assistant, Detective-Sergeant Anjic, from the outer office.

He was very familiar with the people living in the little villages of his district, and he was aware that their sense of time was not the same as people accustomed to clocking in and out at work. For all he knew, Emin Ibrahimovic's sister could have been murdered and disembowelled the previous year and this was the first time that Emin had managed to get into town to report it.

"Yesterday," said Emin. "Before noon. She was cold when I found her."

Detective-Sergeant Anjic stepped quietly into the office. "Call Dr Fallavic, Kasim," said the inspector. "We are going to Jusic in connection with a murder."

The Department of Criminal Investigations did have transport, and a little over a half hour later, the three members of the murder squad and Emin Ibrahimovic were standing in the living room of the small house where Alija Hodzic had lived.

Alija was laid out on a bier made of some planks laid over two saw-horses and covered with black cloth. She was clean. Her hair was combed. And she was wearing her best dress and shoes.

"This is very irregular," said Dr Brod Fallavic. "The body has been washed and prepared for burial. It should have been left where it was found or, at worst, brought to the morgue in Tuzla."

"I do not want my sister taken to Tuzla," said Emin evenly.

The inspector shrugged. "Then the doctor must examine her here," he said. "We must know how she was killed and what else may have been done to her. If you do not agree to that, we will go back to Tuzla and your sister will never be revenged because no one will ever know who killed her."

This was all quite untrue. The inspector was a public official and he could not simply walk away from a murder case. However, he was accustomed to dealing with the people in his area and he knew how to manipulate them.

As usual, his strategy worked and Emin offered no objections to the examination of his sister's body, although he still did not want it transferred to Tuzla which he considered to be a large and wicked place and not suitable for a respectable woman, even if she were dead.

The examination produced nothing of note other than what the villagers had already determined. Alija had been killed by one nine-millimetre-calibre bullet fired into the back of her head at fairly close but not point-blank range. Two further bullets of the same calibre had then been fired into the spine at the nape of the neck, traditional "executioner's shots" to make completely certain that the victim was dead. Following that, she had been turned on her back, and her belly and womb had been carefully slit open, the umbilical cord which attached her to her baby had been cut and the baby itself removed.

"A Caesarean," said the doctor. "Not as a doctor would perform it, but rather the sort of rough surgery that a farmer might carry out on a dead cow in order to save the calf. I have recovered two of the bullets and one is in good enough shape for ballistic comparison if you can find the gun that fired it."

"Who in the village would have a nine-millimetre pistol or rifle?" said the inspector, looking at Emin.

"No one," said Emin automatically. "There are no guns in Jusic."

The inspector raised his eyebrows.

"Almost everyone," said Emin. "But they are not going to let you see them."

"Was there a blood debt?" said the sergeant, who came from a village very similar to Jusic, although it was not Muslim.

Emin hesitated.

"The elders say not," he said finally.

"But what do you think?" said the inspector.

"I am very young. The elders are usually right," said Emin. "Why do you not speak with them yourself? There are blood debts here in the village, yes, but I do not know of any that could have been paid by my sister's life."

"I do not think it could be a blood debt," said the doctor. "The purpose of the murder was obviously to obtain the child."

"That is what the elders say," said Emin. "They say it was a sorcerer."

The three men from the murder squad looked at each other a little uneasily. The suggestion was not so far-fetched as it might have seemed in other parts of the world. The Tuzla Department of Criminal Investigations had never had such a case, but there had been cases involving witchcraft, black magic and worse in other parts of the country. There are some very strange people living in what were once the Balkans, and the old beliefs die hard and, sometimes, not at all.

There were terrible things that a new-born child, torn from its mother's dead womb, could be used for and none of the men liked to think of them, particularly as they could think of no other reason for anyone stealing Alija's baby.

"Perhaps if we went to look at the place where you found her . . .?" said the inspector. "We may be able to see something that will help us understand this murder."

Emin enthusiastically agreed. He knew nothing of police detection practices, but he had great confidence in people who worked for the government. By his standards, they had very good and important jobs and they must therefore be persons of great ability.

Leaving the doctor in the village to speak with the residents and see if he could learn anything of value, the inspector and the sergeant followed Emin to the place on the banks of the Kamenjacka river where he had found Alija's body, but apart from a great deal of blood on the ground, they were unable to find anything.

"This is a long way from the village," remarked the sergeant. "What was she doing here anyway?"

208

Emin looked thoughtful. "I do not know," he said. "I only learned that she was not in the village when her neighbour came to me to say that Alija's other child was crying and that she should come and give it something to eat. The sun was two hands above the south crest at that time, and although I looked everywhere in the village I could not find her, so she must have left before then."

"Come," said the inspector. "We will go back to the village and try to determine what time two hands above the south crest is. This may be important. I think you said your sister was within a day or two of giving birth? It is hard for me to believe that a woman that pregnant would be wandering around in the forest half a mile or more from her house."

"It is hard for me to believe too, now that you mention it," said Emin. "My sister was not a foolish woman. She would not have gone into the forest alone when she was so near to giving birth."

"But as we know that she did go into the forest, she must have gone with someone," said the sergeant. "Who would she have gone with in Jusic?"

"Almost anyone," said Emin. "My sister had no enemies."

The inspector raised his eyebrows.

"No personal enemies," said Emin. "Well, perhaps the Murakovics. They did not like it when she spoke for Emin Brojic after he had killed Hasim Murakovic. However, the debt was paid when Ali cut Brojic's throat. That should have satisfied everyone."

"Everyone but Brojic," said the inspector. "He was her best friend's father?"

Emin nodded. "Shefka Hodzic," he said. "She is the second prettiest girl in the village." He paused and then added sadly, "The prettiest now."

"Is there any reason why the Murakovics might have taken the child if one of them killed your sister?" said the sergeant bluntly.

Emin thought it over.

"I can think of nothing," he said finally, "unless they thought they could trade its life for one of theirs. There are many Murakovics, but there are more Ibrahimovics and the Hodzics also have many full grown men. If one of them did this, we would wipe out their strain. Perhaps they thought that we would not if they had the child."

"But you would anyway," said the sergeant.

"I would," said Emin, "but it would not be my decision. That would be for my father and brothers to decide."

Back at the village, they found that Dr Fallavic had spoken with about half of the villagers and he was convinced that none of them knew anything about the murder. Everyone was of the opinion that the murderer could not possibly be anyone from Jusic and there were not even the usual attempts to make trouble for personal enemies by suggesting that they were involved.

With a little calculating, it was determined that two hands over the south crest of the mountains some twenty miles off was approximately ten-thirty in the morning, and that Alija had, therefore, left the village at not later than ten as it would have required that much time for a highly pregnant woman to walk to the point where she had been murdered.

Why a highly pregnant woman would have taken it into her head to walk off through the forest was something which could not be determined, and, the police party having investigated everything that they could think of to investigate without any success at all, they returned to Tuzla.

"What do we do with the case?" asked the sergeant. "Mark it unsolved?"

"I suppose we shall have to," said the inspector reluctantly. "It is not solved and I haven't the slightest idea of what happened there in Jusic. It is not like any of the other cases that I have had to deal with."

The sergeant shrugged. "I would not be surprised if the villagers solved it themselves," he said. "I come from such a village and it is impossible to keep secrets in such a place for any length of time. Sooner or later, the truth will come out, there will be a flurry of killings and then everything will settle down to normal again."

"But that must not be," said the inspector. "We are not here to preside over a series of tribal massacres. The citizens of a socialist republic are not permitted to murder each other in this manner. We must do something."

"What?" said the sergeant.

"If anyone from Jusic killed this woman, it was, as far as I can make out, someone from the Murakovic family," said the inspector. "They are, however, not as strong as the Ibrahimovics and, if the truth comes out, they will all be killed. You must go back to Jusic and speak with the heads of the family privately. Tell them this. They will realize that it is true."

"And?" said the sergeant.

"Tell them that they must turn over the murderer to the police and the baby must be given back to the Hasanovic family before any more blood is spilled," said the inspector.

"I don't believe they will do this," said the sergeant. "If it were my village, I would not. However, I will go to Jusic and do what you say. Perhaps some good will come of it after all."

Nothing either good or bad came from the sergeant's second visit to Jusic. The Murakovics all swore by everything holy that they had had nothing to do with the murder, that they had no inkling of the whereabouts of the child and that they loved the Hodzics and even the Ibrahimovics like their own brothers.

"The only thing which may be of value is that Baja Murakovic, who is the head of the family, has promised to let me know immediately if any rumours begin to circulate around the village," said the sergeant. "However, he says that he does not believe that the crime will ever be solved because he does not believe that anyone in Jusic is responsible."

"And yet," said the inspector, "Alija Hodzic almost certainly did not go for a walk in the woods alone that day. Someone was with her and, if that person did not actually murder her, then he or she must have a very good idea who did."

"He or she?" said the sergeant.

"More probably she," said the inspector. "There are hardly any active men in the village."

"She would not have gone with a man anyway, unless it was a relative," said the sergeant. "It would have looked bad, even if she was pregnant. It must have been a woman."

"Then perhaps the Murakovics can find out which one," said the inspector. "If they are truly innocent, it is in their interest to help us find out who is guilty."

The sergeant went back to Jusic where the Murakovics assured him of their full cooperation, but repeated what they had said before, that the murder of Alija Hodzic had not been the work of any resident of Jusic.

The sergeant went back to Tuzla, wrote "unsolved" on the file, and put it away in the filing cabinet. He did not think that he would have any further use for it.

However, criminal investigations officers are mistaken as often as anyone else and, a week later, one of the younger members of the Murakovic family appeared in Tuzla, asked to see the inspector and told him that he had been sent by Baja Murakovic to say that Alija Hasanovic had gone for a walk with her best friend on the morning of the day that she had been murdered.

"Who was her best friend?" said the inspector.

"Baja did not tell me to say that," said the young Murakovic.

"But you will say it," said the inspector, "or I shall put you in jail and you will never see Jusic again. However, the food here is very good. We have pork three times a week. Everyone must eat it."

"Shefka Hodzic," said the young man quickly.

"Get Dr Fallavic, Kasim," said the inspector. "We are going to Jusic."

Upon their arrival in the village, they found Shefka Hodzic sitting in front of her house and nursing her new baby. She had given birth three days earlier. The baby was a boy and had straight black hair and black eyes – in other words, it looked exactly like every baby that had ever been born or would ever be born in Jusic.

"You went for a walk with Alija Hasanovic on the morning of the day she was killed," said the inspector without preamble. "What have you done with her baby?"

"It is a lie," said Shefka Hodzic sullenly. "Someone is trying to harm me."

The baby was fussing and fretting and Dr Fallavic suddenly bent forward and pulled its mouth away from the nipple.

"You have no milk," he said.

"He has already drunk it all," said Shefka, her eyes

widening and her hands suddenly clutching the child as if she feared it would be taken away.

"You have no milk," repeated the doctor. "Is that your child?"

The inspector and the sergeant were staring at the woman in a mixture of amazement and horror, although their features revealed little of their feelings.

"Examine her!" snapped the inspector suddenly. "See if she has just given birth."

"No!" screamed Shefka, jumping to her feet and trying to run away.

The sergeant caught her expertly by the arms and held her motionless. Although technically a court order was required for a physical examination without the suspect's consent, she was marched into her own house and the doctor proceeded to carry out a brief but thorough gynaecological check, the sergeant turning his head modestly to one side and the inspector remaining outside the door.

When the doctor summoned him to enter the room, he found Shefka Hodzic crouched on the floor with her face buried in her hands.

"Oh, the shame!" she wept. "I cannot bear the shame! That I, the most beautiful woman in Jusic can have no children! Everyone will know! Everyone will know!"

"There is more than shame involved," said the inspector. He pointed to the baby, which the sergeant was now holding. "That is the child of Alija Hasanovic, your best friend. You killed her and stole the child from her belly!"

"I had no choice," sobbed Shefka. "Don't you understand? The shame! The shame!"

Whether the inspector understood or not, the jury, made up, of course, of local persons, did.

Premeditation was clearly established by the fact that Shefka had been stuffing her clothes with rags to simulate a pregnancy for the full nine months that her friend was actually pregnant. However, the jury decided that the shame of being unable to have children, in a village where this was the most important function of any married woman, was an extenuating circumstance and handed down the relatively

213

mild sentence of eight years' imprisonment.

When it is completed, Shefka will be able to return to her village without fear of retribution. The life of a woman can neither be taken nor given in the settlement of a blood debt.

FIFTEEN

LITTLE GIRL STEW

On Saturday, July 3, 1976, a young man with dark-blond, curly hair, a broad, honest face and a physique so square and massive that he looked as if he had been carved from a single block of something solid staggered backwards out of a narrow, smelly toilet on the fourth floor of a block of flats in Laar, West Germany and fainted into a fifteen-stone heap.

This was astonishing, for the man was Detective-Sergeant Max Riese of the Duisburg police and, if there is any place in Germany where police officers are not inclined to fainting spells, it is the Ruhr which is where Duisburg is located.

Often referred to as the Iron Triangle, the Ruhr represents one of the greatest industrial and mining complexes in Europe and encompasses fifty cities ranging from the giants such as Duisburg and Essen down to little communities such as Laar. It is a heavily populated, incredibly polluted region where soot and sulphuric acid fall from the sky, the lifeless streams run chrome yellow and verdigris green, and flinging open a window to take a deep breath of air can put you in hospital.

The Germans are very proud of the area, for the Ruhr produces a great deal of wealth.

It also produces some remarkable people and it was one of these who had caused a very tough, very experienced police sergeant to swoon like a dieting teenager. Even in the Ruhr, there are not many crimes horrible enough to do that.

Such an exploit is, of course, the result of a combination of talent and practice and the person responsible possessed both, the practice in particular stretching back over a period of more than twenty years.

Or more?

No one knows precisely. Joachim Kroll was forty-three years old and he may well have begun his career at a very early age. However, twenty years is a long time and Kroll does not remember everything.

Only the more exciting ones, the ones he had liked and whom he had patiently followed for hours, for days, sometimes for weeks to find the perfect moment, the perfect place to carry out his obsession.

Obsession, yes, but not such an obsession that the sly will for self-preservation was ignored. It was always Kroll who was in charge, not the obsession. Kroll was patient. Kroll could wait. Kroll accepted only ideal circumstances.

And because of this, for over twenty years a five-foot-four-inch tall washroom attendant at the Thyssen Steel Works could hunt and rape and kill and, sometimes, eat the women and girls of the Ruhr without the police ever once suspecting his existence.

How many women and girls?

There again, nobody knows. Once he had finished with them, Joachim Kroll was no longer interested in his victims. He did not read about their deaths in the newspapers. He did not attend their funerals where the criminal police were discreetly photographing any strangers who might turn up.

As a matter of fact, Joachim Kroll could hardly read at all. He had had only three years of schooling and he had had to repeat the third year a second time. That had been in Hindenberg, the town in Oberschlesien where he and his four brothers and sisters had been born. In 1947, his mother had moved from the communist east zone to West Germany.

This was going to save Joachim's life thirty years later. East Germany had capital punishment. West Germany does not.

A few years after the move, the mother had died. The father was already long dead. Joachim was not close to his brothers and sisters. They drifted apart and he was alone.

He was not, however, lonely. At the time, he was living in the Thyssen Steel Works bachelor quarters and he had many friends. A small, balding man with a triangular face and large, melting brown eyes, he was soft-spoken, friendly and

216

fond of a joke. It was true that he did not shave or bathe very regularly, but then neither did most of the people with whom he associated. These were exclusively men. As Joachim Kroll was later to tell the officers of the Duisburg Department of Criminal Investigations, he had only ever had one intimate relationship with a woman in his life and that had come to nothing.

With a living woman, that is. Joachim Kroll had had some remarkably intimate relationships with dead women and little girls. In some cases, it could be said that they had literally become one with him.

No one knew about this, however – absolutely no one, and even the director of the Thyssen bachelors' home, Arnold Schulze, did not suspect for a moment that there was anything criminal about the occupant of the room on the first floor. Schulze thought that he was a little strange. After all, he was a grown man and what would a grown man be doing with dolls?

Joachim Kroll had a great collection of dolls, dolls of all sizes and shapes, and only one of them made any sense to Schulze who knew exactly what all the occupants of the building kept in their rooms.

It was a life-sized rubber sex doll such as are sold in German sex shops or through mail-order sex houses, not a particularly expensive model, and it had seen a good deal of usage. Schulze could understand what a single man like Kroll might want with a rubber sex doll. He was not the only man in the building who owned one.

As for the other dolls, Kroll may have wanted them for his little friends. He was very popular with all the little girls in the neighbourhood and they came to take him for walks on Sunday and called him Uncle Joachim. Sometimes, Uncle Joachim tried to smuggle one of his little friends up to his room, but this was always circumvented by the alert Schulze. Regulations forbade female visitors and, like any true German, Arnold Schulze held to the regulations.

In the end, after having lived for over twelve years in the bachelors' quarters, Kroll was kicked out for trying yet again to smuggle a young girl into his room.

Were these little girls in danger? Would Uncle Joachim

have torn off their clothing, strangled them to death, raped them, cut them up for his pressure cooker with a few choice cuts to be stored away in his small deep-freezer?

No one knows, but perhaps not. Out of eleven confessed murders, one attempted murder and a dozen or so which he was not quite sure about, Kroll only carried out one attack in his own room.

It is logical that he would not. No killer was ever more cautious. The *modus operandi* was incredibly drawn-out, incredibly patient and, if no opportunity presented itself within a varying period of time, Kroll would abandon his chosen victim and move on to another. There are undoubtedly dozens, possibly hundreds, of women and girls walking around alive today because of this inordinate caution on the part of Joachim Kroll.

When he finally did strike, he was as deadly as a cobra. There was no fumbling, no hesitation, no waste movement. Kroll knew exactly what he wanted and he knew exactly how to get it. The victim was seized, preferably from the rear, and thrown to the ground. Kroll's hands locked about her throat and his thumbs sank into the arteries carrying blood to the brain. Loss of consciousness followed within a matter of a minute or two, but Kroll did not relax his grip. He held on until the victim was definitely dead and he never made a mistake in this. The only victim ever to escape was ten-year-old Gabriele Puettmann and he had not yet laid his hands upon her.

Once the victim was dead, Kroll removed her clothes rather carelessly, taking them off where they would come easily and tearing them where they would not. He then subjected the dead but still warm and pliable body to sexual intercourse, using the missionary position and taking some care in the insertion of his slightly above average size penis, particularly in the case of the smaller girls, the youngest of which was only four. He invariably ejaculated inside the victim's vagina and usually followed this by masturbating over the body. Some idea of his sexual capacities can be grasped from his confession that, upon arriving home following one of his murders, he invariably masturbated and performed sex with his rubber doll again.

218

While still at the scene, however, once he had slaked his sexual thirst at least temporarily, his thoughts sometimes turned to other appetites and, using the long, folding knife which he always carried with him, he would cut off steaks, chops and even small roasts to take home with him, carefully wrapped in the same waxed paper in which he wrapped his lunches.

The bout with the rubber doll eliminated the last of the sexual tension which had been building in him since he began to follow that particular victim and, for Joachim Kroll, that was the end of the matter. He was no longer interested, rarely knew the name of the victim and took no perverse pleasure in eating her flesh.

It was quite simply that fresh meat is expensive in Germany and Kroll hated to see it wasted. He was basically a thrifty man.

It is because of this lack of interest in his victims that it will never be known how many women and girls Joachim Kroll murdered. All that he could remember was the approximate time and the place and, if the girl pleased him particularly, then something of her appearance. Shown a picture of the victim, he could usually identify her and name the place where he ended her life. On the other hand, it often happened that, as the police were taking him to the scene of one of his crimes, he would suddenly stop on the way and announce that he remembered killing someone at that particular place.

The police then looked through the unsolved sex-murder files and Kroll was invariably right.

Sometimes, however, they had to look through the solved cases as well. Over the period during which he was active, no less than six innocent men were sentenced for crimes committed by Joachim Kroll. Two of these committed suicide.

It might seem impossible that a man should rape, kill and devour little girls and women for over twenty years within an area less than fifty miles long by twenty miles wide without anyone realizing that this was the work of a single man. Moreover, as his crimes were nearly always committed outdoors in patches of forest or fields of high grain, they were concentrated largely in the summer months. Not only were there fewer victims about in the winter, but Kroll appears to have been sensitive to cold. Over half of the murders took place in June, July and August.

The police did not, however, connect these various crimes because, to begin with, Kroll was not by any means the only sex criminal murdering women and children in the Ruhr. He had a great deal of competition and, as he had no particularly conspicuous *modus operandi*, his crimes closely resembled those of his competitors. Kroll was probably the only sex criminal who was also a cannibal, but the police did not know this and, furthermore, Kroll did not always eat his victims.

Secondly, Kroll was invisible. In the great anonymous masses of our modern society where every effort is bent towards reducing the individual to a five-digit number in the memory of some computer bank, a small, shabby workman does not stand out. Kroll often followed women for days on end and there is no evidence that any of them ever noticed him. Had he been large and fierce-looking or remarkably handsome, he might well have come under suspicion long before, but he was neither of these. Not big enough to look dangerous, not handsome enough to attract attention, Joachim Kroll moved through the drifting tides of the hundreds of thousands very much like him in appearance like a fish in water. The only thing that made him different was not apparent to the eye.

The most striking aspect of Kroll the Cannibal's personality was his utter reasonableness. He was not a clever man nor an erratic one. Everything which he did was for a reason. He ate the flesh of his victims because it was good, fresh meat and meat is expensive. He murdered and raped his victims because it was the only way in which he could satisfy his abnormally strong sex drive. According to his statements, he first discovered this when he was in his teens and was witness to the butchering of some pigs. The sight had excited him sexually and it had only been a single step to substitute humans for pigs. Here again, he was ruthlessly logical. He not only obtained a sexual stimulus from the act of killing, but he also eliminated any possible witness. Joachim Kroll was very careful about witnesses.

Finally, even the dolls in his room had their purpose. Kroll used them to practise strangling children.

Undoubtedly, Kroll's crimes took place within such a circumscribed area simply because he was dependent upon public transport. Joachim Kroll rode to his murders on the bus or train in exactly the same way that he rode to work.

Usually, he did not have to ride far. Spotted on a map, the scenes of Kroll's crimes form a rough horseshoe with its rounded upper edge lying directly on and in one case across the Rhine river. The open end of the horseshoe points north-east and some fifty miles in this direction lies Walstedde, the scene of what is believed to be Kroll's first murder and the only one to take place outside the Ruhr. It was also the only murder to take place in really cold weather.

Walstedde is no more than a village, lying on the southern fringe of Muensterland to the north of the Ruhr district. The nearest town of any size is Ahlen, and it was from Ahlen that the police arrived following the discovery of the body of Irmgard Strehl in the forest to the south of the village.

The date was February 8, 1955. Irmgard was nineteen years old, an attractive, well-built, vivacious girl and had last been seen walking down the main road to the neighbouring village of Herrenstein, less than a mile away.

She had not arrived in Herrenstein and, when she failed to return home in time for lunch, her parents began to look for her. Nearly every other able-bodied person in the village joined in.

The search did not last long. By three in the afternoon, Irmgard Stehl's body had been found amidst the snow-covered brush a hundred yards from the road. She had been stripped naked, raped and murdered. Her attacker had ripped up her stomach very much in the same manner in which pigs are gutted after butchering. Joachim Kroll was reliving one of the experiences of his not-so-far-off youth. At the time, he must have been twenty-two years old.

The police, summoned from Ahlen as Walstedde has no more than a village constable, knew nothing about Joachim Kroll, but they concluded very rightly this was a sex murder.

"Except that I have never heard of sex murderers working as a team," said Dr Otto Knopf, the Ahlen police medical

221

expert, "I would almost think that it was two men. There is a great quantity of sperm inside the vagina and even more on the lower part of the abdomen and the pubic hair."

He was a small, worried-looking man who now looked more worried than ever. The Ahlen district is not a place where there are very many sex murders.

Inspector Ralf Peterssen, chief of the small Ahlen murder squad, was large, blond and calm.

"We'll get him," he said confidently. "A pervert like that, somebody'll surely have noticed him around here. He'd have to be a stranger. Did he gut her while she was still conscious or did he knock her out?"

"After she was dead, I think," said the doctor. "Unless I'm mistaken, the actual cause of death was strangulation and both the rape and the cutting took place afterwards."

The doctor was not mistaken, but the inspector was. No one in the entire area had seen any suspicious-looking stranger, presumably a rather large man driving a car, on that day.

Joachim Kroll was, of course, a small man and he was using public transport, having apparently taken the train to the city of Hamm which lies due south of Herrenstein and Walstedde and then continued either on foot or by bus.

Actually, Kroll does not remember how he got to what he insists is the scene of his first murder. If it was, it did not make a very strong impression on him. He never knew the victim's name and he does not recall cutting open her stomach. He was, however, able to pinpoint the place without the slightest prompting and he was even able to describe how the corpse had lain in the snow on top of her clothing with her thighs spread and the blood trickling from between them on to the snow.

Considering the force of Joachim Kroll's sex drive and the fact that his later companion, the rubber sex doll, was not at that time available, it is very difficult to believe that he followed this success by complete abstinence for over four years. However, the next case which he has been able to remember took place on June 17, 1959, in the town of Rheinhausen, and was the only case which took him to the west of the Rhine.

The police do not believe this and they are convinced that

222

Kroll committed an unknown number of murders between 1955 and 1959, probably on the east bank of the Rhine, but perhaps on the west bank as well. The confirmation of this may be years in coming. Not only every unsolved sex murder has to be dug out of the old files, but every solved case as well. Kroll can then be questioned about them and, if he is guilty, he will admit it. A man who has already confessed to eleven murders has nothing to lose, and besides, Joachim Kroll is an obliging, cooperative man who has no desire to give the police any more work than necessary.

The victim in Rheinhausen was twenty-four, and her name was Klara F. Tesmer. She was a pretty woman, blonde and well-built. Kroll apparently had no preference in hair colour, but he liked pretty women and girls and even his oldest known victim (who was sixty-one) was a handsome woman.

Like Irmgard Strehl, Klara Tesmer was found in a patch of woods outside the city limits, and also like her, she had been strangled, raped and mutilated. Parts of her buttocks and thighs were missing.

There was no reason to connect this murder with the Strehl murder in Walstedde four years earlier and no such connection was made. Instead, a thirty-seven-year-old motor-mechanic named Heinrich Ott was arrested and charged with the crime.

Ott was believed also to be the author of a number of other sex murders which had taken place in Rheinhausen, a considerably larger city than Walstedde, over the preceding few years and, when he committed suicide by hanging himself in the detention cells, this was regarded as proof positive and all of the cases were closed.

Now it is known that Kroll was responsible for the Tesmer murder and possibly for some others of which Ott was accused. On the other hand, Ott was, presumably, not completely innocent and was also a murderer, if not as cautious a one as Joachim Kroll.

The Rheinhausen murder being regarded as solved, it was not strange that Kroll's next crime, which took place only a little more than a month later on July 26, 1959, in the town of Bredeney, some twenty miles to the east, was not connected with it.

The victim this time was sixteen-year-old Manuela Knodt who went for a walk on Sunday afternoon in the city forest of Essen which lies just to the north of Bredeney. She was never seen alive again. Her dead body, naked, strangled and raped, was found among the bushes and the murderer had masturbated not only over her pubic area, but her face and hair as well.

Because of this, the medical expert from the Essen police Department of Criminal Investigations was of the opinion that the crime had been carried out by at least two men and possibly more. In this respect he was in agreement with Dr Knopf in Walstedde, although neither man knew this, and he was just as wrong.

Manuela Knodt was not murdered by a gang of young perverts, but by the sexually abnormal Joachim Kroll.

Bredeney is the only known exception to Kroll's apparently invariable rule of never striking twice in the same community. Over seven years later, he would return to the little town for another kill.

Kroll does not remember his murders for 1960 or 1961. There is not much doubt that he committed some. Medical experts are of the opinion that it would have been impossible for him to go for such a long period without slaking his lust on something more exciting than the rubber sex doll.

Nor are the police short on unsolved sex murders for the period. The question is merely which ones are Kroll's? He did not commit them all, for the times and places make that physically impossible. Also, some of these crimes were solved, officially at least, and men are still serving sentences for them. Not all of them confessed. Are some of these men innocent?

It can be seen what a great deal of trouble a man like Joachim Kroll can make for overworked police departments, public prosecutors and the courts in general.

Kroll's next known murder is a perfect example of this.

On April 23, 1962, which happened to be Easter Monday, thirteen-year-old Petra Giese was strangled, raped and partially cut up in the forest outside the little town of Bruckhausen on the northern edge of Duisburg. Her body was found by a search party the following day.

224

The Duisburg Department of Criminal Investigations was called in and a team consisting of Inspector Heinz Bulle, Detective-Sergeant Kurt Ball and Dr Karl Onkel proceeded to the scene of the crime. Fourteen years later, Detective-Sergeant Ball would be the inspector in charge of investigations when his replacement, Detective-Sergeant Max Riese, staggered out of the toilet in Duisburg to fall in a faint. Both Inspector Bulle and Dr Onkel would be retired by this time.

Although the police did not faint this time, they were highly revolted by the details of Petra's murder.

"This," said Dr Onkel, making a report on the findings of the post-mortem in Inspector Bulle's office, "is one of the worst sex crimes I have seen. Its only redeeming factor is that the murderer does not appear to be sadistically inclined. The child was raped and cut up after she was dead, not before."

"Thank God for that, at least," said Inspector Bulle, a greying, kindly man in his early fifties. He was of a generation that still believed that God took an interest in such matters. "Are you quite sure?"

"Yes," said the doctor, taking off his heavy horn-rimmed spectacles and wiping them nervously with his handkerchief. "If she had been alive at the time, she would have struggled so violently that she would be covered with bruises. Actually, there's not a bruise on her with the exception of her throat."

"The pieces that were cut away," said Detective-Sergeant Ball, a slender, dark-haired and olive-skinned man who looked more like an Italian than a German. "Why? What did he do with them?"

The doctor shrugged and looked more nervous than ever.

"It wasn't her sex organs or her breasts," he pursued the sergeant when the doctor failed to answer. "A fetish . . .? It was the meaty parts of the body . . . Surely he couldn't have wanted to . . .?"

The doctor looked at his fingers and said nothing. On the other side of the desk, the inspector swallowed hard and gazed first at the medical expert and then at his assistant with a look of horror on his face.

"Good God, man!" he suddenly shouted. "You're not suggesting that he cut her up for meat?"

The doctor abruptly got up and left the office without

saying another word. Behind him, the inspector and the sergeant sat silently staring at each other. Even if no one had actually said the word, the thought of cannibalism was in all three minds and fourteen years later, the sergeant, by that time Inspector Ball, would remember that scene in the office.

In 1962, however, there was no concrete evidence that Petra Giese had been the victim of not only a murdering rapist, but also a cannibal, and the murderer, when he was caught, vigorously denied it.

As a matter of fact, he denied being the murderer altogether, but he was convicted and sentenced anyway. There were a number of things against him and he could not explain any of them.

To begin with, Vinzenz Kuehn, a fifty-two-year-old unmarried miner, drove a Goggomobile Isar, which was a rather unusual sort of vehicle, an ill-conceived cross between an automobile and a motorcycle, and these were not common. As a matter of fact, there were exactly 522 Goggo Isars in the entire area.

All of them were checked following a report by a farmer that he had seen a Goggo Isar in the vicinity of the scene of the crime on the day of the murder. Kuehn was the only owner of such a vehicle who could not account for his time on that day.

Secondly, Kuehn had a record, an unfortunate record for the type of crime with which he was charged. Kuehn was fond of little girls. He waited for them in the parks and other places where he was not likely to be disturbed and he offered them candy or, if they preferred, money to let him take off their panties and give them lessons in masturbation. He followed this by applying the same techniques to himself and there was no question but that he had practised his perversion on many more little girls than ever came to the attention of the police or their parents either for that matter. Kuehn had a way with little girls but, prior to the case of Petra Giese, he had never been known to injure one physically. Moreover, he rarely approached a girl as old as Petra had been.

Balanced against this was the matter of the Goggo Isar, the fact that Kuehn had no alibi for the time in question and the belief of the medical experts that any man engaging in such activities with young girls would or, at least, could find himself carried away one day and end up a rapist and a murderer. Kuehn, it was suggested, had lost control of himself, and raped Petra and then, realizing what he had done, had killed her and mutilated the body to simulate a sadistic sex murder.

Incredibly, the official post-mortem report showing that Petra had been killed first and then raped was ignored. Perhaps the jurors felt that it was better to have Kuehn out of harm's way whether he was guilty of this particular murder or not. The thinking may have been that even if he wasn't guilty this time, he soon would be.

That might also explain the lightness of the sentence. Although convicted of rape and murder of a female minor, Kuehn was only sentenced to twelve years' imprisonment and a course of psychiatric treatment designed to rid him of his unnatural interest in little girls and convert him to a useful member of society.

He was given the psychiatric treatment, released after six years and is believed by the police to be continuing his activities with female minors, though much more cautiously.

In a way, Kuehn was fortunate, for had he not been in police custody on June 4, 1962 when Monika Tafel was raped and murdered, he would surely have been blamed for it.

Monika was twelve, one year younger than Petra, and she was murdered just outside her home town of Walsum which is only a stone's throw to the north of Bruckhausen. Her body was not found until June 11 by a police helicopter. It was not hidden, but it was lying in a part of the forest that none of the search parties had happened to pass through.

Perhaps if the Tafel case had been handled by the Duisburg Department of Criminal Investigations, the parallels to the Petra Giese case might have been noticed and Vinzenz Kuehn spared six years in prison, but it lay just far enough to the north that the investigation was handled out of Bottrop, another larger city to the north-east of Duisburg.

As in the case of Petra Giese, the investigators found that Monika had been strangled to death, stripped naked, subjected to sexual intercourse, masturbated over and

227

robbed of some of the more fleshy parts of her body. Like their Duisburg colleagues, they were puzzled and secretly horrified at their own suspicions. These were not, however, officially voiced for, again like Duisburg, they soon captured the murderer.

There was no conviction in this case because the police lacked the evidence to even charge the suspect. Walter Quicker, a thirty-four-year-old steel worker and former French Foreign Legionnaire, was arrested on the basis of statements by witnesses that they had seen him in the area on the day in question in the company of a young girl.

Quicker denied this, but the investigations showed that he was well-known in the community for his interest in little girls and that many thought his actions towards them suspicious.

Quicker admitted that he was fond of little girls, but insisted that he had no sexual interest in them and that he had always wanted a daughter of his own.

Dozens of little girls in Walsum were questioned and all maintained that Quicker's attitude towards them had been perfectly correct. No child could be found to whom Quicker had made sexual advances of any kind.

This ruined the police case and, although they still believed Quicker to be guilty, they were forced to release him. His prosecution was then taken over by his neighbours and his wife who filed for a divorce on the grounds that she could not stand the disgrace of being married to a child-molester. The divorce was granted.

The neighbours stopped speaking to Quicker completely and the local shops refused to serve him. When he came out of his house, younger residents of the neighbourhood would run behind him, asking if he had raped any young girls that day. This was considered screamingly funny by their elders.

Walter Quicker did not find it screamingly funny. On October 5, 1962, he went into the forest with a washing-line and hung himself.

The police considered this proof positive of his guilt in the Monika Tafel murder and the case was closed.

The real murderer was, however, Joachim Kroll and he had now succeeded in murdering (or causing the death of) a man he had never seen or even heard of. With, of course, a little help from Mrs Quicker, the neighbours and, regretfully, the police.

Joachim's next known victim was also a man, although it was surely not the next victim for the murder took place on August 22, 1965, more than three years after the murder of Monika Tafel. Kroll could not possibly have gone that long without the stimulus of intercourse with a fresh corpse. Also, he would have had to buy meat during that time.

However, he was unable to remember any specific murders during that period and the police collected reports of sex murders, preferably those in which some parts of the body were missing, to boost his memory.

Joachim Kroll did remember the case of Hermann Schmitz very well because, as he says, this was the only man that he ever killed. He is probably telling the truth for Kroll's interests were purely heterosexual. He was not interested in men and he did not kill Hermann Schmitz in order to rape him, but merely because he was in his way.

The Schmitz case is different in another way as well. There was a witness to the murder, his eighteen-year-old fiancée, Marion Veen.

On the night of the murder, Hermann and Marion had driven to the shore of an extensive artificial lake which filled the excavation of an old gravel pit and there, beneath a romantic August moon, they were engaged in some rather passionate necking.

The place was Grossenbaum, a village to the south of Duisburg, the day was Sunday and the time was approximately nine o'clock.

Joachim Kroll had arrived in Grossenbaum by tram. He had left his room in the Thyssen bachelor quarters at shortly after six and, ever since, he had been prowling the streets, following first this young woman or little girl and then, as an opportunity failed to present itself, another. He was in a state of considerable sexual excitement and he was becoming impatient.

Kroll knew about the gravel-pit lake at Grossenbaum because he had, at one time, lived in the village of Huckingen, less than half a mile distant. He also knew what went on at the lake and, as a matter of fact, he had occasionally taken part. Not as a participant, of course, but as a spectator. In addition to his other problems, Kroll was an accomplished Peeping Tom who enjoyed masturbating outside the cars while the occupants made love within.

A harmless perversion, perhaps, but on this particular Sunday evening, Kroll was not prepared to settle for masturbation and watching. Creeping silently up to the car in which the twenty-five-year-old student engineer and his fiancee were sitting, he drove the long, sharp, folding knife which he always carried into the right-hand front tyre of Schmitz's car.

His reason for doing this was, according to his own statements, to prevent Schmitz from driving off and, at the same time, to lure him out of the car. In his straightforward, matter-of-fact, insanely logical way, Kroll intended to kill the young man so that he would then be able to kill and rape Marion Veen who, as he later said, he found exceptionally attractive.

Hermann Schmitz, however, failed to react as anticipated. Although he apparently realized that the car had a flat tyre, he started the engine and drove off. If he had known the area better, he would have saved his life.

He did not, however, and there now took place a series of tragic errors. To begin with, Schmitz missed his turn and entered a dead-end road less than a hundred yards from where he had been parked. Arriving at the end and realizing his mistake, he turned the car around and headed back out again.

At the end of the road, there stood Joachim Kroll, jumping up and down and waving his arms in the headlights!

Whereupon, Hermann Schmitz made his second and final mistake. He was a large man in perfect health and something of an amateur athlete. The shabby, unshaven little workman leaping about in front of the car came barely to his shoulder and he looked as dangerous as an anaemic field mouse. Schmitz stopped the car and got out.

Through the windscreen, Marion Veen watched her fiancé walk forward to where the little man was waiting. The two men appeared to exchange a few words and then, suddenly,

230

something flashed in the stranger's hand. Her eyes wide with horror and astonishment, she actually saw the blood spurt as the killer drove his long knife repeatedly into Hermann's chest.

So far, Joachim Kroll's plans were working out perfectly. The man was eliminated. All that remained was to murder and rape the girl.

Marion Veen had other plans, however. She had an astonishingly cool head and she reacted so quickly and forcefully that Kroll himself nearly lost his life.

Sliding into the driver's seat, she threw the car into gear, slammed the accelerator to the floorboards and went roaring down on Joachim Kroll like an avenging fury.

The little killer was barely able to scramble out of the way and, corresponding to his extremely cautious nature, he immediately ran off and disappeared into the darkness. He had no stomach for pursuing victims who defended themselves.

Marion Veen swung the car around so that the body of her fiancé was in the headlights, wedged a hair-clip into the horn button so that it began to sound continuously and, with great courage, for she had no way of knowing how far the killer had gone or whether he was still waiting in the shadows, got out of the car and ran to where Schmitz lay.

He had collapsed instantly when the knife was driven into his chest and the post-mortem would later show that the very first stab must have pierced his heart. Nonetheless, he was still alive and, as Marion fell to her knees and lifted his head, he tried to say something. All that came out, however, was a cross between a gasp and a groan and his head fell forward.

When the first couples from the other cars that had been parked at the lake arrived, attracted by the steadily blowing horn, they found Marion, the front of her dress soaked with her fiancé's blood, sitting in the road and holding his head against her breast. He was quite dead.

Grossenbaum also belonged to the Duisburg police district and it was they who carried out the investigations. There was not very much investigating to do. All they had was a somewhat sketchy description of the murderer from Marion who had seen him briefly in the headlights, and some casts of the shape of the knife-blade taken from the wounds in Herman's chest.

A number of men known to frequent lovers' lanes were picked up and questioned, and a very hard look was taken at not only Schmitz's friends and acquaintances, but also those of Marion Veen. The police had no way of knowing the motive for the killing and they suspected that it might have been the work of a disappointed boyfriend of the girl.

No such boyfriend was found. None of the lovers' lane peekers corresponded in any way to Miss Veen's description of the murderer. The case was sent to the unsolved files. It was not put down as a sex murder. It was not connected with any of Kroll's previous crimes.

In any case, his next crime, if it was his next crime, took place a good distance away and completely outside the Duisburg police district. It was, in a way, a classic example of Kroll's work.

One Tuesday afternoon, after he had finished work, Kroll took the train to Marl, a town some forty miles to the northeast of Duisburg, where he began to prowl the streets looking for suitable prey. By shortly before seven o'clock he had found none and he went to hide and wait in a park known as the Foersterbusch. He was, by now, highly aroused and he would take any victim regardless of age or appearance so long as she was female.

As chance would have it, he was to get a very young and lovely one.

At a few minutes after seven in the evening of September 13, 1966, twenty-year-old Ursula Rohling left the Capri Ice-cream Parlour in suburb Marl. She had spent the last hour and a half there with her fiancé, twenty-seven-year-old Adolf Schickel, discussing plans for their forthcoming marriage. It was now time to go home and the shortest way was through Foersterbusch Park.

There is now only one person alive who knows what happened next, but he is remarkably frank about it.

"I saw this woman in the park," said Joachim Kroll, making his confession to Inspector Kurt Ball of the Duisburg police. "She was young, with short hair. I spoke to her. Then I grabbed her around the neck with my right arm

232

and dragged her into the bushes. I threw her on the ground on her back and choked her."

"Why?" asked Inspector Ball. "Why did you have to choke her to death?"

"She could have fought me," says Kroll. "Then I couldn't have done it. Anyway, she could have told it was me. I choked her until she stopped moving. Then I took off her pants and her other things and I did it to her.

"I left her lying there and took the train back to Duisburg. When I got home, I was still hot, and I had it with the doll and did it with my hand a couple of times."

The following morning, Joachim Kroll had gone off to work in the Thyssen steel plant washroom as calmly as if nothing whatsoever had taken place. He had never been in Marl before. He did not know the name of the girl that he had murdered. He did not even bother to look in the newspaper to see if the murder was reported.

As a matter of fact, it was not. When Ursula had failed to come home that evening, her parents had first contacted Adolf Schickel and finding that he knew nothing of her whereabouts, had called the police at shortly after ten o'clock. A search was immediately undertaken, but it was only two days later that the corpse was found by a municipal park employee.

Although there was not the slightest trace of a motive, Adolf Schickel was immediately taken into custody and held for over three weeks under continuous interrogation. During all this time, his reply never varied.

"Why would I kill Ursula?" he said. "I loved her. We were going to get married. Why would I do such a thing?"

"For sex," said the police. "She refused to let you have sex with her until you were married so you raped her and killed her."

This accusation was at complete variance with the facts. To begin with, the post-mortem had shown that Ursula had been dead when the rape took place. Secondly, it was not true that she had refused to have sex with her fiancé until after the wedding. There were witnesses who could testify that she and Adolf had spent more than one night together.

Nonetheless, when Schickel was released, it was simply

because the police could find no legal grounds for holding him longer. They still considered him guilty and so too did almost everyone in Marl.

Like Walter Quicker before him, Schickel was persecuted, ostracized and eventually chased out of Marl. On January 4, 1967, depressed by the death of his fiancée and the false accusations which had been levelled against him, he drowned himself in the Main river near Wiesbaden.

Joachim Kroll, who believed that he had only killed one man in his life, had just caused the death of the third, again with a little help from the public and the police.

On the other hand, the police are not to be too strongly condemned. Kroll was one of the most elusive murderers of all time, at least, of all the murderers who were ever detected at all. He was extremely cautious, utterly ruthless, in no way interested in his victims once he had finished with them, seldom struck twice in the same area and never had the slightest contact with any of the victims prior to the actual murder. How could such a man be traced or even his very existence suspected?

When to this is added the fact of his innocuous appearance and the cloaking factor of the dozens or even hundreds of other sex criminals operating in the same area, it is a marvel that he was ever apprehended at all.

Even before Adolf Schickel had had time to commit suicide over a crime which he had not committed, Kroll had carried out his next murder, this time on a five-year-old girl named Ilona Harke.

The date was December 22, 1966, only slightly more than three months after the murder of Ursula Rohling, and the scene was the little town of Bredeney on the southern outskirts of Essen. Kroll had been there for the last time in 1959 when he had raped and murdered sixteen-year-old Manuela Knodt. However, the body was found in a small patch of forest near the city of Wuppertal, nearly twenty miles further south.

This was typical of Kroll's murders. Normally, he never struck twice in the same city, but this time he did. Normally, the murder was carried out wherever he happened to find the victim. This time, he must have persuaded the girl to

234

accompany him on the train to another city.

The most remarkable thing about the criminal career of Joachim Kroll was its lack of consistency. Sex criminals usually follow a rigid pattern in the performance of their crimes. Kroll never did.

With, of course, the exception of the raping, stripping, strangling and cutting up for meat in the case of the younger victims. Ilona Harke was a very young victim. Kroll ate several pounds of her flesh.

The case was thoroughly investigated by the Essen police who interrogated hundreds of suspects and hundreds of potential witnesses who might have seen a little blonde girl with a man on the train between Bredeney and Wuppertal on the day of the murder.

Nothing could be proven against any of the suspects and nobody remembered seeing any girl who looked like Ilona Harke. The case went to the unsolved files.

1967 was remarkable in that it produced Joachim Kroll's second known failure, for he had not really succeeded in the case of Marion Veen. Although he had murdered Hermann Schmitz, this had not been his primary objective. Schmitz merely had to be removed in order that he could murder and rape Marion Veen and in this he had not succeeded.

The proposed victim on June 22, 1967, was not a determined young woman like Marion, but an innocent, trusting, little girl who knew Uncle Joachim and thought he was a fine fellow.

The girl's name was Gabriele Puettmann, she was ten years old and she lived in the little town of Grafenhausen, a few miles to the north of Bottrop. At the time, Joachim Kroll was living in Grafenwald, another small town very near to Grafenhausen.

The attempt took place in neither town, but in the open country halfway between the two. It was a Thursday and Kroll should have been at work, but was taking a few days off on sick leave. Gabriele had been to school in the morning, but it was now afternoon and German schools do not have afternoon classes.

Joachim Kroll was well-known and popular among the little girls of the district. He had a way with children and he was always good for sweets or an ice-cream cone. It was not at all uncommon for him to take a walk with some little girl.

Unquestionably, many of the parents knew this and saw nothing objectionable in it. Kroll was a gentle, soft-spoken man who appeared completely normal to everyone who met him. Moreover, nothing had happened to any of these little girls who had gone for walks with Joachim Kroll.

And why not? Here again, nobody knows. Was it merely that no absolutely safe opportunity presented itself? Considering the extreme caution which Kroll almost invariably showed, it seems likely that, so long as someone knew that he had gone for a walk with a little girl, then that little girl was safe. Unlike most sex criminals, Joachim Kroll could apparently control himself whenever it was necessary for his own protection.

On that June afternoon, it seems he was convinced that no one knew that he and Gabriele Puettmann had gone for a walk along the road leading from Grafenhausen to Grafenwald, and somewhere along that road they reached a point where no one else was in sight.

Joachim Kroll took Gabriele by the hand and led her into the field of ripening wheat beside the road. He had, he said, something to show her.

And, indeed, he did. A collection of pornographic cartoon booklets.

Gabriele was more bewildered than shocked, and it was a few minutes before she realized what the people in the pictures were doing.

This realization, however, embarrassed her terribly and she threw her hands over her eyes. Joachim Kroll laid his hand on her shoulder near her throat.

As Gabriele now remembers it, she was not frightened nor did she think that Kroll might harm her. She was merely ashamed and confused and she jumped to her feet and ran out of the wheatfield and down the road as fast as she could go. Typically, Kroll made no effort to follow her. He was much too cautious for that.

Gabriele Puettmann ran all the way home and she never went near Joachim Kroll again. On the other hand, she told no one of her experience, neither her parents nor her school-

236

friends. She was ashamed to and it was only when Joachim Kroll was finally revealed as the raping, murdering cannibal that he was that she came forward with her story.

Had she done so earlier, she might have saved the lives of several people, but then again, perhaps not. Kroll would have been charged, at the most, with molesting children and would have been given a light sentence or, possibly, none at all. There was no reason to connect him with any of the murders that had taken place.

There were, of course, sex murders in the Ruhr during 1968, but which of these were the work of Joachim Kroll is not known. Kroll thinks he may have killed one or two people that year, but he cannot remember where or what age they were. The only thing certain is that they were female.

But not, necessarily, young. Kroll's victim for 1969 was sixty-one years old. Her name was Maria Hettgen, she was a widow and, on July 12, 1969, Joachim Kroll strangled her to death, removed her clothing and raped her in precisely the same manner that he had strangled, stripped and raped the five-year-old Ilona Harke.

But although Mrs Hettgen was a plump woman, Kroll did not cut off and carry away so much as a chop. The folding knife stayed in his pocket.

And yet, he had gone to a good deal of trouble to locate this victim. The crime took place in the woods outside Hueckeswagen, a village nearly forty miles to the south-east of Duisburg.

The following year, on May 21, 1970, Kroll added a pretty thirteen-year-old to his trophy list and, incidentally, sent another innocent man to prison.

Not that Kroll knew this of course. He neither read about the crime in the newspaper nor did he attend the funeral where plain-clothes detectives were secretly photographing all strangers present. A good many murderers have been caught this way, but not Joachim Kroll.

It was only in 1976 when Kroll was being led to the scene of another of his crimes that he halted suddenly near a wood on the outskirts of Breitscheid, a small town to the south of Grossenbaum where Hermann Schmitz had been stabbed to death, and remarked, "I choked a girl in this place once."

The police listened carefully. It was not the first time that Joachim Kroll had made such an observation and he had always been right.

The girl in this case turned out to be Jutta Rahn who was on her way home from school, one Thursday afternoon. Kroll spotted her at the railway station and followed her along the road through the woods. Although it was raining heavily, it failed to cool his passions and he seized the girl, dragged her into the forest, strangled her to death, removed her clothes, raped her and masturbated over her pubic area. He then got the uneasy feeling that she might not be dead after all so he tied her red brassiere very tightly around her neck and went home to Duisburg and the rubber sex doll.

Jutta's father found her body nearly six hours later. He and his neighbours had been searching ever since Jutta failed to return home from school.

A search for the murderer was also begun and, after checking out over twelve hundred clues and leads in vain, the police hit upon Peter Schay, the twenty-year-old son of one of the Rahn's neighbours.

Schay's only previous offence had been a charge for petty theft on which he had not been tried or convicted, but red fibres matching those from Jutta Rahn's brassiere were found on his clothing and his blood group was AB, the same type as that shown by the traces of sperm in Jutta's torn vagina and in her pubic hair.

For fifteen months, Schay sat in pre-trial detention, denying constantly and truthfully that he had had anything to do with the murder. When he was finally brought to trial, the defence was able to show that there were garments in the Schay household with identical red fibres to Jutta Rahn's brassiere. Witnesses were also produced who swore to having seen Schay in his own home within minutes of the time when the crime had taken place and in completely dry clothing although it was raining buckets outside.

The case was thrown out for lack of evidence and Schay returned home a free man. Both he and his family received the same treatment as had Walter Quicker and Adolf Schickel. Schay was henceforth called "Murderer" as if it was his given name and his family was known as "The

238

Murder Gang". This treatment continued until Kroll's confession to the murder in 1976.

From May 1970 to July 1976 is a long time for a man to go without satisfying his sexual needs, but Joachim Kroll maintains that he managed during this period with nothing more than masturbation and the faithful sex doll. The police do not believe it. They have a list of more than fifteen unsolved sex murders, most of them children and most of them from the Ruhr district, which they are slowly and methodically checking out. They are quite certain that some of these are the handiwork of Joachim Kroll.

But here too, Kroll demonstrates that strange lack of consistency which made him so hard to catch. Although he freely admits to murders much longer ago, calmly furnishing the most gruesome details and even volunteering information on murders that he was not previously suspected of committing, he stubbornly denies all connection with any of the crimes during this more recent period.

All, of course, except Monika Kettner, for it was she who put an end to Joachim Kroll's career and presented the police with the solution to one of the longest series of sex murders ever recorded in Germany, a series which they did not, incidentally, even know was going on.

The date was July 2, 1976, and the place was Laar on the northern outskirts of Duisburg. Joachim Kroll was living in an attic room at 24 Friesen Street.

Monika Kettner was also living in Friesen Street. She was a four-year-old blonde girl and, that afternoon being hot, she was wearing nothing but her panties.

At approximately four o'clock, Mrs Hella Kettner discovered that Monika was missing. She searched briefly, spoke with some of the other children playing in the street and then called the police.

The police came, spoke also with the children, none of whom knew where Monika had gone, and then began a house to house search, paying particular attention to the basements.

They were still doing this when Oscar Muller, who occupied another attic room at 24 Friesen Street, came down to where they were searching and asked them to take a look

239

at the toilet on his floor. It was a common toilet for the whole floor and it was blocked up. Mr Muller would not say what he thought it was blocked with, but he was yellowish-green in the face and kept swallowing convulsively all the time that he was talking to the police.

His manner, if not his information, was convincing and the uniformed officers from the patrol cars, dispatched by police headquarters to investigate the report, followed him to the fourth-floor toilet.

What they found there left them nearly as upset as Mr Muller had been. The toilet bowl was half filled with a red liquid which looked like a mixture of blood and water, and there were strange, horrible things floating in it. Worst of all, perhaps, were some strands of blonde hair. It must be remembered that the officers were looking for a little blonde girl.

While one of the officers remained to guard the door to the toilet, the other went to summon the searchers from the other patrol cars at the scene. The house was immediately surrounded and no one allowed in or out.

Police headquarters was notified and, a short time later, Inspector Ball, Detective-Sergeant Riese and the department's medical expert, Dr Johann Haut, arrived and went immediately to the toilet on the fourth floor.

As they had been informed of the circumstances, they had brought tools with them and the sergeant quickly removed the toilet bowl from its mounting and turned it upside down over a plastic tub.

It was when the sergeant lifted away the bowl and saw what was in the tub that he staggered out of the toilet and fainted.

Lying in the bloody water was a complete but tiny set of human entrails – a heart, lungs, kidneys and liver. There were also some other scraps of freshly cut flesh and long strands of fine blonde hair.

The rest of Monika was found in Joachim Kroll's room, some parts neatly wrapped and in the deep freeze, others on plates in the refrigerator for immediate use. Stiff with horror, the inspector lifted the lid of the pot cooking on the stove. In the boiling stew he found a complete tiny hand from which the thoroughly cooked flesh had begun to peel away.

Joachim Kroll had not yet had his dinner.

240